# THE
## LESS-THAN-PERFECT
# HORSE

'A most helpful and well-thought-out book which will stand the test of time.' **Ian Stark**

'This valuable reference book is the result of her experiences with problem horses ... and gives her tried and tested solutions.' *The Times*

'The concise and practical approach to schooling the horse makes this book easy to read but no less informative. Jane Wallace writes from obvious practical experience and readers will be able to relate to her sympathetic approach.' **Chris Bartle**

'Informative, clear and extremely easy to read.' *Horse and Hound*

**JANE WALLACE** was born in Cambridge and started riding at an early age. She was soon spotted as showing talent and rode many of the top show ponies in the 1960s, winning at all the major shows including the Horse of the Year show.

She went on to win and be placed point-to-pointing and in 1974 started her own yard, initially producing young show jumpers. In 1982 she turned to eventing and won Windsor three-day event that year on Marsh Heron, coming eighth at their first attempt at Badminton in 1986.

Jane was selected for the British team in Poland on King's Jester in 1986 and for the European Championships in Luhmühlen in 1987. She won Bramham three-day event on King's Jester in 1987 and 1988, during which year she was shortlisted for the British team for the Olympic Games and won Burghley three-day event.

In 1989 Jane won the individual silver medal at the European Championships at Burghley and was ranked third lady rider in the world.

In addition to eventing, Jane is on the HIS Hunter Judging Panel, has been a member of the Senior Selection Committee for the British three-day event teams, is a steward at point-to-points and an adjudicator for the FEI Fellowship exams. She is much in demand as a teacher both in the UK and abroad. She is married with two sons and lives in Leicestershire with her husband Malcolm Wallace.

# JANE WALLACE

# THE
# LESS-THAN-PERFECT
# HORSE

Problems Encountered and Solutions Explained

*Illustrations by Fiona Silver*

KENILWORTH PRESS

First published in Great Britain by
Kenilworth Press Ltd
Addington
Buckingham
MK18 2JR

First published in Great Britain in 1987 by Methuen London Ltd
Reprinted 1991 by the Kingswood Press
First published in paperback in 1993 by Methuen London
Reprinted 1999 by Kenilworth Press

**Disclaimer of Liability**
The authors and publisher shall have neither liability nor responsibility
to any person or entity with respect to any loss or damage caused or
alleged to be caused directly or indirectly by the information contained
in this book. While the book is as accurate as the author can make it,
there may be errors, omissions, and inaccuracies.

**British Library Cataloguing in Publication Data**
A CIP record for this book is available from the British Library

ISBN 1-872119-13-1

Printed in Great Britain by Hillman Printers (Frome) Ltd

For all those whose brains
I have picked over the years!

# Contents

# List of Illustrations

## Acknowledgements

I would like to thank Peter Green MRCVS for the time and effort he took in clarifying a few points which I thought required a professional comment.

Heartfelt thanks go to my sister, Anne Parker, who spent many hours poring over my script, eradicating the myriads of unnecessary commas and correcting the endless grammatical errors; to Jenny Brightwell, who not only typed, edited and deciphered my inserts and deletions, but also withstood my irritable moods without once grumbling; and to my husband John, who sat me down in front of the typewriter – almost handcuffing me to it when I displayed signs of disillusionment and despair – and insisted that I had to a go at writing this book, giving me enormous support, encouragement and lots of helpful suggestions at every verse end, rarely moaning when I grizzled and complained. Without these people I would never have had the courage nor the initiative to continue, let alone finish! The book would not be complete without the illustrations, and I am very grateful to Fiona Silver for her excellent pictorial interpretation of my words.

I would like to mention my mother, for without her unfailing generosity in transporting me all over the country as a child, I would have been unable to reap the benefits of Davina Whiteman's invaluable training. I must also mention Liz Pickard, who was not only the instigator of my early enthusiasm, but also organised my first point-to-point ride many years later.

Finally, I must thank John and Maryan Huntridge for providing us with wonderful horses to event, especially Marsh Heron and King's Jester, who allowed me to fulfil ambitions beyond my wildest dreams.

## Foreword

To write a book takes a great deal of time, dedication and courage. It does not surprise me, therefore, that Jane Wallace has added to her already accomplished life by becoming an authoress!

I highly recommend this volume of facts, ideas, technique and simplicity, all geared towards the most valuable part of the horse's training – the basics!

Jane is a true professional. Her results in three-day eventing prove her to be one of the talented stars of this marvellous sport. This book is a credit to her, and will be of great value to the reader.

*Virginia Elliot*

# *Preface*

I read with amusement in John Francome's autobiography, *Born Lucky*, that he spent the majority of his English lessons gazing out of the window at a young, attractive schoolgirl during her games lessons, and was rather suffering the effects of his inattentiveness when he came to write his book. Well, I know how he must have felt, because although I was not gazing out of the window at boys (or girls for that matter!), I passed most of the time in my English lessons either chattering, or wondering who had won the 2.30 at Cheltenham (I was racing mad then and still am), or doodling horses endlessly in my rough book. I now realise that drawing horses in such detail was definitely of benefit to me when it came to assessing a horse's good and bad points of conformation . . . but I am not so sure that John Francome's study stood him in particularly good stead for his chosen career!

# Introduction

I have always thought that there has been a lack of equestrian books dealing with the schooling and training of the non-perfect horse. It is true that most books do have a chapter or so on some problems which one might expect to encounter, but on the whole all the books which I have read on the subject seem only to cover the training of the non-complicated horse. Since few of us will ever be sufficiently privileged to own such an animal, I am hoping that this book will be of great value to the reader in the understanding of, and therefore the means of coping with, any difficulties that may occur in the production and education of the 'ordinary' horse. The very easy horse is the exception, so one should never feel alone in thinking that troubles are confined to one's own horse! For anyone involved with the training and schooling of horses, this book will, I hope, be of interest and assistance as regards the reasons underlying the problems experienced on the long road to a well-schooled horse. Even for the more experienced rider or trainer, this book should be stimulating for I have tried to cover problems from different angles, many of which could be new to readers.

One of the most fascinating aspects of horses and riding must be the fact that there is no rigid rule for what is right and what is wrong in the training of a horse, provided that there is an understanding within the partnership of horse and rider. This can be seen clearly in the very varied styles of riding – particularly in this country, where everyone adopts, to a large degree, an individual way of riding. With this in mind, John and I feel that we are qualified to voice our opinions on how to train a range of horses who fit into the category of non-perfection. Having had many years' experience in various fields of riding, we have pooled our knowledge and practical experience, and together we feel able to comprehend more fully why so many horses have difficulty in the different phases of competition. Our viewpoint, together with any theory we have proposed, is based on the results achieved from having spent twenty years or so working with hundreds of very individual horses. We will be looking mainly from the eventing point of view, but, as eventing is the most comprehensive test of horse and rider, of course virtually every aspect of training the horse will be covered. We are not setting out any hard-and-fast rules by any means, but merely relating what *we* have found to be the most successful way of training from scratch, or re-training a horse with a problem.

When dealing with any horse, the first thing to analyse is its conformation, because conformation=soundness=performance. Colonel 'Handy' Hurrell once gave a lecture to our Pony Club on conformation, and told us something I shall never forget; he said that the horse with the most perfect conformation that he had ever seen was Arkle. That, to my mind, sums up my previous statement. Arkle remains undisputedly the best steeplechaser of all time. Conformation will be discussed at greater length in the first chapter, but basically we believe that the root of any difficulty incurred in training a horse is closely connected with its conformation, whether this be a physically or mentally related problem. A horse who finds his work easy will be easy to train, but if he finds that you are asking him to do something beyond his present capabilities, he is going to tell you, and the form that this resistance takes will depend greatly on the character of the horse. This is the most important point to understand, as until it can be ascertained why a horse is behaving in a particular way, it will not be possible to find a way to improve him.

The use of gadgets such as Chambons or side-reins, can undoubtedly be of great assistance in re-training a horse, provided that they are not merely used as a short-cut. There is no short-cut in schooling. Similarly, there is no quick way of getting a horse fit, or a human being for that matter: muscles take time to strengthen and become more elastic. In order for a horse to withstand half an hour's schooling, he must be physically fit in the specific muscles necessary for that work. It is interesting to note how a fit hunter will puff and sweat when made to work in a confined space – i.e. using muscles unaccustomed to working in a particular way – even though he may be very fit for hunting. The horse is an athlete and must be prepared for the specific activity in which he is going to participate. A mis-used gadget will only exacerbate problems, therefore, by forcing a horse into a shape before his muscles are sufficiently strong. It can, in fact, damage the muscles by making them work harder than they are capable of at the time: at the same time that the discomfort is created, a physical reaction will occur which will be mentally connected with pain. It takes a long time for the horse to recover both physically and mentally. However, the use of this equipment on the lunge will sometimes help both horse and rider: very often a resistance from the horse is aggravated by the rider's weight on his back – especially in the case of the less experienced rider, who may return the resistance by being a little insensitive in the hand. This will be covered in more detail when discussing individual problems.

The perfect horse being rare, a myriad of set-backs are likely to be encountered *en route* to success. Although there are many books written dealing with general training, this book is devoted to corrective training, or how to live with a problem, for it is rarely possible to sell the problem horse at the drop of a hat. For one thing, it may be very difficult to sell the horse to the right home. For another, it is a defeatist attitude and there is nothing more rewarding than overcoming moments of despair, provided that the horse is capable, to an extent, of doing what is asked of him. Also, horses are often the objects of great emotion, and success with a particular horse often becomes the sole aim of an owner or rider. However ambitious one is, it is always a challenge to teach and improve a living being: with this end constantly in sight, schooling improves the obedience of the horse and therefore increases the rider's enjoyment . . . and this is, after all, what riding is all about – a happy partnership created out of trust and understanding.

Somebody once described us to John's father as the people who make good horses out of bad ones. Although we do not really believe that this is possible, it does underline that our theories, when put into practice, show that a horse is not necessarily bad, but is probably misunderstood, and the extent to which it can be improved towards the point of being a 'good' horse is largely dependant upon the horse's natural ability – as the old saying goes, 'You can teach a cow to jump four feet.' By understanding the basis of the 'bad' horse, it is possible to persuade it to give of its best. Very often what appears to be the most difficult horse will turn out to be the best in the end – so have patience!

The book is divided into three main sections. Conformation is discussed first, as the horse's performance is entirely determined by his make and shape, and the various defects in that make and shape are examined to show why they make problems for the horse in his work. A horse with a bull neck, for instance, will never be comfortable with his head and neck in a 'round outline', because his neck would be forced into a shape which is quite unnatural for that horse, and which may also restrict his air-flow. This is just one example of many defects and their results. Understanding why a horse resists what is being asked of him is the beginning of how to train him to cope with his particular problem.

The second section of the book is the 'Blueprint' where I have explained the steps to be taken in the training of the horse and the reasons behind them. Many of the problems which occur are caused by asking the horse to perform some exercise which he is not physically or mentally prepared to do. Laying down an exact order of achievements in terms of training should avoid these pitfalls. It should also explain at what point the horse should be asked particular questions, as, obviously, in order to progress in training, the horse has to be asked to work a little harder each time, and, in so doing, to perform more complicated movements each time too. So many people are diffident to ask a question of a horse, and in consequence ask nothing at all. This in itself can cause problems because the horse becomes bored and therefore reluctant to concentrate, providing his own entertainment in ways that are irritating to the rider: shying, bucking and being generally excitable, for example. Of course, experience plays a large part in knowing when to ask a new question without upsetting the horse, but I hope that by describing the exact stages one should expect to achieve in training, it will be made clear precisely where the various problems have originated, and thus to which stage one must return to gain access to progress once more. Often one has to go back two stages in order to progress to the next one.

A typical training session will be covered in this section too, although the main purpose of having a 'Blueprint' chapter is to try to avoid repetition when discussing the actual evasions and resistances in specific instances. These are featured in the third section of the book, where symptoms, causes and treatment of problems faced in dressage and show-jumping and jumping at speed in cross-country and steeplechase are examined. This is the main part of the book, where I have explained in detail the underlying reasons behind each individual problem and the different approaches to dealing with them. It is shown how conformation defects tie in closely with many of the problems, and also how best to compromise in various cases. I have set each problem out alphabetically for easy reference in a symptoms/causes/cure format. Having ironed out a particular problem, the reader is then referred back to the Blueprint section to start again from whichever stage is suggested.

Obviously the extent of success cannot be determined and I am not saying that every horse can be made into a top-class performer, but it is safe to say that any correct training can only be of benefit to any horse, whatever is required of him and whatever problems he may have. On the whole, there are few horses who are completely hopeless cases, and treated with patience and understanding they should be capable of giving their owners a great deal of pleasure.

It is impossible to give a riding lesson on paper so when the aids for various movements are explained, the rider must experiment until he learns the best way of obtaining the correct response from his horse. Trial and error play a large part in the training of a horse so, as a rider, one must never be afraid to try something different.

# ONE

## *Conformation*

To study a horse's conformation is to see how he is put together, appraising his ability and soundness to perform the necessary tasks. Before going on to talk about the conformation defects that can affect the performance of a horse, it is important to establish exactly what should be sought in the ideal competition horse. The general impression of a horse should be of balance and symmetry. A horse is like a finely tuned machine, and should any part of that machine be unsynchronised, then the whole will malfunction. The horse can be compared to a car. In a high-performance car a driver requires power steering, power-assisted brakes and fuel-injection acceleration. The rider requires the same precision performance from a horse, and the higher the standard of performance needed, the more precise the initial response must be. This can only be achieved when the horse is sufficiently well balanced in himself to allow him to be tuned to this fine degree.

On seeing a horse for the first time, try to take in the whole picture and try to imagine him in equal parts – i.e. the length of the back end should be in proportion to the length of front, length from loins to tail, and length of leg: the ideal type of horse should fill a square with a leg at each of the bottom corners (*see* diag. 1, p. 2). Do not be swayed by your immediate reaction to, for instance, an attractive colour or a pretty head – these are merely cosmetic aspects. Some horses do have natural presence, but presence can also develop as the horse matures and progresses in his training. However, the horse must be in proportion. A huge front on a horse can make him a very comfortable ride, with a good length of rein, but it is far more difficult for the horse to lift this big front over a fence, unless of course he is matched in strength behind. The risk then is that the horse may be rather long and so lacking in nimbleness. A big front is desirable for the show-ring and hunting, but does create problems for the event horse. However, although one does not wish for an exceptionally big shoulder, one that is too small will restrict movement: whereas a good front will recover from a blunder on landing over a fence, a poor one with a straight shoulder will often fall. Some length of back is necessary for fast work, but a long

**1 A good type of horse fits into a square**

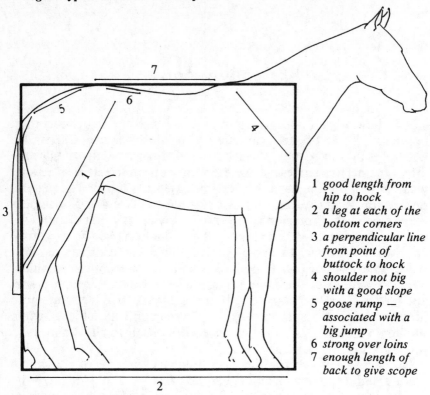

1 *good length from hip to hock*
2 *a leg at each of the bottom corners*
3 *a perpendicular line from point of buttock to hock*
4 *shoulder not big with a good slope*
5 *goose rump — associated with a big jump*
6 *strong over loins*
7 *enough length of back to give scope*

back is weak, and a short-backed horse will lack scope, both in stride and jump.

It is most important to study the structure of the hindleg, for this is the engine and lever. It is by bringing this hindleg underneath him and pushing with it that he is able to balance himself, move rhythmically in all paces, slow down, accelerate, collect and lengthen and, of course, jump. When looking at the hind limb from the side, a perpendicular line dropped from the hip-joint should meet the ground midway between the toe and the heel. The hindquarters should be strong and well-muscled, and although a goose rump may not appear very attractive, it is usually a sign of a good jumper. This is because a goose-rumped horse usually is long – relatively speaking – from hip to hock, and this length is vital as regards the leverage. A straight hindleg lacks the strength to cope with its long leverage and the horse will not have the necessary push from behind. The point of the hock should be below the point of the buttock in a good hindleg. It is rare to see a top-class jumper with a bad hindleg, and although an event horse is not required to jump enormous fences, he does have to use his hindleg to a high degree not only when jumping and galloping, but particularly in the dressage when the demand on his weight-bearing hocks is probably greatest. Some people do not object to curbs, but they are a weakness: although the curb itself may cause no trouble, it is a sign of a poor hindleg, whichever way one looks at it. There are many good racehorses with poor hindlegs, but I have yet to see a top-class jumper with weak hocks and, after all, it is jumping which is all important in eventing.

Having assimilated the symmetry of the horse from the side, and studied his hindleg from that angle, stand behind the horse and look at the symmetry of his hindquarters (*see* diagram 2). A perpendicular line dropped from the point of the buttock should divide the leg and foot into two equal parts. Also, the hips should be level with equal muscle on either side. The width between the hips is all-important, for remember this is the horse's motor; a horse with narrow hips is inevitably weak – bear in mind the saying 'Head like a lady and farewell like a cook.' However, the width must be evaluated in relation to the general stamp of the horse. A horse which is lightly

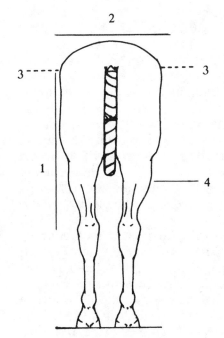

**2 The symmetry and proportions of the hindquarters**

1 *well let-down hock*
2 *good width between hips*
3 *level hips*
4 *well muscled thigh*

made but in proportion will require only the width necessary to lift his weight and, similarly, a horse with a big front will need enormous width to allow for the leverage necessary to lift it. If the horse appears to be slightly bandy-legged behind, this is often a sign of strength, but a cow-hocked horse will be weak in action as this fault causes the limb to move outwards instead of forwards in a straight line, and so he will lack drive. Although horses do cope with shortcomings in their hindleg conformation, the correct hindleg is infinitely preferable, as this leg will be in perfect balance in action, therefore throwing no strain and stress on any one point.

The pasterns must not be too upright, for this will cause jarring, or too long, as this will put strain on the whole leg – this applies front and back. The upright pastern in front will tend to give a short choppy action and, although the long pastern gives a very springy, comfortable ride, it does throw enormous strain on the tendons. However, the pasterns do need sufficient length to give some spring in the stride.

When considering the athletic horse, the other important aspect to look at is the way in which the head and neck join the shoulder. The horse's head-carriage can only be considered in conjunction with the neck. A neck which is poorly set on can result in it being unnatural for the horse to work in a correct shape. A bull-neck makes it uncomfortable for the horse to flex at the poll because it restricts the air-flow. A swan-neck is rather weak and tends to result in the horse being 'rubber necked', with an ability to bring his head very high, and invariably into the rider's face! The head itself should not be too big for balance reasons, and the horse should have an intelligent expression. From the bitting angle, the jaw formation is something to notice: it is important that its structure permits the comfortable accommodation of a bit in his mouth. We once had a horse with a malformed lower jaw, with teeth growing in unusual places, and he was always very difficult to bit. A horse will obviously never accept the bit without resistance if he is in perpetual discomfort. Although malformations of the jaw are relatively uncommon, horses do vary in the size and shape of their jaw and it is important to find a correctly fitting bit.

Scope of movement is one of the prime factors in the determination of a good horse and this depends, to a large extent, on the angle of the horse's shoulder. As vital as the shoulder, though, is the amount of freedom at the elbow. This freedom of movement is paramount, for if the horse is tied in at the elbow, he will be unable to lengthen his stride sufficiently. However much drive the horse produces, there must be room for action, and if the horse is restricted in his elbow room, he will never have the necessary agility and scope.

It will be noticed that the appraisal of the front leg has been left until last, whereas from a soundness viewpoint, the first adage is 'No foot, no horse', and this always refers to the front feet. From the training aspect it is the hindlegs which are important, for it is they which create propulsion (the lack of which causes problems), but the front leg does take sixty per cent of the standing weight of the horse. A poor front leg is unlikely in itself to cause a horse to be stiff or resistant, but related problems stemming from a poor shoulder, bad feet or upright pasterns, can cause discomfort from concussion and jarring. The physical training problems are connected in virtually all instances with the horse not using himself behind, either in his back or his hocks, or being stiff in his muscles. Soreness in his feet, front legs or shoulders will show up in a horse's reluctance to stride out and jump, particularly any fence with a drop. The problems incurred in the front leg are therefore veterinary ones – damaged tendons, fetlocks or foot trouble – caused by the rigours of eventing or competing in general. If the horse does not carry himself on his hocks, then the strain of the extra weight on his forelegs can aggravate any potential damage. Obviously, it is better to avoid buying a horse with a very weak front leg, as there is nothing more disappointing than putting hours of work into a horse for him only to let you down at the crucial moment by going lame. Having said that, many horses cope with eventing with poor front legs and the best of forelegs can suffer from problems. Getting the horse properly fit can be the key to avoiding many troubles, but all too often a strained tendon is in fact caused by a knock, which is either not noticed, or not treated, and which will then develop into a 'leg'. Many people worry about 'bone', or lack of it, in a horse, the measurement being taken around the cannon bone and tendons immediately below the knee. We did an interesting experiment one day by sending our working pupils round the yard with a tape-measure, asking them to measure the bone of all the horses in the yard. It was fascinating to compare the actual measurements of all the various horses: in some cases the inches sounded impressive, and yet when compared with the horse concerned, there was not sufficient bone in comparison with body size, and, similarly, some horses which had good front legs measured comparatively small. *The Irish Stallion Guide* lists bone and girth size of each stallion, which sounds a good idea, but we were told in strong words by a very good Yorkshire dealer that it was not representative, and having done this little test ourselves, we were able to understand why he said what he did! The size of bone is dependent upon how heavily 'topped' the horse is (his body to 'bone' ratio), and also the length and quality of bone.

Good conformation must be associated with good movement. When assessing a horse's action, study carefully the walk, as this will normally reflect all his other paces. In order to be a good mover, the horse must be athletic and vice versa. By good, it is not meant that he should have a great, long, low action with no bend in the knee, even if this should make him the most blissfully comfortable ride. Watching the horse move, he should have a stride with plenty of spring in it, with a good hock flexion and also some knee action. If the horse does not naturally bend his knee in his basic movement, then he will find it difficult to bend his knee when he jumps, and certainly he will never be very 'sharp in front' – i.e. he will not 'snap' his front legs over a fence. The problems associated with this will be covered in detail in the jumping chapters. A rolling action is to be avoided, as this invariably means that the horse is not pushing from behind, although, of course, with training this can be improved; a straight action is preferable as it indicates that the horse is propelling himself straight forward. Although dishing to a small degree will not cause training problems, it is unsightly for the dressage judge sitting at C, and can present difficulties in lateral work. We have found that the slightly pigeon-toed horse is far quicker in front than the splay-footed horse, who is prone to be 'flat-footed'. The overall impression created when the horse moves should be one of agility, activity, athleticism, power and yet lightness of foot. If a horse is heavy on his feet, he will lack the sharpness necessary for speedy reactions. Cast your mind back to your school days, and those games lessons: it was always quite obvious from the general movements around the schoolroom, and the physique of the classmates, who was going to be good at games, and who was not. By studying horses, it will soon become apparent which will have a chance of making a top-class horse, and which will be average or below.

The one aspect which nobody can tell in advance is aptitude – in the schoolgirl's case, how hard she is prepared to work at games, and how much she enjoys it. Exactly the same attitude is necessary in a horse, but bravery comes into account too in the case of jumping, and in eventing in particular. Bravery can easily be abused, and by indiscreet riding, or an unfortunate accident, this confidence can easily be destroyed. It is then questionable whether the horse will ever regain his original faith either in the rider or his own ability.

Horses come in all shapes and sizes, but closer analysis of the top-class horses reveals that their engineering is invariably as near perfect as it is possible to get. There are horses who possess excellent conformation who are disappointing performers because of their lack of mental competitiveness; conversely, there are horses whose mental attitude and 'heart' compensate for their physical defects. As already stated, the horse's physique should suggest power, agility and an honest outward-looking personality. Temperament plays a big part in a horse's performance, but a willingness to please is further enhanced by correct training and an understanding attitude on the part of his rider. A horse's character depends a lot on his physical ability and it cannot be stressed strongly enough that the easy horse to train will be the one who understands what he is being asked, and who finds his work well within his capabilities, and therefore enjoyable. For example, if he is asked to perform a ten-metre circle before his muscles are sufficiently supple, he will swing his quarters, lose his rhythm, or resist in his mouth, and will then associate that movement – and possibly dressage generally – with discomfort. He cannot tell you in words that something hurts, so he will show you in other ways that he is unable to do what is being asked of him, and if he is an honest horse, he usually becomes upset and tense. If a person was made to touch his toes first thing in the morning, without being given a chance to loosen up, he would probably react in a very violent way! A bad-back sufferer might well understand just why a horse will complain when he is asked to perform similar exercises. Direct flexion is demanding the same movement from the spine as toe-touching does for humans (*see*

**3 A comparison between toe-touching and direct flexion** — *both demand the same longitudinal stretch from the spine*

diagram 3). After many years of 'grinning and bearing' pain in my own back, I really thought it was time that I consulted a specialist. Basically, I have lost the cushioning between a couple of my vertebrae and I was given the choice between an operation to fuse them (the chances of success being far too slim to my mind), and a programme of swimming to build up the muscles either side of my spine in order to strengthen it enough to compensate for the damage inside. Initially I swam every day for about twenty minutes, and now I maintain my fitness by swimming about twice a week. Although my back is still far from pain-free, I am able to live a very energetic and active life, and therefore I see no reason why, by strengthening a horse's back, he should not be able to cope as well.

Although it is not only discomfort in the back that can cause a horse to be 'temperamental', back problems are very common and are caused by many factors. First, the horse was never designed to be ridden, and placing a relatively heavy weight on his back, usually at an immature age before the horse is fully developed, can only cause strain. Secondly, badly fitting saddles and pressure from rollers add to the complication. . . . And then there is always the risk of damage from a fall. Watching some of the bad falls, it always strikes me as a miracle that more severe damage is not suffered. We always have our horses checked over by our veterinary surgeon should they have a fall, or even 'lose their back-end' over a fence in a way that could cause damage to their back. We feel that it is a wise precaution, just in case there is an injury which is not immediately visible or apparent; we are well aware of the cost, but feel that our horses are of such value to us, and the demands we place on them so great, that it is the correct action to take. Far better to treat the horse for a minor problem than to carry on working, only to exacerbate the condition and to necessitate a long rest, or even to cause permanent damage.

The controversial subject of conformation can be discussed *ad infinitum*, but of course if there were concrete rules for the perfect horse, then showing would no longer exist, for the horses would always be in the same order of merit in the ring. The discrepancies, arguments and endless discussions created by different judges only make the subject more fascinating and interesting for everyone, both competitor and spectator. It does sometimes appear to be a monopoly at the top of the showing world, but there will always be one judge who will be brave enough to stick his neck out and cause a sensation by completely reversing 'form'. That really does cause a stir! As a judge, I know that it is *your* opinion on the day that counts, and it is up to the individual to be honest and courageous in his opinion and not be swayed by popular belief.

In this chapter the various conformation defects which can adversely affect the competition horse have been mentioned, but of course there is always the exception to make us all swallow our words. It is these instances which show that a narrow-minded approach to a horse's make and shape is altogether wrong, and every horse being different, that it is possible to learn a little from every one. Also, in order to give every horse a fair chance, never be a horsy snob! John and I had bought a horse called Danby Wiske in Yorkshire as a hairy five-year-old, with only hunting experience behind him, and he was therefore 'green broke' (as the Americans so beautifully put it). He was inspected by the Pony Club B test fraternity, and when they had all assessed him, they decided that he would be adequate for hunting and a little Pony Club work; the following year he represented GB in the Junior European Championships at Rotherfield Park with his owner Clair Sankey! He was never the speediest, but his jumping ability, courage and athleticism compensated for his lack in that respect. So, never sweep aside a horse just because he does not instantly strike you as being impressive. Always analyse the levers, the physical strength and agility before casting him aside as a no-hoper.

Correct conformation in a horse is something which can only be appreciated after many years of study, and even then it does not necessarily mean that just anyone will be able to understand fully what they are looking for in a well-put-together horse. I do strongly believe that there is such a thing as an 'eye for a horse', and I think that this can be described as an artistic appreciation or a feeling for the right attributes in a horse's make-up. I know many people who will tell you that they know a horse which is beautifully put together – the perfect stamp to go eventing – and when you eventually see this animal, it is conformationally so incorrect that not only will it have no chance of becoming a very successful competition horse, but it will also be most unlikely to jump with any ability whatsoever. It is so very difficult to explain to someone who cannot 'see' exactly why this particular horse is not made the right way, for they obviously cannot see the defects which may be very subtle. The blatant defects, such as curbs or a long back, can be seen by all, but it is the total symmetry and mechanical leverage of the hindquarters and hindlegs which are so difficult to explain to someone who does not really understand what they are looking for, someone who does not have the 'feel'. This is why I say that one of the best ways of learning the mechanics of conformation is to study hard the top-class horse in any field of competition, and try to assimilate all the details which explain exactly why that horse is so talented; study the symmetry, the angles and the general impression, and also look for any defects. Learn from these horses that it is still possible to be highly successful in spite of faults. This is when judging becomes very difficult, as it is always easy to find the winners in the class, but it is deciding between various lesser evils in the minor placed horses which is so hard. I love to look at any picture of a well-put-together horse, whether it be Thoroughbred or otherwise, as these horses are so difficult to find and one must appreciate them when you see them. One cannot ever beat quality, and the sight of a beautifully built Thoroughbred which is strong, fit and well is a vision really to pull at the heart-strings!

However, having said that, bear in mind the old saying, 'All that glisters is not gold.' But also remember one of my dear Grandmother's favourite expressions which I find springs to mind so often (and not just in connection with horses!), 'You can't make a silk purse out of a sow's ear.' How very true!

TWO

# *Blueprint*

Before moving on to the problems experienced in training the horse, it is important to make clear exactly what the aim of training should be. What precisely is the rider hoping to achieve from his horse?

The goal of any rider in the training of his horse must be to produce a horse who is completely and instantaneously obedient to the rider's aids. Most people, when asked what they are aiming for, will say that they want a well-balanced and supple horse with a good mouth. I am in complete agreement, for in order for a horse to carry out his rider's commands at the precise moment that they are given, he HAS to be extremely well-balanced and very supple. It must never be forgotten that the horse only resists when he is unable to perform – at that exact moment – what is being asked of him. For example, to ask a horse to turn and jump a fence from a gallop and then to turn immediately afterwards, requires maximum balance, suppleness and agility, and unless the horse has been trained to cope with these situations he is going to be incapable of responding correctly. I am sure the reader can picture in his mind the untrained horse asked such a demanding question: the horse with head high in the air and mouth wide open, taking great sweeping turns both into and away from the fence and the rider with a somewhat desperate expression on his face! This horse's behaviour has little to do with his mouth; it is a result of the horse's lack of training which would enable him to adjust his balance quickly, carrying his weight on his hocks. The way that he shows this gap in his education is in his mouth – by being unresponsive to the rider's aids and trying to free his head and neck in order to balance himself. So, it should be the target of schooling to produce a horse with the lightest and most responsive of reactions to the rider's aids. Obedience in a horse can be enjoyed in whatever activity in which the horse is partaking, and merely enhances the pleasure: the happy horse is the obedient horse as the happy dog is the obedient dog. With obedience comes total trust and respect – again from both sides – and, as with any animal, this mutual harmony cannot be won by bullying or aggression but by patient yet firm treatment. Having had no children of my own, I perhaps have no right to speak with authority on the subject of raising them, but, from an outsider's point of view, it does strike me that the happiest children are the ones who receive firm discipline from their parents, yet are not ruled with an oppressive rod of iron, which only seems to provoke rebellion at a later stage. We all know how obnoxious the thoroughly spoilt child can be, so one must obviously strike the happy medium to obtain respect without fear. Fear can easily lead to anger in any species of animal, whether it be from an inherent fear of something or an acquired fear created by another species: a cowardly, repressed Alsatian, for example, is an animal to beware of, as I have learnt to my cost! With this in mind, I do not deal with vice in this book apart from to mention that if a horse is going forward from the leg in an obedient and happy manner there is no cause or opportunity for him to nap. Nappiness stems either from naughtiness, which infers disobedience, or from nerves, in which case the horse has been pushed too quickly in his training. The reasons behind the nappiness – which may take the form of bucking, rearing or jibbing – must be understood before the rider can deal with it and the answer to disciplining the horse is rarely a big stick but firm, correct riding.

So, having determined exactly what is required from the horse, the question remains of how to achieve this standard of training. The initial schooling steps are precisely the same for whatever activity the horse is required to do (be it hunting, dressage, or eventing), but variations will occur in the final stages of his training in a specific discipline, the more technical demands only becoming apparent at this higher standard. If the basics are sound and correct, the continuation of training to more advanced levels should run smoothly: it is most commonly the case that problems encountered at a later stage are the result of some fault which has either passed unnoticed or been ignored in the early phases of training.

When I am training a horse, I tend to divide his progress into six stages of basic training, with the goal being self-carriage. The length of time it takes to reach each stage depends upon the individual horse, and provided that the horse is working in an established manner in one stage, he may then be worked towards the next one. There is no exact moment when the horse passes from one stage to another so the process of moving through the stages will be a gradual progression. Until each stage has been firmly established within the training routine, it is not possible to proceed to the next stage without coming across a problem later on. There are no short-cuts, remember, so the correct foundations laid down in schooling are vital. Provided the foundations of self-carriage are correct, the progression, through advanced training, to collection should present no major problems, and this book concentrates on laying this ground work.

It is necessary at times to ask the horse to work a little harder and, in so doing, he may be asked to try to move on to the next stage, if only to assist in the achievement of the preceding one. This is perfectly acceptable, as long as the horse does not resent the extra work in such a way as to make it obvious that he really is not ready to move on – by becoming upset and tense. Within a schooling session, ten minutes gentle persuasion asking the horse to progress a little cannot do any harm.

These six stages of training apply to any horse, whether newly broken or in the process of being re-schooled, and they also set the pattern for a schooling session, forming the order for warming up too. Once the pattern has been absorbed and understood, the endless ever-decreasing circles and the feeling of 'Well now, what should we do now?' should have been ousted by a process of schooling with a more definite goal.

In the compilation of the stages of training, I have borne in mind the fact that the horse is to perform as a complete athlete, and therefore that every schooling session must be thought of in terms of aerobic bend-and-stretch exercises. Picture an athlete limbering up before his particular race, and that is what we must try to reproduce in the horse: each stage of this limbering-up session must be progressive, gradually introducing the more demanding exercises (*see* diag. 4, p. 14). This is, in effect, the same as schooling. Schooling does not necessarily mean correction, but covers the working and exercising of the muscles in preparation for concentrated effort: as will be shown in detail as each stage is discussed, the exercises do all follow each other in a logical warm-up sequence. Going back to the human athlete, he does not spend hours preparing himself for exertion, but long enough to loosen up all his muscles in order that he may use them to maximum efficiency. If he allowed this period to become too long, he would begin to utilise energy which he will need for the demanding time ahead. Obviously the exact time required for warming up varies for every person and every horse, and this is where knowing one's horse is crucial. For example, any horse which is prone to 'tying up' or which has ever shown signs of azoturia should always be warmed up very gradually and he should have at least twenty minutes walking with perhaps some gentle trotting before he is asked to work. This primes the muscles for the work ahead by loosening them up and so making cramp less likely. The workload for this type of horse must always be increased

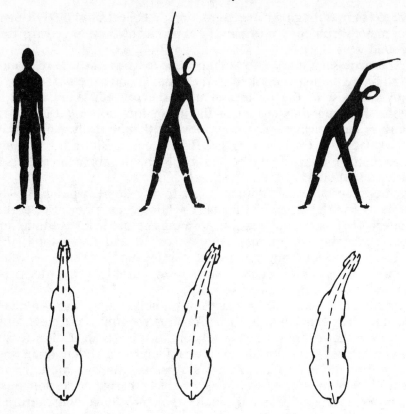

**4 A comparison between human limbering-up exercises and indirect flexion in the horse** — *in both cases the body is stretched laterally, and increasingly so, as it warms up*

gradually as any exertion when the horse is unfit will cause him to tie up.

If the horse is not given enough preparatory work he will not give of his best, but the same will be true if he is overworked. A little exuberance will give the horse added presence and elevation in his dressage test whereas, if he goes 'over the top', he will appear listless and, despite an accurate and obedient test, he will not gain such good marks as the horse with some spark: the horse who performs his tests happily with ears pricked will always score more marks than the miserable animal with ears back and a dull or resentful expression. My ideal warming-up time before a dressage test is probably between thirty and forty-five minutes. This time also applies to an actual schooling session, or to work preceding jumping either at home or competitively. Provided that the horse has been schooled at home in a disciplined manner and is used to his regular 'work-out' period, he should be quite conditioned to concentrating for that length of time. Horses are very much creatures of habit, and this we can use to our advantage in training them. If your horse is used to being allowed to play around for the first ten minutes of his schooling sessions, then this will become an annoying habit which will appear even more frustrating on the day of a competition. By all means allow the horse to be exuberant, as presumably this proves that he is happy to be ridden; but channel his energy into something worthwhile, such as medium trot or an improved springy rhythm, so that he is being taught a lesson at the same time. After all, your ultimate aim is to produce and contain energy, so the fact that the horse is producing his own energy can be enjoyed by the rider, who in turn can reward the horse by allowing him to utilise this energy in a productive fashion – rather than hanging on for dear life and praying for the horse to settle down! The older horse who understands discipline will probably benefit from a hack at walk to limber him up before schooling, but on the whole I am against the practice of taking a horse out for a hack prior to a schooling session in order to 'calm him down a bit'. To my mind, this shows a lack of proper discipline in training, and indeed may only make matters more difficult for the rider: on a hack he will be travelling in straight lines, his muscles will not be stretched in the required way, and he will probably come home rather fatigued and tight; this may make the horse even more reluctant to work than he was before. It is far better to put him on the lunge instead, where he is asked to work in a round shape, within the terms of discipline, and where he can use his exuberance to a beneficial end. His muscles can loosen up without the weight of the rider to cause any tenseness. At a competition this is even more helpful as normally the rider is somewhat nervous and tight (you know the feeling – when the limbs seem to lose all co-ordination and strength!), and of course the horse, who is feeling much the same, will take advantage of this in a very big way! After fifteen minutes or so on the lunge with side-reins of a length to keep the horse in a longish outline, both horse and rider should be in a more relaxed frame of mind to work together in a harmonious manner. I have found this method to be the most successful, but, even so, the total length of time involved would probably not exceed forty-five minutes. Particularly at a one-day event, there is not enough time to spend hours riding in, especially if more than one horse is to be ridden, and a long journey is involved. Also I like to feel that I will still have plenty of petrol in the tank at the end of the cross-country and if the horse has already had about two hours' work, he is bound to feel somewhat weary, unless he is super fit, in which case he may be too fit for a one-day event. Whatever you do, train and condition the horse to a set time pattern, and there should be no problem, as horses enjoy a regular routine.

Before we progress any further I would like to say a few words on the subject of martingales. A martingale is an artificial aid and when correctly fitted may be of benefit at certain times. Any martingale should only come into effect when the horse raises his head to such an extent that the rider experiences loss of control. If fitted any tighter than this a martingale will be restrictive, while, if it is fitted any looser, it will be of no practical use. The standing martingale is not allowed under BHS or FEI rules for either eventing or show-jumping, and its use has become less fashionable. It may be useful helping to control a young horse, and it provides the rider with the all-important neck-strap to grab. It will also protect the rider's face from injury should the horse fling its head up; but it cannot be termed a cure for this problem as the horse will still throw his head but within the restriction of the martingale. Its advantage is that there is no attachment to the rein which means it does not alter the rider's contact, but it may restrict the freedom of the horse's neck, particularly when jumping.

The Market Harborough falls into the category of a 'short-cut aid' by forcing the horse into a shape, causing him to tighten in his neck and back, not permitting him to stretch. It does not, to my mind, have a place in the training of horses.

The Irish martingale holds the reins together under the horse's neck to prevent both reins ending up on the same side of the neck should the horse peck after a fence or buck violently. (This is an alarming feeling, I remember, as I cast my mind back to one occasion with a horse that wore no martingale!) The drawback of an Irish martingale is that, by keeping the reins together, it does not permit the rider to open his inside hand for turning.

The running martingale is most widely used and accepted as, for much of the time, it is redundant and only comes into action if the horse raises his head so far that the rider loses control. It is used as a prevention and a precaution; it does not restrict the freedom of the horse's head and neck; and it has the added advantage of keeping the reins either side of the horse's neck in an emergency. Some people feel that it does at times break the direct contact between horse and rider, and in so doing may jeopardise the balance of the horse landing awkwardly over a fence. One danger of it arises if a horse catches hold of one of the rings or straps of the running martingale, as he will quite likely panic and sometimes even rear over backwards. A bib martingale, where the two straps are connected by a triangular piece of leather, will lessen the chances of this happening, but this has the same drawback as the Irish martingale.

There are points both for and against the use of a martingale, but, broadly speaking, we would use no martingale for flat work, although we would advocate the use of a breastplate as a safeguard for keeping the saddle in place. We might use a running martingale on a fresh or young horse for additional control and a neck-strap to grab in anxious moments. We advise the use of a running martingale for jumping, fitted only as a precaution; the martingale will rarely come into play, but will act as a reminder should the horse momentarily try to evade hand and leg. Some horses may resist still further if they feel the restriction of the martingale, a situation often caused initially by an over-tightly fitted martingale. Whether a martingale is employed or not depends on the individual horse and preference of the rider and is often a matter of trial and error. Martingales will rarely be mentioned again in this book: remember that they may help in the short-run, but are not curing any basic problem which will only be improved by training. It is similar to a seat-belt in a car which we all hope we will never need, but which will not stop the driver crashing the car!

I will now move on to the sequence of stages, and having covered all the stages, I will give some examples of typical schooling sessions first on the flat and then incorporating some jumping exercises. Flat work and jumping go hand in hand. Exactly the same principles apply, but any faults already existing on the flat will be exaggerated when jumping. It is safe to say that virtually all problems associated with jumping originate from incorrect basic flat work, which is why it is so vital that the initial ground work is thorough and correct. I am not saying, though, that the horse cannot be asked to start jumping before he can go perfectly on the flat. The horse can only achieve this perfection by learning to carry himself in a balanced way, and this takes practice over all types of terrain, and over all kinds of obstacles.

The initial ground work consists of stages 1 to 4 and these are the stages that are constantly retraced in the re-schooling of the horse. All through the book it will be seen how I emphasise the importance of maintaining these stages: if they are correct the subsequent stages of training will happen almost automatically.

### 1. Calmness

This can be one of the most difficult stages, particularly in an older horse. The young horse, provided that he has accepted the rider in the saddle, is normally far more phlegmatic about his schooling as he has not yet been exposed to the exciting aspects of life, and all he knows is being ridden quietly, having been lunged and backed in familiar surroundings, either in a manège or a field which he has grown to trust as an environment. The older horse has probably been 'out and about' and learnt how exciting life can be at a show, or in the hunting field, or whatever aspect of life to which he has been subjected. In exposing a horse to 'outside interests' we are stimulating his mind enormously, and many horses do find it very difficult to cope with this. It is very important, in my opinion, that the young horse is really quite obedient to the aids before he is allowed to go to a show, or hunting, so that, even if he does find it all too exciting, he is sufficiently responsive to the aids that the rider can still control him, teaching him that even if he is excited, he must still do as he is told. This may sound easier said than done, for trying to control a large, very enthusiastic horse is not easy, but it is a great deal more difficult – nigh impossible – if he is totally uneducated.

If the horse is rather fresh, nervous or excited, the easiest way to obtain calmness is to occupy his mind by giving him exercises to do, such as circles, changes of direction and/or transitions, so that he starts to concentrate on what the rider is asking him to do rather than on his own ideas. The rider's voice is an invaluable assistant in many ways, both to encourage the horse forward and to soothe him. It can be of enormous help as an extra aid, and is never more helpful than in moments of potential crisis – the little click when jumping a fiddly fence, just to make the horse realise that he must keep going forward, or otherwise a firm 'Whoa' when the rider is experiencing difficulty in slowing down. Depending on the occasion, the voice must be sometimes authoritative, and other times just a steadying influence. Lungeing obviously trains the horse to respond to the voice aids, as does any loose work, and this response must be maintained throughout the horse's training, so that he learns to keep the habit of listening to his rider. I had a fall cross-country one day with a horse whom we had broken ourselves, and who was very responsive to the voice. It was only as he was galloping across the field towards home, and Clair Sankey (who was with us as a pupil at the time) called out, 'Whoa boy, whoa Paddy' or some such similar words, that we realised just how responsive he was. He stopped dead, and allowed Clair just to walk up and catch him! I am not saying that there are many horses who would do that, or even that if the same thing happened again, he would do it a second time, but it is worth trying at least.

In order to obtain stage 1, and so progress onwards, it is sometimes necessary to ask for stages 2, 3 and 4 to make him relax and settle to his work.

The main reason for the horse to be calm, is that he must be relaxed in his muscles. If he is tense or excited, then the muscles will be rigid, and because the main muscles are all connected with the back, it will be impossible for him to be supple enough to carry out the aerobic and athletic exercises absolutely necessary for training.

## 2. Free Forward Movement

With the newly-broken horse, once he has decided that he has no intentions of immediately removing the rider, free forward movement is the beginning of his real education. As those of you who have been involved in breaking horses will know only too well, the last thing in a youngster's mind is to go forward. It requires very enthusiastic, strong riding to get most newly-ridden horses going at all: they weave around with no idea where they are supposed to go once they are free from the security of the lunge and the rider has to be very positive in his riding to give the horse encouragement and confidence to carry on round the school on his own. A horse is a herd animal, and to be on his own is a most unnatural thing for him, and therefore, as trainers, we must never forget this very important aspect, particularly when the horse shows signs of insecurity. We must always reassure him in a firm way that what he is being asked to do, or where he is being asked to go, is perfectly safe for him, and that he must trust his rider. It is in the horse's earliest stages of training that he is likely to exhibit signs of fear and lack of confidence. If, during this time, he is misunderstood and, as a result, dealt with in either too harsh or too lenient a manner, troubles in the form of napping or severe hanging can develop. It is so very important that he learns always to think forwards, and to be responsive to the rider's driving leg. This driving leg must be a distinct aid from the rider. In any upward transition or forward aid the rider's leg should be on the girth, and vibrating slightly to encourage the horse to move forwards, while the rider's hand must allow the motion to flow forwards and not restrict it in any way. The downward transition aid is a different leg aid, in that it is a 'dead' squeeze with the leg, to drive the horse's hocks underneath him, so that he can slow himself down by using his hocks and hindquarters. These two leg aids must be clearly different for the horse to be able to differentiate between the two commands. If, during a downward transition, the horse slows down too abruptly, the leg can squeeze and vibrate simultaneously in order to drive the horse forward in his transition. He will soon learn which leg aid is which by voice association. If he ignores the upward aid, give a little click as you nudge; if he ignores that, squeeze again, giving him a smart tap with your whip just behind your leg, so that he associates the nudge or squeeze with a reprimand if he does not obey it. The aid should be definite and momentary: if the pressure of the rider's leg is just gradually increased when the horse does not respond, it will merely have a deadening effect. If necessary, the leg should be taken off and re-applied. Try to avoid a 'nagging' with the leg, however, because the horse will soon start to ignore this – use the nudge–click–smack method to prevent that. The very green horse, of course, has no idea what is needed from him at all, and it will take time for him to understand the rider's leg, but with the assistance of the person in the middle, who has been lungeing him using his voice and holding the lunge whip if need be, and helped by the rider's voice too, the horse will soon associate voice aids with leg aids. The speed with which a horse can learn is very rewarding, but this can also work against the trainer, for it also means that he will pick up incorrect habits just as quickly. Needless to say, this should be avoided if at all possible. Although the horse is infinitely stronger than we are, our brain is (we hope!) superior, and it is up to us to anticipate how the horse will react in a certain situation and prevent his response, rather than wait for a resistance and then try to cure it.

Once the young horse is sufficiently obedient to the basic aids to be taken out for rides, to encourage him to go forward will become far easier. The company of another horse will give him more courage and he will learn to enjoy being ridden out. Hunting experience will enhance this enthusiasm, but as I have already stated, it is important to ensure that his education will not be hindered by taking him out hunting before he is sufficiently obedient to the aids. If he is taken hunting too soon, he may be quite uncontrollable, thus proving a hazard not only to himself and his rider, but to other people as well. It is far better to risk the chance of boredom at home (although this is more in the rider's mind than the horse's!) than to expose the horse to stimulants with which he may not be able to cope at this stage. We always prefer to take our young horses to a couple of shows – preferably indoor – before exposing them to the delights of the hunting field. Although the first show can prove exciting to them, after they have jumped a couple of rounds, or done a dressage test, they cease to find it all so thrilling, and settle down quite quickly. The number of other horses cantering around usually causes some excitement but, if the horse gets accustomed to this hubbub at shows, the number of horses encountered out hunting does not seem quite so mind-boggling. There is time at a show to ride the horse in until he has settled – i.e. setting the pattern for the future, and teaching him that however excited he may be, he will have to settle and behave sensibly – whereas out hunting standing around at the meet is not ideal, and although a long hack to the meet will tire him, this does not necessarily improve matters – often, the more tired the horse becomes, the sillier he behaves, as he has not yet learnt to cope with the situation of aching muscles. These aching muscles can make him appear more excited, in the same way that children become hyper-active when they are very tired.

It is amazing to notice the improvement in the forward-thinking attitude of a horse once he has been to a show. All of a sudden, it seems that the horse realises that there is a purpose to being ridden, and is much keener to 'go somewhere' than worry about what the rider is doing. Some horses do take a long time before they are able to concentrate on other things and are perpetually looking backwards at their rider: by taking him to shows and then hunting, you will give him something else to think about, and his fear of and interest in the rider's changing weight will seem quite trivial in such varied surroundings. To subject the young horse to the rigours of a collecting ring full of horses jumping, or the hassle of the hunting field is wonderful experience. It progresses his education by leaps and bounds and although it is possible to bring on horses without these outside influences, it certainly does speed up the process quite considerably – they suddenly seem to 'grow-up'.

Most people are aware of the necessity to make a young horse go forward in a positive way, but often lose sight of this important aspect once the horse has progressed a little way in his training. Unfortunately, thinking that they must 'get their horse on the bit', they stop riding forward and end up 'collecting' the horse up from the front. This promotes endless problems both on the flat and particularly later on over fences. (These will be covered at length in the sections which follow.) Whatever standard rider and horse have attained in their training, this vital stage of free forward movement must be established before any more serious demands are made.

### 3.  Rhythm

This follows on quite logically from the free forward movement. Once the horse is moving forward from the leg, he must be taught to maintain a rhythmical stride in whatever pace he is working. We aim to achieve this firstly in trot, because trot is the easiest pace in which to learn rhythm – it is only two-time, so he just has to swing along from diagonal to diagonal. At the same time, by changing the rein and changing diagonal we can develop his muscles evenly. Also, we can ride the horse forward most strongly in the rising trot, as our body is slightly inclined forward, thus urging him onwards. The canter, being three-time, is the next pace to concentrate on, although it is interesting to note how the rhythm of the canter improves automatically as the rhythm of the trot improves. The horse's walk is by far the most difficult pace to work on, and is best left as natural as possible. The walk is all too easily spoilt – if the rider shortens the stride, or the horse tenses and tends therefore to jog. The walk is best worked at out on a ride as the horse is more likely to stride out then in a relaxed manner. Nonetheless, some work should be done at walk, but with the emphasis being on the rhythm and light contact with the horse's mouth, so there is no danger of the horse shortening his natural stride.

By ensuring that a steady rhythm is maintained throughout the movements carried out, we are teaching the horse to balance himself, and use his hocks. In order to execute a circle in rhythm, the horse must use his hocks to control his pace, thereby keeping his balance: here, already, is the beginning of the lesson in the use of the hindleg. So, at this stage, the horse is merely required to carry out simple exercises in the school, maintaining his free forward movement and, at the same time, keeping an even rhythm throughout. The more naturally balanced horse will find keeping the rhythm far easier than the poorer moving horse, and the rider must be very positive in his riding to encourage the horse to obtain the objective. In the pursuance of a good rhythm, circles, changes of rein and transitions should be practised, to accustom the horse to altering his balance in order to carry himself and his rider. The effect of the rider's weight upon the horse is to make him feel that he is going to fall down onto his nose at any moment (*see* diagram 5). His weight-carrying ratio is altered, and it is only by bringing his centre of balance further back – i.e. by carrying his weight on his back end, or, as it is termed, 'on his hocks' – that he can adjust his carrying capacity . . . and thence gain mobility and agility. We all know how a heavy knapsack can

**5  The effect of the rider's weight on the horse's balance**

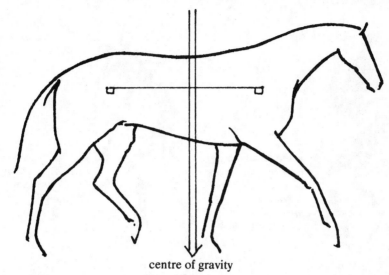

centre of gravity

a  *naturally balanced, hocks stepping under the body*

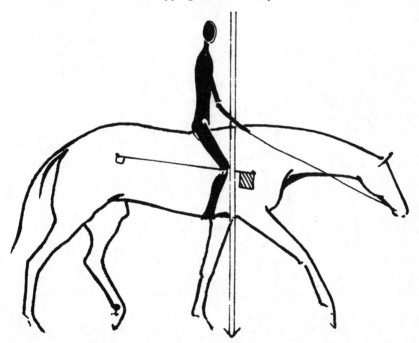

b  *with the addition of the rider, the forehand is carrying more weight and the hocks are trailing*

**6  A comparison between the weight-bearing techniques of the human and the horse**

a  *if the burden is not over the centre of gravity and the back is hollow it is very difficult and uncomfortable to carry*

b  *it is much easier to carry a weight over the natural centre of gravity*

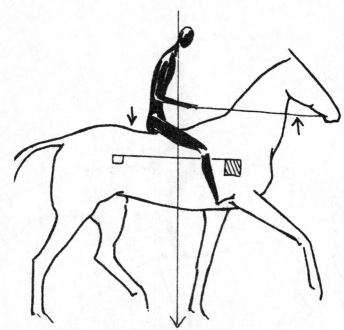

centre of gravity moved forward

c  *if the rider is sitting too far back and is not in balance, his apparent weight is heavier than his actual weight and the horse resists by hollowing his back. The horse remains on his forehand, although the rider is behind the centre of gravity: his head is up, his back hollow and his hocks are trailing*

greatly affect our balance until we adjust ourselves to it, yet the horse has the added complication; our weight moves on his back, and sometimes out of balance (*see* diagram 6)!

Trotting poles are valuable in helping the horse improve his rhythm. The trotting poles make the horse lift his legs a little higher, and maintain an even stride at the same time. This obviously makes the hocks more active for a few strides at least, and trying to maintain this impulsion around the school helps in the attempt to find an established steady rhythm. Indeed, trotting poles are of great benefit throughout training as they make the horse use himself, forcing him to stretch and become more supple. Later on in his training, the horse can be made to trot over raised trotting poles. The poles can be raised a few inches quite easily by using two pieces of planking with notches cut in at the requisite distance of about 1.5

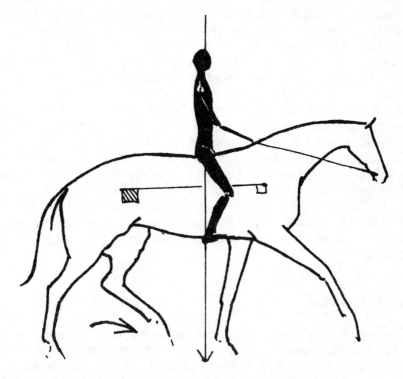

7 **The readjustment of the horse's centre of gravity to maintain balance, mobility and agility** — *as the hocks step further under the horse's body, the hindquarters carry more weight and his centre of gravity moves back to resume its natural position. The horse's back rounds upwards to meet the rider's weight.*

metres (4½ – 5 feet). The extra height really makes the horse work hard, as he has to lift his legs quite high in order to clear the poles. The horse should maintain his rhythm and stretch a little in his outline, but not too much, as all he is being asked to do is lift his legs higher, not make the shape of jumping a fence. Trotting poles are designed to assist in establishing rhythm by improving the pushing and carrying capacity of the hocks, but if the horse stretches his neck in an exaggerated fashion, he will shift his weight too far onto his forehand. However, he must be allowed to lengthen and round his outline and so stretch the muscles over his back (*see* diag. 7, p. 25). To encourage the horse to bring his hocks underneath him, and to round his back, the rider should be in rising trot over the poles, or even stand up in the stirrups. Unless the horse is advanced in his training and very strong in his back, and therefore able to cope with the rider's weight, a sitting trot over poles will probably cause him to hollow and tense his back muscles in his efforts to clear the poles, rather than to round and use the muscles. An interesting exercise to test this theory is to trot for several minutes standing up in your stirrups from a rising trot when out on road-work and then resume rising; it is incredible how much the horse's back will have raised itself during the respite. This is noticeable even with older horses, and it is a good idea to give every horse a break from the rider's weight when on long exercising, to allow him to round his back.

High on the list of priorities on a dressage sheet is the word rhythm, and high it must be in the rider's mind too. It matters not whether it concerns a working trot, a gallop, jumping or hacking, the horse will only be able to use himself to maximum efficiency if he learns to maintain rhythm whatever he is doing, as he will maintain his balance and be able to adjust easily as required. Rhythm and balance are key words in the correct training of horse and rider.

## 4. Straightness

This can be defined as the horse following with his hindlegs the track his front legs are tracing, whether it be on a straight line or on a circle. In other words, the horse must be straight on the straight and bent around the corners. (Another word for the bend of the horse is indirect flexion.) Imagine looking down on an electric train set on an oval track (*see* diagram 8). The wheels of the train must follow the rails, and on the corners the train appears to bend around, like a flexible tube. The horse's feet are equivalent to the

**8 A comparison between the horse and a train, with regard to maintaining a degree of straightness around a bend** — *The horse's hooves mimic the wheels of the train, as long as the hocks are working, while the muscles along the back allow him to be flexible around the corner like the train.*

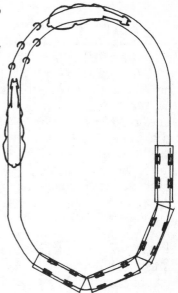

wheels of the train and the suppleness of the muscles along his back allow him to emulate the flexibility of the train on the corners. So, in order to follow the track of his front legs on a circle, the horse must bend his hocks to track up, otherwise, by trailing his hocks or swinging his quarters, he will lose the rhythm; and he must also bend around the corner, and so be supple in his back muscles. The size of the circle affects the amount of effort required from the horse to track up for, in a working trot, not only must the horse follow the shape of the track traced by the front legs, but his hind feet should actually step into the marks left by the front feet. If the horse can, at this stage, trot a 20-metre circle on each rein, going calmly but freely forward in a good rhythm, and tracking up, then the training has been correct.

Note that no mention has been made so far of the head position of the horse. This is because the head position is dependent on the placement of the hindleg, which forms stage 5. Presuming that the young horse has been correctly lunged, he should have learnt to accept the side-reins quite happily and to carry himself in a long outline on a light contact. The rider's hand should reproduce that light contact and the changing of bend and direction should prompt the horse to give in his mouth, in order to follow the rider's aids and therefore remain in a round shape: the reasons for him evading this outline will be covered in the problem chapter. For the moment, we are assuming that there are no problems in training.

A young horse does find straight lines very difficult, however, and so most of his schooling has been carried out on circles (starting with the lunge). Gradually the horse must be asked to come off the circles, and in a school he has the sides of the school to guide him. To teach him to be able to cope with straight lines in open spaces, he should be asked to go straight several feet away from the school sides, and then to do some diagonals and centre lines. Straight lines are difficult – up the centre being one of the most difficult movements – as the horse must be pushing forward equally with both hocks to maintain equilibrium. As soon as the horse stops going forward the line becomes wiggly, so again, that free forward movement is vital. The need for the horse to be supple evenly is important too – i.e. not stronger on one side than another – otherwise he will not be able to remain balanced in that straight line. He must push equally from behind and he learns to do that on circles, where each hindleg takes its turn on the inside to be the carrying leg, so strengthening its weight-bearing capacity. It is important to realise how vital it is that the horse does carry himself straight, as when the time comes to ask for medium or extended work, problems will occur if the horse does not push forward straight from behind. Similarly with jumping, he cannot jump a fence from a crooked position very easily, and if the fence is big and the horse tired, it will be impossible for him.

Rhythm is impossible if the horse is not straight, and sometimes if a difficulty in maintaining a rhythm is experienced, then straightness should be concentrated upon and it will be found that a rhythm will follow once the horse is more supple and pushing equally from behind – then the rhythm must be concentrated upon. The rider must not be tempted to think that he can move on to the next stage permanently, even if the present stage proves to be difficult. Many times must one take two steps forward only to take one step back and be patient.

Stage 4 in a horse's education is critical because it is the first time that the horse is actually asked a question. Up until this point the rider should be quite satisfied if the horse is moving forward in a good rhythm, and to the majority of horses this poses no great problem. Once the rider starts to ask the horse to bend around his corners, the rider in effect is beginning to interfere with the natural way the horse is going. It is imperative that the rider does not fall into the all-too-common trap of incorrect riding at this point. The aids must be correct otherwise problems will be created which will become only too apparent in later stages of training. I cannot stress too strongly the importance of correct riding from this stage forward.

To ask the horse to bend around a corner, the rider must use a strong inside leg with an inward action, as if he is trying to slice the horse in half with his inside leg. He must prevent the horse from swinging his quarters over with the outside leg behind the girth. The rider must be careful not to collapse the inside hip when working hard with the inside leg on a corner. If he does, then his weight will shift over onto the outside seat-bone, which will mean that the rider is not sitting in balance with the horse. The rider's weight must always be centrally placed over 'the engine' and because the inside hindleg is working harder than the outside hindleg on a corner, the rider's weight should be a little more on the inside seat-bone, and certainly not on the outside one. I do not think that one should concern oneself overmuch with theory in matters of this sort, as I believe too much theory can spoil a rider's natural riding instinct, but sitting too heavily to the outside on a corner *is* a fault to be corrected as the horse's balance can be severely affected. (A transition to canter is very dependent on the rider's weight distribution: his weight must be on the inside for the horse to be correctly balanced to strike off on the right leg. It is the same principle of weight ratio – the horse must carry extra weight on the inside hindleg in the strike-off, so the rider must retain a balance by placing extra weight on his inside seat-bone or heel. At first the horse will not understand the aid of the inside leg to canter and will either ignore the nudge or try to go faster.) The rider must insist with his inside leg, and guide him round with the inside hand, preventing him from losing his rhythm and balance with the outside hand. As the rider increases the use of the inside leg, not only is he asking for a bend, but he is also asking the horse to bring his hocks underneath him, for, as I mentioned earlier, the horse cannot bend around the track and maintain his rhythm unless he bends his hocks sufficiently to track up. We are, therefore, unwittingly asking the horse to bring his hocks underneath him. The inside leg is doing two things. On the girth it is maintaining the forward movement, thereby creating impulsion and also asking for a bend. The outside leg, behind the girth, is controlling the hindquarters, preventing them from swinging outwards. The inside hand guides and directs the horse on the circle, and therefore asks the horse to bend and also to yield in his mouth, for unless the horse gives to the feel of the rider's hand he will be resistant on the turn. The outside hand controls the forehand – it is the 'balance' rein, controlling and containing the energy created by the inside leg. Hence the expression, 'inside leg up to the outside hand' – the gathering of energy in the horse. Stage 4 is the initiation of the horse to this feeling.

Probably the most common fault to be found in riding is the use of the inside hand as a means not only of creating but also of protecting the bend, with consequently little or no contact being taken by the outside hand. This has the immediate result of a total lack of control of the forehand and, worse still, stops the forward movement completely. All too often one can see a solid inside hand, with the rider's outside hand 'wiggling' on the rein asking the horse to drop his nose. This horse will not be going forward and will have no assistance from the rider in the adjustment of his balance. A good analogy, which John thought of, to make this clear in the rider's mind, is to imagine that you are riding a horse down a long tunnel, with the reins as the tunnel walls (*see* diagram 9). The horse has no idea how long this tunnel is, nor where it is going, so the rider has to drive him along strongly, keeping him within the walls without knocking the sides of the tunnel. When a bend in the tunnel appears, the rider must guide the horse with his inside hand slightly opened, in order not to close the wall in the horse's face, and follow the line of the tunnel with the outside hand without allowing the horse to knock his shoulder on the wall. If the inside hand is crossed over, it will have the effect of shutting off the tunnel – halting the horse in its tracks, and stopping all forward movement. It is quite obvious from this example how important it is to ride up to the outside hand and not restrict with the inside hand. In the early stages of training, the inside hand may be exaggerated in its guiding line and brought inwards towards the rider's knee to encourage the horse to turn. At no point must it ever be brought backwards, otherwise again the forward movement will be stopped. If the horse proves to be very unwilling to move away from the rider's inside leg, and persists in cutting the corners, the rider may use an open outside rein to guide him into the corner, but the inside leg must be working very strongly in conjunction with the open rein, so that the horse associates bending into the corner with an aid from the leg, rather than with one from the hand. It is impossible to make the horse bend in his body by just using the hand as this will only cause him to bend in his neck (*see* diagram 10). Opening the inside hand (by which I mean moving the inside hand towards the centre of the school or circle) (*see* diag. 11, p. 32) is a good way to check whether the training is correct. If the bend is being protected by the inside hand, the horse will immediately fall in round the corners, whereas, if the bend has been created by the inside leg, the horse will retain

**9  John's Tunnel — the rider's influence on a bend**

a  *straight*        b  *right hand open —*        c  *right hand crossing*
                        *tunnel open —*               *neck — tunnel*
                        *correct bend*                *shut off*

**10  Riding the bend incorrectly — common turning faults**

a  *If the rider pulls back on the inside*        b  *If the rider closes and pulls back*
   *rein, he might turn the horse's head*            *on the inside rein, he will also twist*
   *and neck but there will be no bend*              *to the outside and will be out of*
   *through the body and the outside*                *balance. The horse will be unable*
   *shoulder will not be supported.*                 *to go forward.*
   *The rider will sit to the outside and*
   *the horse's head will tilt.*

**11 The use of the open rein to guide the horse**

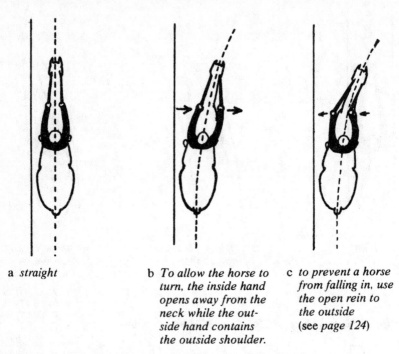

a *straight*

b *To allow the horse to turn, the inside hand opens away from the neck while the outside hand contains the outside shoulder.*

c *to prevent a horse from falling in, use the open rein to the outside (see page 124)*

*Note.* On both occasions the hands remain the same distance apart, never pulling back, and the rider's weight should be to the inside

his bend, by being contained between the inside leg and the outside hand and leg. The temptation to hold the bend with the inside hand is great, because the hand really does protect the bend, and give the impression that the horse actually is bending around the corner. However, the success of this method of cheating will only be short-lived, as the inside hand will be restricting the forward movement and so preventing the horse from bringing his inside hindleg (the main carrying leg on the turn) underneath him: this reaction will, of course, prevent progress and indeed will cause retrograde steps in the training programme.

Circles, changes of bend, serpentines and demi-voltes are all useful exercises for teaching the horse suppleness and therefore straightness. The continuation of training stems from this point. Provided the training up until now has been correct, the horse should be an obedient and pleasant ride, because he will have established a good forward rhythm and be able to maintain this while bending correctly around his corners.

## 5.   Placement of the hindleg

Note that I use the expression 'placement of the hindleg', rather than just the horse 'using his hocks'. The reason is that it is the whole of the hindleg which is necessary in the carrying capacity of the hocks. All the joints connected with the back end of the horse must be supple, strong and active. If the horse is rigid in his back, stifle or fetlock, it will have the same effect as if he is inactive in his hocks – i.e. he will be unable to carry sufficient weight on his hindquarters and hindlegs to balance himself correctly or propel himself forward. The general term for the activity of the hindquarters is 'engagement of the hocks'. Although for ease one talks of the horse using his hocks, this does not indicate to what extent they are working, so it is better to think in terms of placement of the hindleg, or how far the horse has his hocks underneath him. The further under the horse are the hocks, the more he can use them to balance himself and alter pace with maximum speed and efficiency. So, depending on the standard of training attained, the hocks should be as far under the horse in his work as is necessary for the movements he is required to perform. In order to progress from walk to trot to canter and back again, execute 20-metre circles and similar such undemanding exercises, the horse needs to use his hocks to a moderate degree. However, if he is required to perform half-passes, 10-metre circles, canter to halt transitions and similarly difficult exercises, then he must have his hocks well underneath him, and working hard. Initially the horse's hocks will be inactive and will trail, but gradually, by the schooling procedure mapped out in this chapter, the horse will learn to bring his hocks under him in order to use them for propulsion, deceleration, and exploiting their carrying capacity to improve balance. Whilst asking for the bend, the increased activity of the inside leg has also been demanding work from the hocks, and, as has already been explained, in order for the horse to be straight and rhythmical around a corner or circle, he must track up. The smaller the circle, the more he must bend his hocks to stay within the one track traced. Changes of bend in such movements as serpentines are all invaluable schooling exercises, for they cause the horse to alter the weight-bearing hindleg within two or three strides as it is the inside hindleg which carries more weight on the turn than the outside leg. As the horse has to trace a smaller track with the inside leg than with the outside one, and in order to keep in rhythm and on that track, the horse has to bend all those inside hind joints more than the outside ones. Inevitably horses find it easier to flex one way rather than another, but by the constant change of bend, the horse is asked to flex from one way to another, making him use his hindlegs alternately and making him as supple as possible.

The shoulder-in is another helpful schooling movement, and should be introduced as soon as the horse understands the fundamentals of a bend. In this movement, where the forehand is brought off the track and the hindlegs remain on it, the inside hindleg is made to work very hard by carrying even more weight as well as by having to bend throughout its length in order to keep the rhythm in the movement. To carry out this movement, the horse can be taught to move away from the rider's inside leg, first at walk and then at trot. The rider merely increases the inwards pushing motion of the inside leg, whilst guiding the horse's forehand with the outside hand, being careful not to restrict with the inside hand. A give-and-take action with the inside hand will keep the horse's head bent in the required direction − to the inside − without stopping the forward movement. An opened inside rein will prevent any inclination on the rider's behalf to protect the bend with the hand. The rider will then have to use his leg very strongly to obtain the required response from the horse. This movement can be carried out in either rising or sitting trot − start in rising and then progress to sitting. (In the early stages of training, sitting should be avoided as the horse will not be strong enough to cope with the rider's weight, and as a result will become tense in his back muscles and drop away from the rider.) By all means sit for a few strides every so often to teach the horse that he must not alter his rhythm despite your change from rising to sitting trot and vice versa, and also that he must not immediately associate sitting trot with a change of pace. Sitting trot is not required until Intermediate eventing dressage test level and so there is no rush to burden the horse with the rider's weight. Whilst on the subject of sitting trot and the rider's weight in the saddle, I do strongly believe that the English horse is not, on the whole, very strong in his back, unlike the warm-bloods (such as the German, Dutch and other European breeds) and many problems are caused by the rider trying to 'use his seat'. The use of the seat is vital as an aid in the motivation of the German horse, but the lighter type of English horse just cannot cope with this excess seat and merely becomes more and more tense and hollow.

Initially the horse will only be able to carry out a few strides of shoulder-in, but eventually he will be able to cope with the entire length of the school. Even if at first he finds it difficult, the fact that the rider is asking him to attempt it will benefit him; it will increase the activity of the hindleg, which in turn will help in bringing the hocks further underneath him.

The leg-yield is a similar exercise to increase activity in the hocks. The horse remains straight in his body, with a slight bend in his neck away from the direction in which he is going, and moves away from the inside leg. The easiest place to do a leg-yield is to change the rein across the diagonal, then leg-yield from X to the quarter-marker. In order to move away from the rider's leg, the horse must bend his legs, and cross them over, so increasing agility.

The counter-canter is a useful suppling exercise but is demanding and should only be asked for when the horse is physically able to perform it. It can aid training by making the horse carry more weight on his outside hindleg than he would of his own volition (*see* Hocks Trailing, p. 131, and Canter Problems, pp. 117, 125, 166). One must bear in mind that 'outside' refers to the outside of the bend and not the outside of the direction, so that in a counter-canter to the right, the right hindleg is still the outside, even though it is on the inside of a circle.

The counter-canter should be introduced by executing demi-voltes in canter, rejoining the track before the quarter marker and trotting on reaching it, and also by riding loops in from the long side of the school which can be gradually increased in size until the horse performs the canter serpentine. The horse must remain bent to the inside throughout the three loops and must retain his rhythm and balance.

It must be remembered that virtually any resistance in the horse's mouth is caused by lack of engagement of the hindleg (back and hindquarters included). If the horse is using his hocks the requisite amount for the question asked by the rider, then the front end of the horse will be quite free to be manipulated and the horse easy to steer. This leads us on to stage 6.

### 6. Relaxation of the lower jaw

A great amount of work has been done already before it is considered that the horse is ready to relax his jaw completely, and so fully accept the rider's hand. It must be understood that before the horse can relax in his jaw, he must be carrying himself on his hocks and therefore sufficiently well balanced to be able to perform the movements asked of him without resisting in his mouth; indeed, ninety-nine per cent of any resistance in the mouth is due to the horse not using his back, hindquarters, or, to use the general term, hocks. If he is very light in his mouth without his hocks underneath him, then he will be behind the bit, and not going forward. When he is carrying his weight on his hocks in such a way that he can use himself to the maximum, he is at the point when he can be considered 'on the bit'. To most people, on the bit means that the horse is going along with his nose nicely tucked in, moving smoothly from one pace to another. There is another term to describe on the bit, which is 'direct flexion', and to me this better explains what is required from the horse at this stage. Direct flexion consists of three components which must all exist at the same time, all the time, before a horse can be described as being on the bit. First, the horse must be straight (*see* stage 4); secondly the horse must be pushing forward from behind with his hocks underneath him (*see* stage 5); and finally, he must be relaxed in his jaw (*see* stage 6). These three requirements must be present all the time, whatever movement is being performed before it can be stated that the horse is truly on the bit, and in order to attain stages 4, 5 and 6, stages 1, 2 and 3 must be well established. A vertical nose does not mean that the horse is on the bit, although plenty of people on the ground may be fooled by it. The proof of the matter will be when the horse remains the same obedient horse when jumping or going cross-country. It is always quite staggering to me how so many horses who obtain excellent dressage marks appear to be so totally undisciplined in the jumping phases. Dressage and jumping go hand in hand and the horse who is capable of producing a very good test should be able to produce an equally good show-jumping and cross-country round. At the lower levels of dressage it is possible to hide a certain number of faults, as the standard of test is very basic, but at the higher levels these imperfections will inevitably be pin-pointed and any short-cuts discovered. It is so important to train from the very beginning in a correct way, in order to avoid the all-too-common situation of saying, 'He was fine at Novice level, but we are having *x* number of problems now that we are upgraded.' If the training is correct, these problems should not occur, as the level of training should be in advance of the level of competition. It is very important that the horse is not always asked to carry out the most difficult tasks in actual competition. He should be asked sufficiently complicated questions at home that he is perfectly confident, at an event, to perform whatever is asked of him despite a myriad of outside distractions. He will soon come to associate a competition with something to be nervous about if he is always made to do something there which is more arduous than he is used to. I am not suggesting that he should be jumped over huge cross-country fences at home, but he should be jumping the equivalent dimensions either in the form of exercises or single fences to teach him to have confidence in his agility and his ability to jump whatever is in front of him. Many people dislike jumping in cold blood, mostly because they lack confidence, and the only way to overcome this fear is to jump with the help of an understanding person on the ground. The rider must have total faith in this ground person, and must begin to understand the fundamentals of jumping in order to learn that jumping is indeed a continuation of flat work.

If the flat work has progressed correctly, the horse will automatically be relaxed in his jaw. However, there is normally some stage where the horse will try to ignore the bit, and will 'run through the rider's hand'. The horse must be as respectful of the rider's hand as he is of the leg, otherwise, as the rider increases the leg to create impulsion, he will just go faster instead of responding by bringing his hocks underneath him. At no time must the rider ever pull backwards should the horse disregard the hand; he should merely increase the squash of the leg, and block with the hand. This is called a blockade – a very strong half-halt. The more the horse tries to run through the hand, the stronger the leg must be. The strength of the blocking hand can be as strong as the leg used, but no more. Thus, the more leg is applied, the more definite the hand may be without any fear of pulling backwards and therefore causing resistance. As soon as the rider's hand is stronger than his leg, the horse will resist in his mouth and all forward movement will be halted. With the use of the blockade and the half-halt, the horse's balance will be assisted and, as his training progresses, the half-halt will even prevent the cause of the horse running through the hand, which is that he is not carrying his weight sufficiently on his hocks. Never forget, I emphasise, that ninety-nine per cent of problems in the mouth are connected with the back end, and that is why the horse is not expected to be relaxed in his jaw until quite late in his training. Until this time, his head carriage should be as natural to the horse's own balance as possible, with the horse carrying himself and not relying on the rider's hand for his balance. With some horses with poor conformation, however, this 'natural' head carriage must be cultivated. The swan-necked horse must be encouraged to lengthen his outline by strong forward driving, an open inside hand asking him to lower his head and neck at the same time. The short-necked horse must also be encouraged to stretch his neck, otherwise the muscles will develop in such a way that it will be almost impossible for him to carry himself in a round outline later on. As long as the horse is stretching the base of his neck and holding the bit lightly, as the training progresses he will automatically be in the right shape without the rider having to think, 'Ah today, we will go on the bit.' The correctly produced horse will come onto the bit in time and without any resistance.

### Self-carriage — the goal of stages 1—6

When stage 6 has been attained, the horse should then have attained self-carriage. He should be able to carry out all basic movements with consummate ease, in perfect balance and harmony with his rider. This state of self-carriage means that the horse is on a contact with the rider's hand which is such that the reins could be made of thread, and that this light contact is retained in whatever pace or transition the horse is in. The progression on from self-carriage is

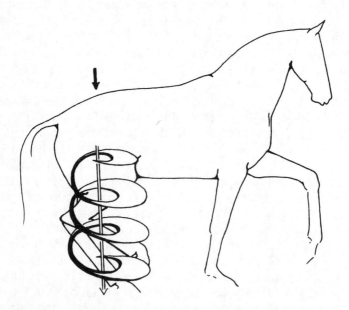

12 **Storing potential energy in the hocks** — *Quarters lower as hindlegs step further under the horse's body, and the hocks are flexed. The forehand lightens and potential energy is stored like a compressed spring.*

the ability to produce true collection and full extension. This means that the horse must have potential energy stored in his hocks (*see* diagram 12), and the rider will contain that energy in his hand, until the horse is asked to extend, for instance, when the spring is released, his hocks come well underneath him, and he can stride forward on a powerful long stride (*see* diagram 13).

This is the point of schooling where the rider is continually trying to create and maintain impulsion and potential energy. From rhythm, one moves to cadence in the stride – cadence can be defined as rhythm with a bang. This means that the horse has more spring in his stride, and is very positive about his steps. Cadence in the young horse will only come with training, strengthening him up and reaching stage 6 of his programme. In the older horse, who may have grown a little idle in his schooling, this will be obtained by schooling exercises specifically chosen to make him more active – transitions, half-halts, shoulder-ins, shoulder-outs, half-pass or any other exercises to make him engage his hind-quarters to a greater extent.

This phase of self-carriage must not be missed out. All too often, horses are persuaded by their riders to move strongly up into the

**13 The potential release of stored energy from the hocks — extension —**
*the spring is released and the horse travels forward on a powerful long stride, his hocks coming well under the body.*

rider's hand before they have had a chance to find their own proper balance. The result is that the horse is running along, relying on the rider's hand to balance himself rather than learning to use his hocks to provide himself with a balancing pole. It must be remembered that it is the horse which takes the contact and not the rider, therefore the rider must not take – in return – more than the horse is willing to give. There is a vast difference between the horse which is running along on his rider's hand, and the one working strongly up to the rider's hand because of the potential energy in the hindquarters which needs containing until it is required, for example, in lengthened strides, half-pass or jumping. The higher the degree of training required, the more energy needs to be created and stored, and as this energy is used in various movements, so it needs to be replaced by more. So, the rider has to use a vibrating leg constantly to create that energy without letting it all flow away through his hand.

All those horses who are capable of having a large amount of energy stored are also capable of working in total self-carriage on a very light contact. When the highly-trained horse begins a schooling session he will be in this state of self-carriage, and then, as the rider starts to build up the schooling exercises, he will use his hocks more strongly and so create energy which the rider will keep contained in his hand. A horse working at Advanced level will actually be quite strong in the rider's hand but only because the horse's hocks are pounding away creating all this energy, which unless contained, will be utilised.

So, following on from the self-carriage in a progressive way comes the state of collection from the containing of energy in the horse's hocks. In order to obtain collection, the schooling of the horse must be hitherto unhindered, and so this book will concentrate merely on the stages up to and including the state of self-carriage.

**Typical schooling sessions**

At all times, schooling sessions should have a point to them, and what the rider is trying to achieve should be clear. If the horse learns his lesson very well, and you feel that you are satisfied with his performance, even if he has only been in the school for twenty minutes, it is far better to finish on a good note – so that the horse has his reward – and then either do something different, such as give him a quick jump or take him out for a ride. To plug on when you have achieved a good result is only asking for trouble. I am not saying that as soon as the horse does as he is told, you should stop work, but over-drilling is the commonest cause of lack of enthusiasm on the part of both horse and rider, and enthusiasm on both sides is so important in achieving results. Work should be enjoyed by both parties, and the enjoyment is partly gained from the mutual understanding between horse and rider in their relationship. It should be exhilarating to do a medium trot, there should be a feeling almost of smugness in a good transition, a feeling of elegance in a half-pass, and a great thrill and enjoyment when jumping a fence, whether it be an exercise or a single fence. The wonderful feeling of a horse really springing over a fence and fully using himself in the air is quite indescribable, but I know that it always makes me smile, and surely being happy with your horse must be one of the most vital aspects of a successful partnership.

It can be seen that the main objective of training, once the horse has reached stage 4, it to make him use his hocks as much as possible, and within a schooling session, as many exercises as possible should be incorporated which will encourage the horse to do just that. This does not mean that the whole repertoire of exercises should be repeated every single session, but a variety introduced into the schooling time will not only advance his progress but also keep the horse's interest, for nothing is more boring for a horse than to go round in endless, tedious circles, with no specific purpose in mind. A horse likes to be kept interested, and should learn to enjoy his work: in fact to maintain the horse's enthusiasm (and the rider's!) is half the battle in flat work. 'I hate dressage' is the eternal cry from a great many event riders, and I can well understand their feelings if dressage to them means hours of struggle with an unco-operative horse. A half-hour session two, three, or even four times a week is surely within the mental and physical capabilities of any horse and rider, but the prospect of hours of purgatory in the form of sitting trot and non-purposeful work is enough to put dread into the heart of the most ardent dressage fan! So much of the 'dressage schooling' can be incorporated into a jumping session that there is no reason why a horse should become bored with dressage, and it is up to the rider to make sure that the horse's mind is kept sufficiently active and occupied to prevent any tedium creeping into his work. Horses want to please, with the odd exception of course, and, as trainers, we must be careful never to give the horse the chance to become disgruntled with his daily routine by overdoing his schooling, by underworking him, or by confusing him, so creating unnecessary problems which could have been avoided with a little thought.

Before discussing some schooling sessions, now might be the

moment to discuss transitions and the aids and preparations for these – including the half-halt. As was mentioned in stage 5 (Placement of the hindleg), the horse must use his hocks in his upward and downward transitions. If he fails to do so, he will then try to use his head and neck instead to alter his balance, which is a resistance the rider tries to avoid. The horse, by trying to raise his head, will, of course, fight the bit and, unless the rider responds by using a strong leg to engage the horse's hocks while asking with the inside hand to relax the jaw again, a poor transition will be the result. The most important part of any successful transition, or indeed any movement at all, is the rider's preparation of the horse. The horse must always be between hand and leg and ready to carry out the requisite movements, yet without anticipating. It is very important when schooling to avoid giving the horse the opportunity to anticipate, and this is best achieved by alternating movements rather than sticking to a set pattern. Many people stick rigidly to the walk – trot – canter routine, and finish their session after the canter work. Try to vary the order of work each session and the way that one movement follows on from another. The horse will soon come to remember the dressage tests he does regularly, so it is very important to make him do different patterns of the same or similar movements at home. By preparing the horse for particular movements, the fact that his hocks are being driven strongly underneath him in the series of half-halts in the preparatory period means that he is more under control, and this should help the rider to prevent him from anticipating, basically by making him more obedient. (Remember, the horse can only be made to obey if he is absolutely between the rider's hand and leg.) The different forms of preparation for different movements are covered in more detail under individual sections on problems encountered in transitions, but, briefly, all movements should be preceded by one or several half-halts, to shift the horse's weight further back onto his hocks and so lighten the forehand. The half-halt is a message between rider and horse which is barely visible to the onlooker, except in the cases of a blockade, where the horse is visibly slowed down in a series of very strong half-halts. (The use of the blockade is covered under various problems.) The half-halt is a combination/sequence of aids in which the rider closes the leg in a downward transition squeeze, and blocks with his hand just enough for the horse to start to slow down, but instead of actually allowing the pace to alter, the rider relaxes his hand, without throwing away the contact, and drives the horse forward again – very positively, with a more engaged hock. In a half-halt the rider must beware of stopping the forward movement of the horse by using too much hand and insufficient leg, which will merely slow the pace down instead of creating the desired effect of shifting the horse's balance back a little onto more active and weight-bearing hocks. If the rider loses the contact as he drives the horse forward, then all the energy he has created by the use of his legs, and the consequent bending of the horse's hocks in readiness for the transition, will be allowed to flow away and the benefit of the half-halt will be lost; instead of the horse's hocks remaining underneath him, they will return to where they were before the half-halt, so nothing will have been achieved. The higher the standard of training of the horse, the finer the half-halt message will need to be, while the unschooled horse will need a far clearer message, and probably several of them in quick succession.

All these transitions and half-halts improve the horse's self-carriage, but the rider must be careful not to confuse the horse with indistinct aids, particularly the canter aid. Walk to canter as an exercise is helpful in making the horse engage his hocks, although it must be interspersed with walk to trot, in order to avoid any possibility of anticipation by the horse. If the rider's aids are clear, however, this should not be a problem, but it is worth steering clear of any potential confusion.

The aid to canter must be distinct, as, if the aid given is either rather woolly or incorrect, problems will then ensue when half-pass is introduced. The aid to canter is outside leg behind the girth, inside leg on the girth, and since this is normally given on the corner, the horse is bent in the direction in which he is going. The aid for the half-pass is given when the horse is bent in the direction in which he is going and involves inside leg on the girth, outside leg behind the girth – virtually identical to the aid given for canter. So, how do the two aids differ so that the horse knows what he is expected to do?

First, the aids for the half-pass – for example, from the quarter-marker after the corner to X. The rider asks the horse for a bend, as if he is asking the horse to do a shoulder-in. He then guides the horse towards X with his inside hand, maintaining the bend and forward movement with his inside leg, moving the horse obliquely across with his outside leg behind the girth and the outside hand controlling the outside shoulder. On no account should the rider try to cross the inside hand to keep the bend, but he should use an increased inside leg. Initially a few strides will be all the horse can manage, and he should then be straightened up, driven forward for a few strides, then re-positioned and asked again. The positioning of the horse is all important, otherwise the horse will tend either to lead with, or trail, his quarters. Both the rider's hands and legs play a vital part in the half-pass and if one hand, or one leg, is not giving the correct aid or support, the half-pass cannot be performed correctly. For instance, if the horse tries to lead with his quarters, the rider must use both his hands to bring the forehand across, for if just the inside hand is used, the horse will merely bend in his neck and the shoulder will be lost. The rider's weight must remain central; he must not slip to the outside by collapsing the inside hip. His hips and shoulders must stay parallel to the horse's hips and shoulders to remain in balance, and to help maintain forward movement, he must look where he is going. As soon as the rider looks down, the forward movement will lapse, and this applies whatever the rider is asking the horse to do. The comparison of driving a car may be used again here to demonstrate the point. It is totally against one's nature to put one's foot on the accelerator of a car whilst looking anywhere other than through the windscreen in the direction in which one is driving. It is obvious that if you cannot see where you are going, you are hardly going to want to get there any faster! The same is true of a rider on a horse, for even though he feels that he is riding forward, if he is looking down, then there is an underlying reluctance really to drive forward.

The aid to canter from trot are as follows: the rider, from a sitting trot, moves his outside leg a little further back, without applying it any more strongly (otherwise the horse, if trained to do so, will move his quarters over in response), and then gives the horse a positive nudge with the inside leg on the girth, or even a little in front of it for clarity. As he does so, the rider must ensure that his weight is on his inside seat-bone to push the horse forward into canter on the inside lead. If this aid is given, then there will be no problem when the rider comes to ask the horse to canter on a named lead on a straight line. Many times when the horse strikes off on the wrong leg, it is because the rider is allowing the outside shoulder to swing outwards, thereby freeing the outside front leg for the horse to lead with: this problem is dealt with at length later (in the section on canter leads). Although the outside hindleg is the first beat of the canter stride, it is the rider's inside leg which is the main leg of the aid actually driving the horse forward into canter.

All these transitions may be practised on any horse whatever his stage of training, but obviously the greener he is, the more preparation he must be given prior to the transition, and the longer he must be given actually to perform the transition – i.e. the less he uses his hocks (or knows how to use them), the longer it will take him to change from one pace to another. The fact that he is changing pace makes him use his hocks, however, so these transitions and preparations for them are invaluable to include in any schooling session.

To give examples of typical schooling sessions is somewhat difficult, as so much depends upon the stage that the individual horse has reached, but here are a few fairly typical exercises to include – approximately thirty minutes of schooling – for the average Novice/Intermediate standard horse with no specific short-comings but who needs a general work-out to remain supple and obedient. These schooling sessions do not need to be restricted to a manège or an indoor school, although obviously four walls are helpful and may be necessary for the accuracy required for some movements, such as precise circles. But schooling should also be undertaken in different places, such as out on rides, or in open spaces, both to give variation, and so that you can show that you can insist upon discipline at all times.

Bearing in mind the order of training, the first ten to fifteen minutes must be spent in settling the horse down to his work and the best way to relieve him of his high spirits is to ride him strongly forward in a good working trot. Within this gait it is advisable to incorporate plenty of turns and circles to keep his mind on what you are asking him to do, at the same time gently beginning to supple him both laterally and directly. As the inside leg asks for the bend, it is also – by using it in conjunction with the outside hand – creating impulsion, by driving the horse's hocks underneath him. In the initial stages of the warm-up, the rider should encourage the horse's head-carriage to be fairly long and low, ensuring that his muscles along his top line are being stretched, in much the same way as his outside muscles are stretched on a bend. The stretching and contracting of the muscles, and their easy ability to do so, are the foundations of suppleness. Trotting round on a loose rein serves no purpose at all as, apart from going through the motions of the trot, the horse is unlikely to be in a round shape; his head may be stretched out, but he is more likely to be stretching the underside of his neck rather than the top. By all means ride on a long rein with a very light contact so that the horse is carrying himself, but a loose rein means that the rider has nothing between his hand and leg: the horse's hocks will be out behind him as a result, and so he is free to do whatever he wants. Apart from the fact that if he is fresh, he has every opportunity to buck, or whip round, and easily remove his rider, he is not being made to work at all, and is even actively encouraged either to slop along, or to misbehave. He will have to be on a contact eventually, so it is far better to start with a light contact in order to establish the pattern immediately.

After about ten minutes, the horse should have settled into his work, performing his 20-metre circles in a supple manner, with a good forward-going stride and even rhythm. Then is the time to start to work him a little harder to improve the standard of the work-out, and it depends on each individual horse's requirements as to what exercises are needed to help him to become more supple and obedient. So, here are several different movements and exercises which may be incorporated into schooling sessions.

Smaller circles ask the horse to bend more, and also to bring his hocks further under him; these smaller circles can then be incorporated into serpentines which have the added benefit of changing the bend from one way to another. Serpentines are difficult for the horse, as he has to change his bend twice in a short space of time whilst maintaining the same rhythm. Until the horse is thoroughly warmed-up it is best to work in rising trot, and I personally think that the more time the horse's back is without the rider's weight, the more it will be kept supple and relaxed. If the horse has reached Intermediate Event standard, then obviously he must be allowed to grow accustomed to sitting trot, as the dressage tests at that standard require all the trot work to be sitting. However, even an Intermediate dressage test only lasts 'approximately four minutes' and an Advanced one 'approximately five and a half minutes', so the horse really does not need to be subjected to hour upon hour of sitting trot. The amount of sitting trot the rider chooses to do must depend largely upon the individual horse and how the rider feels that he will be best able to produce the correct response in training from that horse.

Following on from the circles and changes of direction are the excellent movement of shoulder-in or shoulder-out. Both are wonderful exercises to increase suppleness and activity; they really help to drive the horse up to the outside hand – with the increased use of the rider's inside leg and the necessary support of the outside hand to prevent the shoulder swinging out. Alternating shoulder-in and shoulder-out along the long side is one of the best suppling movements for the horse, and a circle of ten to fifteen metres followed by a shoulder-in and then another circle makes hard work for both horse and rider. The more questions of this sort that the horse is asked, the better he will carry himself, as he will have to use his hocks in order to perform them. Transitions are a further way of engaging the horse's hocks to a greater extent. In order to slow down or accelerate, the horse must use his hocks as levers; they are both the brakes and the accelerator for the horse. A very good exercise, which is a continuation of this theme, is to work the horse on a circle, and from a working trot, ask him to walk, but just before he breaks into walk, drive him strongly forward into trot again, without losing his round shape, or losing rhythm. This exercise can be repeated several times, and can also be carried out in canter – asking the horse to trot by closing the leg and blocking with the hand. The rider does not actually allow him to break into trot, but drives him very strongly forward in canter on a lightened contact, again without the horse resisting or losing rhythm. The value of this exercise is enormous because the horse will start to lower his croup and bend his hocks in readiness for a change of pace, and while his hocks are underneath like this, he is made really to engage them as the rider drives him forward again. Provided the horse maintains his shape and rhythm, he will then be re-established in the same pace, but with a much more engaged hock action. The horse will become far rounder in his outline as he uses his back to a great degree too, so the whole exercise is of benefit to both lateral and direct flexion. It is far easier to do this exercise on a circle, as the horse is using his hocks more on a circle in the first place. I am sure the reader knows how it is much easier to ride an uneducated horse on a circle than in a straight line; this is due to the fact that the horse has to use his hocks more on the turn, thereby increasing the carrying capacity of the hock. After about fifteen or twenty minutes of these exercises, the horse should be very light on his forehand and carrying himself well on his hocks without the rider having to think to himself, 'When do I ask the horse to come onto the bit?' The horse will automatically come onto the bit – i.e. he will be straight having done all the bends and circles; his hocks will be underneath him from the shoulder-ins, serpentines and transitions; and his jaw will be relaxed from having been asked to turn and flex.

The majority of schooling is done in trot but work must be done in canter as well, although this need not necessarily be in every schooling session. The horse should carry himself very lightly in canter, on a soft contact: on the circle again, the rider can practise giving with both hands for a few strides, allowing the horse to carry himself completely, but giving a series of half-halts if the horse should lose his rhythm or balance. It always seems a pity that so many horses are restricted in the canter and lose the lovely natural spring in their stride as a result. When the canter has lost its spring, it is very difficult for the horse when he comes to jump, as the spring in the jump is often affected. At Novice level, the horse should be left to find his own balance in the canter, and he must not be over-shortened as this is what spoils the basic pace. Moving from trot to canter and back again in quick succession activates the hocks and helps the horse to carry himself more on them, and increase and decrease of the pace itself will also help while, of course, it is vital in training for the jumping phases. If the horse cannot accelerate and decelerate in canter without falling onto his forehand or resisting on the flat, then he will certainly not be able to alter pace when he is confronted with a course of fences. When working on the flat, try to reproduce the sort of exercise which will benefit both horse and rider when it comes to jumping. For instance, placing poles at random on the ground proves invaluable practice for jumping as cantering over them helps to improve balance and rhythm: it is amazing how some horses and riders lose all control when asked to perform this relatively easy exercise. How can that same combination possibly manage to complete a round over fences if they cannot maintain balance and rhythm with poles at ground level? This exercise of cantering over poles may be incorporated into any schooling session; just a single pole on the track can prove quite a challenge, as the rider should aim to keep the canter stride even, without altering the rhythm or forward movement of the canter. It is good practice for the rider's 'eye', and quite fun too to see how soon you can tell whether the horse will meet the pole 'right' or 'wrong'. It is good practice for the horse to adjust his stride within an established rhythm, which he will easily be able to do, as long as he is carrying himself on his hocks.

The increasing and decreasing circle is an exercise that increases suppleness both directly and laterally. This exercise may be performed at any pace, although the most usual is trot, as this pace makes the horse use himself equally, being a symmetrical diagonal movement. Starting with a 20-metre circle, the rider then asks the horse to reduce the size of the circle by guiding him in with the inside hand, supporting the shoulder with the outside hand, driving him inwards with the outside leg behind the girth, and maintaining the bend and the impulsion with the inside leg. Once the horse is tracing a 10-metre circle, the rider pushes him back out to the original figure with the inside leg, containing the horse in the outside hand (same again, inside leg up to the outside hand), maintaining direction with the inside hand, and controlling the quarters with the outside leg. The activity of the hocks is increased by decreasing the circle, as the horse must be more active to maintain his balance and rhythm. The circle is *gradually* decreased in size, so the horse has less chance of evading work by swinging his quarters; if he tries to swing them, the rider can wait until he has controlled them before asking the horse to further decrease the circle. When the horse is pushed out again to the original circle, the inside hindleg will almost be asked to cross over a little, in much the same way as in shoulder-in. The whole exercise has a twofold action, therefore, by making the horse work not only on the decrease but also the increase of the circle. The horse will be bent around the rider's leg to a greater degree in the smaller circle which will increase suppleness in his back. As the length of time that he is asked to trace a small circle is quite short, there is no reason for the horse to become stiff during this exercise. If he is asked to do a 10-metre circle for a longer period and he finds it difficult, there is every opportunity for him to become tight, which of course defeats the object of the exercise completely. The length of time spent on the smaller circle may gradually be built up until the horse is quite happy working on a 10-metre circle. This exercise is a good way to introduce smaller circles to the horse without upsetting him (by subjecting him suddenly to a difficult exercise as well as making him work hard into the bargain).

This exercise may be performed in canter too to help the horse to carry himself on his hocks by activating the outside hindleg. Performed in conjunction with the exercise in which the rider offers the hand forwards for a few strides on the re-established 20-metre circle, the spiralling circle tests whether the horse is on his hocks or relying on the rider's hand to maintain his balance. When the horse is briefly given a loose contact, he should remain in balance and rhythm without dropping onto his forehand and losing his shape: if the horse can retain self-carriage, then he is carrying himself correctly, but if he cannot maintain his rhythm and falls into a shambling canter, or breaks into trot, then it is clear that there is plenty of work still to be done! In canter it is the horse's outside hindleg which must come underneath him to enable him to canter correctly. In trot, it is the inside hind which is the main weight-bearer, but in canter the outside hand has to bear the weight for the first beat, and if the horse does not bring this leg far enough underneath him, then the whole of the canter will suffer and the horse will be very much on his forehand. This explains something which often puzzles many people: why a horse may, for example, be stiffer on the right rein in trot whereas the right canter is far easier than the canter to the left. If this is the horse's weaker leg in trot on the right rein, the inside hind is not engaging sufficiently, and hence the horse will be stiff in his mouth and body. On this rein in canter, the left hind will become the outside carrying leg, and so the right canter will be an easier canter for the horse than the left canter, when it is the weaker right hind which becomes the carrying leg on the outside. During the spiralling circle exercise the horse is made to use both the inside and the outside hindlegs, and this is why this exercise is of such enormous benefit in any training session. As the circle is made smaller (the rider pushing the horse's quarters to the inside with his outside leg), the outside hind as well as the inside hind is activated as the horse is made to move his quarters over – the same sort of response as will be asked for eventually in half-pass – and in order to do this the horse must use his hocks to a far greater degree. When the horse is pushed out to the larger circle, the leg-yielding type of movement emphasises the use of the inside hindleg. Thus, when this exercise is performed on both reins the horse will be worked really quite hard and helped to understand how he can and must use his hocks to carry and therefore to balance himself.

I always think of a horse as a see-saw in this instance. For one end of the see-saw to be raised, or in our case to lighten the horse's forehand, the other end, the horse's croup, must lower (*see* diagram 14). A see-saw cannot bend, and in a similar way the horse cannot lighten his forehand without a weight correction (*see* diags 15 and 16, p. 52). He has to bend his hocks and bring them underneath his body; carrying himself on his hocks, his croup will lower as a result. If you picture the high-class dressage horse, his croup will appear to be very low, and his head and neck very high – thus, the lighter the forehand, the further underneath the horse's body the hocks must be.

Another exercise which will benefit the horse enormously is trotting him over trotting poles that are first laid on the ground and subsequently raised. A line of six or eight poles is probably the best number to use to encourage the horse to swing over the poles in a balanced rhythm, using himself to the maximum. With the young horse, the poles should be introduced gradually, first with just a single pole on the ground, then two, and so on, until he can cope with a full line. The rider must concentrate upon keeping his balance over the poles in order to allow the horse the total freedom of his back and neck. He must also concentrate upon keeping the round shape of the horse without restricting him in any way. The horse must not be allowed to go over the poles in a hollow outline, otherwise the exercise will have little or no benefit to his training, as the muscles along the horse's back will be worked in a detrimental fashion. As has already been stated, a rising trot, or even a standing trot, should be adopted over the poles to encourage the horse to round his back and so bring his hocks well underneath him. Often, after a line of poles, the horse will take rather short strides, which is his way of catching up with any balance he may have lost during the

**14 The horse as a see-saw**

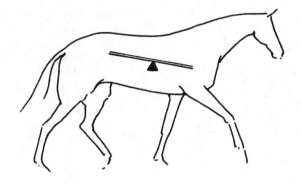

a *horse on forehand, hocks trailing*

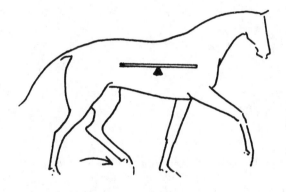

b *balance achieved when the horse steps up under his body and his croup is lowered*

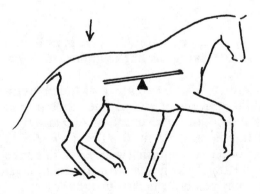

c *if the croup is very much lower and the hocks are well underneath the horse, while the head and neck are high and the forehand is light, the horse is in a state of collection.*

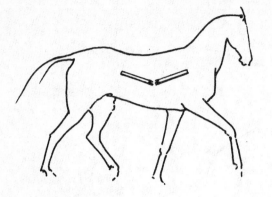

**15  How going hollow will affect the see-saw balance of the horse —** *when the head is up but the forehand is not light and the hindlegs are not coming up under the horse: the horse is hollow and the centre of the see-saw breaks.*

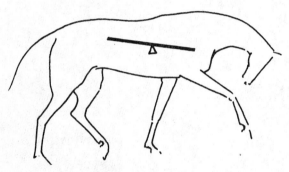

**16  How overbending will affect the see-saw balance of the horse —** *although the horse's head is down and the neck is rounded, the nose is actually behind the vertical and the neck is bending from halfway down: with this 'broken neck' the horse is still on his forehand and his hocks are therefore not stepping under the body.*

line: the rider should help the horse re-establish his normal rhythm by giving a series of half-halts, to bring his hocks underneath him and so readjust his balance.

The raised trotting poles are merely an extension of the poles on the ground, but emphasise the movement and suppleness required for trotting poles. They should be introduced one or two at a time starting with the penultimate pole in the line; the first pole should always be on the ground in order to help the horse over this pole and so into the exercise. Starting and ending with a ground-level pole means that the exercise may be performed from either direction without having to change the poles. So, if eight poles are being used, the sixth and seventh poles would be the first ones to be raised, then the fifth and fourth, and so on, until six poles are raised with the end two on the ground as guide poles. These raised poles can be made in a very simple way by cutting grooves at intervals of 1.25–1.5 metres (4½–5 feet) in pieces of scaffold board, or planking of similar dimensions. Cavaletti may be used but there is a danger in that, for if the horse should hit one of these they do tend to roll and become entangled with the horse's legs, whereas poles balanced on boards will fall to the ground without any risk of damage to the horse. The horse has to work very hard over these raised poles, and they are of great benefit in many ways. The horse is forced to bend every joint in every leg, which requires a vast amount of effort. The horse learns how to bend his legs, and, in so doing, learns that he *can use his hocks*, and he therefore strengthens all the muscles that he will have to employ to carry himself on his hocks and hindquarters. It is an exercise that must be used in moderation as it is strenuous for the horse and it is important not to overdo it. If the poles are used in accordance with the fitness of the horse and his level of training, then they can assist in achieving further fitness in all ways. Even the laziest horse has to work hard, but horses tend to enjoy going down the line of poles, and thus it can re-fire their enthusiasm towards work in general. Learning how to use his legs and muscles by force-flexing them over these poles, the horse can then transfer this acquired knowledge so that he uses his hocks as a source of propulsion and as brakes: it is amazing how the general schooling of the horse will improve once he has learnt just how he can use himself to the greatest advantage. A session using these poles may be incorporated once or twice a week as an athletic exercise to stretch and work many of the muscles required in training. The combination of poles and other exercises which work different muscles – such as the lateral suppling exercises – makes up a very sound foundation of athletic training for dressage or jumping.

It is obvious that difficulties are going to occur in the course of training a horse for dressage and jumping, otherwise this book would never have needed to be written, but at least if the rider has the necessary order of training firmly established in his mind, the paths to follow in order to correct various problems should be slightly clearer when I come to discuss them in the following chapters. Different people have different theories, but the reasoning behind everything I say has been tested on large numbers of very varied types of horse, and the re-schooling of these horses has always followed the six-stage pattern set out in this chapter. I feel, from the rider's point of view, that if, at the end of this phase of the schooling of any horse, he can carry himself in self-carriage without you having to hang on to his head to preserve this, then you can pride yourself that your training so far has been correct.

## Jumping

Jumping undeniably aids the work on the flat by stretching the back and making the horse use himself to the full. When a horse bascules over a fence he uses his back in a way which may prove difficult to achieve on the flat. Also, by loosening muscles by jumping, the horse will invariably be more supple in his flat work. The two disciplines therefore complement each other to a large degree.

The pattern used to introduce the horse to jumping has the same basic rule as the one applying to flat work. Namely, calmness must be achieved first. If the horse is not calm in his jumping, the jump itself will be tense and the horse will be unable to use himself properly in an athletic way. The approach to the fence will be a problem too, and it will be impossible to achieve and maintain balance and rhythm, which are the keynotes to all jumping and training. Do not, however, confuse the horse's enthusiasm for jumping with his being tense. The horse should want to 'get at' the fence and be quite eager – but in a controlled fashion; he should be well up to the rider's hand, pulling the rider into the fence, but staying in the same rhythm throughout. This is, in fact, what the aim of producing a horse for jumping should be. One is, of course, aiming for exactly the same feeling on the flat, but it just so happens that a fence gives the horse some encouragement to create his own impulsion, whereas on the flat he not only relies on the rider to produce it for him, but sees no particular purpose in it either. The fence gives the horse the reason for an increase in impulsion, and most horses are far easier to ride once there is a fence in the way (that is, those horses whose training has been along the right lines!). The horse must arrive at the fence with potential energy so that he can spring into the air and perform a supple elastic jump with a correct bascule (*see* diags 39–40, pp. 195–196).

Raised trotting poles exaggerate the bending of joints necessary for poles on the ground, particularly in the idle horse: however, in the build-up to jumping, a single pole on the ground is of more benefit than a long line of them, as will be explained later. The horse learns from trotting poles to look at what he is doing; he soon learns not to tread on them which will be of help later when he is required to respect a ground or take-off pole. The whole purpose of a take-off pole at the base of a fence is to give the horse something to make him back off and take off a little further away from the fence, which requires him to shorten his frame and increase his power (*see* diag. 44, p. 214). The reason that upright fences with no ground line, such as planks, are so difficult is that they have nothing to help the horse judge his take-off point.

It is very good practice at any stage of training to canter over a single pole on the ground, concentrating on keeping the same rhythm and stride pattern, aiming in time to be able to canter over any pole anywhere in the school without losing any rhythm or balance. Poles scattered here and there in the school can be cantered over in either direction and are of great value in teaching horse and rider to remain in rhythm. We normally start jumping with a small cross-pole 46 centimetres (1 foot 6 inches) high, which encourages the horse to jump the centre of the fence. A trotting pole placed 2–2.75 metres (7–9 feet) away as a placing pole helps the horse to learn to gather himself and spring over the fence, as it will put him in the correct spot for take-off. On the approach, the rider must concentrate on keeping the horse going forward in a rhythm, and squeeze him strongly into the fence – not pushing him flat, but encouraging him to gather himself and spring high into the air. Note the use of the term 'squeeze the horse into the fence'. This driving squeeze from the rider's legs asks for spring whether it be to jump a fence or to take higher/longer steps; here the rider wants the horse to gather himself, pat the ground with his front feet and spring into the air, and the horse will be unable to do this if he is chased into his fences. A kick or a flick with the whip are reprimands and should only be used in jumping if the horse shows signs of refusing. The effect of a kick will be to make the horse go faster, thus flattening both the jump and the stride. The whip will also make a horse go faster, it will not make him jump higher; hitting a horse over a fence will therefore also have the effect of making the horse jump flat and more likely to knock down the fence. Some horses may require strong riding in the early stages of their jumping career or if presented with a spooky, difficult fence, but eventually the horse must learn to respond to a squeeze in order to jump these fences correctly, as well as the more straightforward ones. There are times when the voice can be used to advantage in jumping as well as in flat work, assuming that the horse has been trained to respond to the voice. A click at a tricky moment, such as when meeting a fence deep, will have the effect of sharpening the horse's reactions, and saying 'steady' if the horse becomes too onward bound will have a calming influence.

On landing, the forward-going rhythm of the approach must be re-established as quickly as possible. The landing of one fence is the approach to another, and the sooner the horse gets into the habit of immediately being back in rhythm, the easier it will be when it comes to riding him over a course of fences. From the cross-pole, the fence can be heightened to approximately 75 centimetres (2 feet 6 inches) by putting the pole straight. A high cross-pole is not a good idea in the early stages, because if the horse makes a slight mistake or tries to run along the fence a little, he can quite easily frighten himself. If he should persist in not going straight, some Vs on the fence should correct that (this will be covered in detail in later chapters). On the whole the horse is required to jump from canter, so the sooner the horse learns to pop over a little fence from canter, the better. Having jumped the fence with a trotting pole from trot, remove the pole and jump the fence a couple of times from canter. The rider must sit quietly to allow the horse to concentrate on the fence, but at the same time must ride him forward and maintain the rhythm. Always ride the horse strongly forward on landing to establish rhythm immediately. Although the horse may still be very green, the little canter fence is of such a size that he can jump it with ease from wherever he takes off. It is easier for the horse if it is a small spread fence. There is more for him to look at, and therefore more from which to judge his take-off point, and it also makes him look at the fence more carefully as there is a more solid-looking obstacle for him to see.

The approach to any fence must be straight, and the rider should aim: a) to jump the fence in the middle, and b) to arrive on a line which meets the fence at right angles (*see* diagram 17). This line is particularly important in an indoor school, where one must leave the security of the school wall in order to meet the fence in the centre. The turn into a fence is similar to the turn up the centre line in a dressage arena – turn too soon, and the horse has to drift to meet the centre line, turn too late and it is missed. The turn onto the approach line to a fence must be smooth and of a depth which allows the horse to maintain his forward movement and rhythm. This basic control is up to the rider, although unless the horse is reasonably obedient in his flat work the rider will be unable to put correct turns into practice when jumping.

The horse must be allowed total freedom in the air over a fence. This does not mean that the reins need to be in festoons, and each horse varies in the lightness of contact he needs in order to bascule over a fence. Some horses do prefer to have no contact at all in the air, otherwise they tend to 'invert' (jump hollow) which means they

## 17  The correct line into a fence

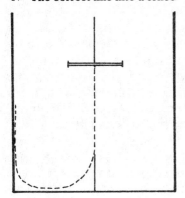 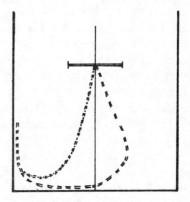

a  *correct — arriving at the fence on a line which meets it at right angles*

b  *incorrect lines of approach:*
   *i  turning too early*
   *ii  turning too late*

c  *the effects on the bend of the horse's body of correct and incorrect turning into a fence:*

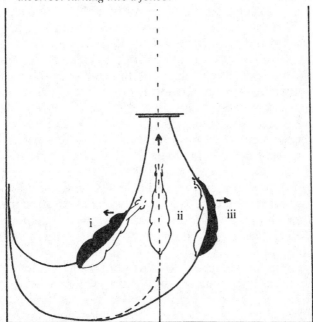

   *i  turn too soon and the left shoulder falls in*
   *ii  turn correctly and the approach is straight and balanced*
   *iii  turn too late and the right shoulder falls out*

are likely to hit the fence. Other horses are quite happy with a light contact in the air, which to my mind is more correct. This is the very slightest of contacts – merely the weight of the rein – but it does maintain continuity, which a totally loose rein does not. Whatever contact is adopted the horse must have complete freedom, as any restriction from the rider's hand will give the horse reason to hit the fence. If he cannot use his head and neck he will jump with a stiff back and, as a result, the jump will lose its fluency, and if he jumps with a hollow back, he is likely to trail his hindlegs and hit the fence. It is tempting to 'lift' the horse over a fence, particularly if one thinks that he is likely to hit it, but the horse is, in fact, less likely to clear the fence. The rider is lifting when he tries to make the horse jump higher over the fence by raising his hand at the point of take-off to try to encourage the horse to give the fence more clearance. The result tends instead to be that the horse jumps the fence unathletically with his head in the air and his back hollow so making it impossible to use himself properly. One fact in its favour is that the rider is not 'dropping' the horse just before the fence – losing contact before take-off – so that the horse is no longer between the rider's hand and leg and can drop onto its forehand at a critical moment. The ideal contact is a steady one all the way to the fence with a slight lightening of the hand as the point of take-off is neared, so that the horse is encouraged to lower his head a little and be soft in his back, ready to carry that shape through over the fence. When a horse jumps loose, he will always lower his head a little just before he takes off; the rider must give the horse the opportunity to reproduce as natural a jump as possible. It is normally when the horse is on his forehand on the approach to a fence that the rider feels the urge to lift the horse over the fence, so it is far more to the point for the rider to sit up straighter, drive the horse's hocks underneath him with a couple of half-halts, and maintain a steady contact to the fence, so that the horse is then well prepared to take off and jump the fence in the correct way. He is far more likely to clear the fence if he is given freedom to do so, than if he is lifted and made to jump hollow.

Many people are reluctant to start cantering at a fence because they feel so uncertain about when the horse will take off (particularly the green horse), but provided the rider controls the balance and rhythm, the horse will sort himself out and learn by any mistakes he might make. It is, nonetheless, important that the horse is able to jump a fence from trot, as there are occasions when he will have to do so. Some cross-country fences have to be jumped from trot – a fence at the bottom of a steep bank, for instance, or a very fiddly fence – while if the horse should break into trot for some reason in front of a fence he must still be able to pop over. A couple of fences in the school, at approximately 60 centimetres (2 feet) high, can be jumped from trot by turning in and popping over without letting the horse break into canter before he takes off; trotting into a fence, and allowing him to canter the last couple of strides may encourage him to rush, so he must be made to remain in trot until he takes off. We strongly recommend, however, that this exercise is only undertaken sparingly, as it is very easy to find the young horse breaking into trot whenever he feels insecure, which is not always convenient! Later on, the horse will be asked to approach fiddly fences such as coffins in a very bouncy canter, and too much trotting at fences will make this extremely difficult. Basically the horse must learn to approach his fences in whatever gait has been requested and to remain in that gait until the point of take-off.

Loose jumping is of enormous assistance in teaching a horse to jump. He is completely on his own without interference from the rider, but has the help of someone on the ground. On no account must the horse be chased, which will only make him jump flat. It is also most important for the horse to be able to concentrate on the fence, and if the ground-man interferes too much, the horse will have half his mind on the person in the middle, and only half his mind on the fence and he will consequently make mistakes. The ground-man must keep the horse going forward in rhythm while talking to him to help maintain a relaxed approach to jumping. A small indoor school is perfect for this sort of work. The horse will soon understand what is required of him, although two people are often necessary to prevent the horse from cutting the corner into the fence. It is better to stick to single fences without placing poles to make the horse use his brain when taking off. Start with a cross-pole to encourage him to jump the centre of the fence, and then build up to whatever size you think the horse is capable of jumping at that stage in his career. Horses will learn to love loose jumping, provided that they are introduced to it properly and have confidence in the person on the ground. A bold horse will come and watch you as you change the fence, and follow you around the school, whereas the anxious horse will stand in a corner, or pace up and down by the door. In time, the horse will not only come to view his loose jumping sessions with enjoyment, but will learn also to become confident about his jumping. The keynote to jumping is confidence in both horse and rider, and all the way through the horse's training this must be preserved at all costs. When a horse is jumping loose, he will make few mistakes, and it is interesting to notice that these mistakes will only occur when the horse is thinking of other things, and mainly if he does not really want to jump the fences. If he is eager to jump the fence, he will always be going forward to it and can therefore correct his stride pattern as necessary. The slightly chicken horse will not be going forward and, consequently, if he meets the fence wrong, he will not be able to put himself right. It is an accepted fact that the chicken horse is far more likely to fall than the bold horse. When jumping over small fences, this type of horse is probably more frightened of the rider than he is of the fence; but when the fences get bigger, his lack of nerve and the resulting half-hearted attempt to jump the fence will invariably end up with his falling. There is nothing worse than setting off on a decent-sized cross-country course on a horse that is not really bold enough.

The diffident rider should gain confidence from watching the horse jumping loose as it shows that he is perfectly able to jump fences from canter. The horse must be able to jump from trot too, but more problems arise if the horse breaks into trot before a fence, than if he remains in canter. A jump is merely an enlarged canter stride and canter is therefore the natural pace from which to jump. They are already patting the ground with their front feet in canter, and so can spring into the air with ease, whereas in trot – working on diagonals – the front legs are further apart and their load is heavier, and it is more difficult for the horse to bring these front feet together and up from that pace.

The use of the placing pole in trot is to make the horse take a little canter stride over the pole so that his front feet are together for take-off, thus encouraging him to 'pat' the ground and 'spring'. Some little fences on a cross-country course may be taken from trot, but it requires much more effort for the horse to jump anything of any size from trot, and in most instances a short bouncy canter is easier and therefore safer.

Teaching the horse to canter over a fence in the early stages is not going to cause him to rush his fences. Indeed, it is probably less likely to than perpetually trotting at them, for he will learn discipline regarding jumping and will take for granted that cantering and jumping are nothing to get excited about.

A line of trotting poles on the approach to a small fence – with the final pole about 2.5 metres (8–9 feet) away from the fence – can, however, be a useful exercise in helping both horse and rider to maintain rhythm and balance. It is particularly revealing for the rider, as any interference, or attempt to push the horse to the fence, alters the rhythm and balance and renders it impossible for the horse to complete the exercise successfully.

Many people feel that the best way to get a horse jumping is to take it hunting. I am very against this because jumping out hunting can teach a horse bad manners, cause him to become excitable, and encourage him to rush his fences. Queueing for a fence, and then making a dash for it when it is your turn is not the best recipe for producing a well-schooled horse. Jumping in a crowd is undoubtedly beneficial in teaching the horse to want to attack his fences, and in jumping all sorts of hairy places, but it does not improve the jump itself – this must be taught at home with exercises. We far prefer to educate a horse at home to jump correctly, and then give him a day or two hunting, just to teach him to jump from all types of going, and to cope with the rough and ready, and also to encourage him to pull into his fences. Having done plenty of basic ground work, this should not mean that all control is lost. Hunting will not make a horse bold 'just like that'. He is either bold or not, but hunting can certainly help give him enthusiasm, and teach him to 'go anywhere' and not bother about mud or puddles or ditches. There are so many horses who will 'jump anything out hunting' but refuse to jump anything of any size in cold blood. Many good event horses whose courage has failed at the higher levels of eventing make the most wonderful hunters, but would most certainly lose heart again should they be taken back to top-flight eventing. Hunting is not the answer to teaching jumping, then, but it is a great help at the right time. To prove my point, both the Advanced horses I ride have only been hunted a couple of times. One was somewhat excitable with his previous owner, and not suitable for hunting at all. The other horse had had one day with the Cambridgeshire Foxhounds, and one with the Drag; this was sufficient to help this one learn to attack his fences with gusto. But they are both naturally bold, which is the vital criterion in the successful event horse. Horses are such valuable animals that often the risk of being kicked or meeting with some other accident outweighs the benefits of the hunting field. There are so many hunter trials now with pair classes, or team chases where these risks are minimised that this is often preferable. For a young horse to follow an older, more experienced horse round a course can often be far more confidence-building than being bumped or jumped across by people in the hunting field. It is a matter of preference which one chooses to do, but we tend to opt for the hunter trial or team chase as an introduction for the young horse. With a safe jumper in front, and a good, steady rhythm maintained, the horse is going to experience a far more educational outing than the hit-and-miss of the hunting field. Having said that, it is undoubtedly a help to buy a horse that has had some hunting experience as, from the schooling point of view, this stage will already have been accomplished, and the horse will not be quite so green when it comes to stepping in puddles and muddy places. He may have bad habits inherited from the hunting field instead, such as boring down on you or tossing his head – habits arising from impatience and tiredness! Probably, in days gone by, when it was possible to 'take your own line' (in the true sense of the word), hunting was invaluable; but with the endless queueing necessary so often nowadays, its benefits have diminished. No doubt all hunting stalwarts will hold their hands up in horror, but this is our opinion, and our preferred method has been successful for us in the production of our young horses.

Once the horse is quite happy about jumping the single fence both from trot, with or without a trot pole, and from canter, he can then be introduced to a jumping exercise, or grid, which is approached in trot. These jumping exercises are all designed for an approach in trot, in which it is easier for the horse to maintain his rhythm (*see* diagram 18). A grid comprising cross-pole to parallel is the one we find the most successful in improving the horse's jump. A cross-pole with a trot-pole 2.5 metres (8 feet) in front of it, then another pole on the ground 2.75 metres (3 yards) away, then finally a small oxer 2.75 metres (3 yards) away from that. The first trot-pole places the horse for the cross-pole. The cross-pole is to guide the horse straight to the centre of the exercise. The second pole keeps the stride short, even and round in the middle, as well as encouraging the horse to land in a round shape by making him look down at the pole. The final parallel teaches him that not only must he go up in the air, but he must also use himself behind too, and open out. It tests the horse in front by showing how he folds his front legs and how quick he is about it, and also makes him use his scope in the width of the fence, and tests his ability to clear the back pole of the fence without cramping his hindlegs. These exercises are invaluable in helping the horse establish a correct jump. The take-off point for the oxer is far closer than most people would aim for usually, but this makes the horse use himself to the full, which is the purpose of all exercises.

Now is the moment to talk about ideal take-off points and related distances, noting that the distances in grids are shorter on purpose than those built in the ring. If we consider a one-stride double of uprights, the distance between the two elements for horses is 7.5 metres (24 feet 6 inches, which is approximately 8 yards): this means that if an average horse's stride is nearly 3.65 metres (4 yards) long,

**18  Basic grids to be approached in trot** — *all distances are suggested, not set . . . if the horse finds them too difficult, lengthen them slightly.*

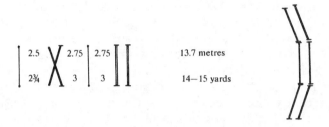

a *basic grid improves the horse's suppleness and rhythm; it increases his athleticism behind, and his neatness and quickness in front.*

b *basic grid with the addition of a small parallel some distance from the original grid, to be approached in an even rhythm from canter, flowing on from landing over the oxer of the grid*

1.9 metres (2 yards) is allowed for landing and 1.9 metres (2 yards) for take-off. The total distance remains approximately the same whatever the height of the fences. When the fences are lower than 100 centimetres (3 feet 3 inches) it does ride rather long on the average horse, but it rides well as the fences increase in size. The higher the fence the rounder the horse's parabola must be and, in relation to the size of the fence, the closer his take-off point. The idea that the higher the fence the further away the horse must take off is in many people's minds, but imagine a puissance competition where the fence may stand over 2 metres (7 feet) high: the rider is, in fact, aiming for a take-off point which is very close to the fence in order to enable the horse to jump it. To jump big fences, a rider must have an accurate eye since the range of take-off points need to be more exact as the fences get bigger. The range of take-off points for fences up to 1.37 metres (4 feet 6 inches) can vary quite considerably and depends upon the speed, impulsion and scope of the horse. This is one reason why eventing is so popular because the accuracy of the rider's eye is not as vital as it is in show-jumping.

A rider should practise striding out yards so that he knows the length of stride he must take on his feet to walk related distances correctly. A related distance may be anything from a bounce to five, six or even seven of the horse's strides between fences. Once the distance exceeds two strides for the horse, the measure reduces by 0.9 metre (1 yard) because the horse's stride length is slightly less than 3.65 metres (4 yards). If a distance between two fences walks 21 metres (23 yards), it means that the horse will take five strides in between: this is worked out by subtracting 3.65 metres (4 yards) for the landing and take-off and dividing the remaining 17.35 metres (19 yards) by 3.65 (the length of the horse's stride), and the answer is five. When it comes to riding related distances it is important to know how much ground your horse makes up and therefore whether he needs to be driven strongly forward on landing over the first element, or whether one should sit quietly.

All the work undertaken in exercises is aiming to make doubles, trebles or related distance fences easy for the horse to negotiate; these grids teach him agility in body and mind and the correct way to jump in rhythm and balance – which is the answer to jumping any combination fences.

The rider's job is to present the horse at an exercise in a forward-going manner, with an even rhythm and on a light contact. He must squeeze the horse into the exercise and then remain very still and in balance throughout, giving the horse maximum freedom with his head and neck, allowing him to find his own balance, and make his own shape over the fences. On no account should the rider try to help the horse to clear the fences by kicking him, or lifting him over. The horse should spring through the exercise without hurrying, but maintaining impulsion and using himself in a truly athletic fashion. Light poles are infinitely better to use for this gymnastic jumping, so that if the horse should hit the fence, he will suffer no injury. It is impossible to make a horse careful. Most horses do not like to hit fences and teaching the horse to jump in a correct shape, in a balanced and rhythmical manner is far more likely to produce a clear round than hitting him with big heavy poles at home, which only result in lumps and bumps. Apart from the exercise already mentioned there are, of course, other variations on the same theme, all designed to build up the athleticism in the horse. The first one is the simplest, and makes the horse use himself in every way – he must be quick in front, spring, and open out behind . . . it is a complete exercise in itself.

Another exercise which concentrates on the front legs and the roundness of the jump, is a trot-pole in front of a vertical, then 2.75 metres (3 yards) to a pole on the ground, 2.75 metres (3 yards) to another vertical, then a pole, then a third vertical. This makes the horse quick in front and makes him stay round, but it does not make him open out behind. A parallel may be introduced as the middle element for variation and this makes the exercise more difficult as the horse must use himself behind, and then be quick enough for the vertical at the end. The poles on the ground keep the stride pattern even, and help to keep the rhythm and stride round and springy.

Grids may consist of a variety of fences at different distances, and depending on the horse's individual requirements, the grid is built for a specific purpose. Different horses will need different exercises to help them with their various problems, and this is where someone on the ground is essential. For one thing, it is impractical to keep dismounting to alter the grid, and for another, a person on the ground will be able to see how the horse is jumping, and whether he is folding his legs, which is something that is impossible to feel from on top, although there are times when one has a shrewd idea that the horse has dangled his legs when he jumps the fence in an exaggerated but doubtful way. One of the most basic grids of all is the cross-pole to parallel which is explained in the blueprint. This grid may then be expanded to make a longer, more difficult grid which incorporates bounces if required (*see* diag. 19, p. 66). A bounce within a grid is beneficial because it teaches the horse not only to be quick-witted and sharp on his feet, but also that he has to use his hocks as well as his front legs to jump a fence. He is unable to rely on the spring off his front legs to jump because having landed over the previous fence he must immediately take off; rather than being able to 'pat' the ground and spring he is therefore merely pushing off.

The event horse must learn how to cope with bounce fences as, even at Novice level, these fences are becoming very popular with course-builders. The majority of horses manage these fences quite easily, although a certain amount of practice at home is necessary. A bounce fence will not help a horse to spring in take off, but will make him bring his hocks well underneath and increases agility. In a bounce fence the need to take off immediately from landing position has the effect of making the horse use his head and neck in an upwards movement in order to raise his shoulders off the ground. He is taking off flat-footed, having had no opportunity to gather himself and spring over the second part. It never feels very comfortable for the rider as there is less fluency in the horse's jump,

### 19 More difficult grids incorporating bounces

| 2.75 | 2.75 | 3 | 3 | metres |
|---|---|---|---|---|
| 3 | 3 | 3¼ | 3¼ | yards |

a *basic canter grid with three uprights — improves technique in front*

| 2.5 | 2.75 | 2.75 | 3.2 | 13.7 metres |
|---|---|---|---|---|
| 2¾ | 3 | 3 | 3½ | 14—15 yards |

b *introduction to the bounce — to be approached in trot — note the slightly long 'last' distance which gives the horse a chance to cope with the bounce in the first instance*

| 2.5 | 2.75 | 2.75 | 2.75 | 13.7 metres |
|---|---|---|---|---|
| 2¾ | 3 | 3 | 3 | 14—15 yards |

c *more advanced bounce grid — the cross-pole becomes parallel cross-poles and the 'last' distance is reduced — working all parts of the horse's body — his ability to stretch and contract — and testing his obedience*

| 2.5 | 2.75 | 2.75 | 2.75 | 2.75 | 10 metres |
|---|---|---|---|---|---|
| 2¾ | 3 | 3 | 3 | 3 | 11 yards |

d *another advanced grid, incorporating one more bounce element — again the horse's athleticism and obedience are tested*

and to stay in balance is difficult. However, the horse must learn how best to cope with these fences, and exercises incorporating a bounce must be brought into the event horse's curriculum.

There is little need to include the bounce in the training of the show-jumper as it is vital that the show-jumper always springs over his fences and indeed, for the size of fence he is expected to jump, he has to. The show-jumper must always be taught to back off his fences and must never be encouraged to try ever to bounce a double or combination. An event horse is expected to jump all sorts of different fences in unexpected places, and so must be ready to jump whenever a fence appears in front of him, however surprising it may be to him. The bounces in a grid will help him learn to think more quickly and be adaptable, but should not be over-used, otherwise the general jump may be spoilt by having made the horse jump flat-footed. A horse who is particularly good behind will find these bounces within a grid very testing as he will feel that his front feet have to leave the ground almost before his back feet have landed, whereas the horse who steps over his fences will find them easier. A stiff-backed horse will also find these exercises difficult and demanding and it is important not to sicken the horse by overdoing the grid work. It depends on the horse, obviously, but once or twice a week should be enough, interspersed with some fences jumped from canter, which will test the benefits of the grid work. The number of times a horse should jump per week is an individual choice, although my motto is that 'a jump a day keeps refusals away'! An old horse will not need too much jumping, just enough to keep his eye in and keep him supple, whereas the young horse at the start of his career has plenty to learn, and needs lessons regularly to progress with his training. Provided that the jumping is done correctly, it will benefit the flat work and give the horse renewed enthusiasm, for, on the whole, horses enjoy jumping more than trotting round in endless circles.

All these varied exercises make the horse look at and think about what he is doing and by changing the format, the rider makes him quick-witted. A trot-pole to a cross-pole bounce approximately 60–90 centimetres (2–3 feet) high and 3.65 metres (4 yards) apart, followed by a parallel 6.4 metres (7 yards) away is a good exercise, which can be altered to a bounce quite easily. For the young horse this can be very small, building up to a height which makes the more experienced horse work quite hard. None of these jumping exercises needs to be enormous, but they do need to be of sufficient proportions to make the horse make an effort. If they are too small the horse will learn little, but of course if they are too big and frighten the horse, then his confidence will be adversely affected, and the exercise will be of detrimental value.

These grids will not only help the horse's athleticism but also help him improve his technique. Once the horse has commenced the grid, he is automatically placed in the correct position to take off for each part of the grid, and, because he can be completely confident that he will be placed correctly to jump the fence, he will be able to concentrate on clearing the fence. A horse who dangles his front legs obviously needs the more upright type of grid to make him tidier. A grid which will help a horse who is untidy in front consists of three uprights starting with a placing pole 2.3–2.75 metres (2½ – 3 yards) from the first upright – to be approached in trot – with poles midway between the elements on the floor to keep the stride even and the horse round in his outline in between the fences. This grid will get the horse up into the air, and, without any spreads, he can concentrate on his front legs (*see* diagram 20). For the horse who is bad behind, which means that he does not use his back end enough in the air and either leaves the hindlegs trailing, or cramps them underneath him, a grid incorporating spread fences will help. The horse should throw his hindlegs up behind him in the air in order to clear the fence (*see* diag. 21, p. 70). The grid should start with the trot-pole to cross-pole, followed by a couple of ascending spread fences, again with the poles on the floor in between.

The distances between the elements of the different grids may vary slightly for different horses, but the short distance is important to make the horse really use himself – under no circumstances allow him to jump flat. A cross-country combination fence with average distances requires as much if not more nimbleness in the horse as this type of grid – shortening the stride from a gallop and trot respectively, the latter in a relatively confined space. Many of the distances in combinations built cross-country today are very short – 5.5 metres (6 yards) is not unusual – so it is very important that the horse learns how to cope with these distances at home from an early age. He will learn there to be quick and athletic and this can then be put into practice in competition. The horse with the slightly dangling action in front needs plenty of exercise to help him learn how to compensate for this imperfection of technique; he has to be extra quick in picking up his front legs if he is rather slow in folding them up in the air. The horse who dangles a lot and who shows no signs of improving his technique despite grids and lots of practice in jumping is probably best allowed to pursue a different career which is less demanding on his jumping ability – or lack of it. If a horse has naturally poor technique and is also slow in reaction, the best rider in the world will be unable to make him tuck up his front legs, and of course if the natural ability is lacking it can never be produced for the horse to work satisfactorily at a high standard.

Throughout all gymnastic jumping, balance and rhythm and free forward movement must be preserved, and this is not just in the

**20 The horse's jumping technique — the position of the forelegs**

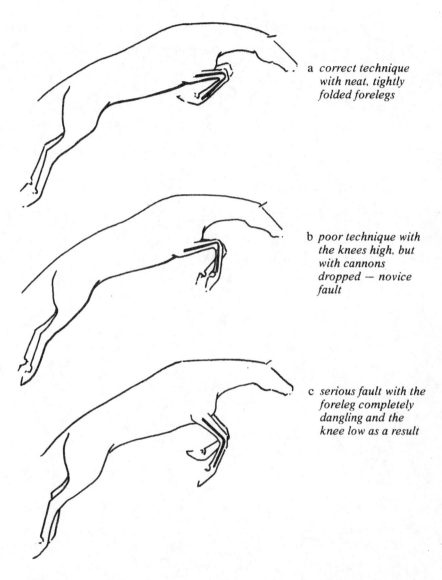

a *correct technique with neat, tightly folded forelegs*

b *poor technique with the knees high, but with cannons dropped — novice fault*

c *serious fault with the foreleg completely dangling and the knee low as a result*

approach to, and over the exercise, but on landing as well. It is a tendency of many riders to feel such a sense of relief when they have successfully negotiated a fence, that they totally forget the importance of re-establishing the rhythm on landing and allow the horse to fall into an unbalanced amble while they are busy patting

**21 The horse's jumping technique — the position of the hindlegs**

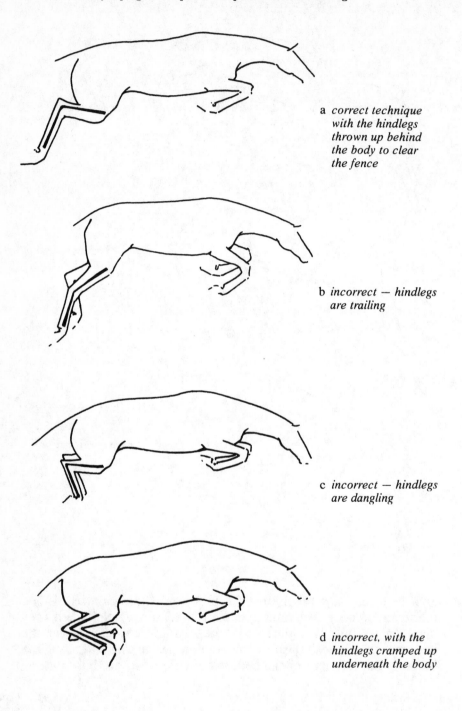

a *correct technique with the hindlegs thrown up behind the body to clear the fence*

b *incorrect — hindlegs are trailing*

c *incorrect — hindlegs are dangling*

d *incorrect, with the hindlegs cramped up underneath the body*

him! These same riders will then wonder why the horse is so difficult to ride round a course of fences. If the pace is always regained as quickly as possible in the early stages of training, it will become automatic for the horse to place and prepare himself for the next fence, but if, every time he jumps a fence, he is permitted to fall into trot, a bad habit will develop which will then need correcting. If the horse drops straight onto his forehand after landing over a fence in a course, he will not have time to readjust his balance before he comes across another fence, and a knock down is likely to ensue. A horse who is particularly extravagant behind will find this readjustment of balance more difficult than the economic jumper, but it is merely a matter of time and training before even the extravagant horse learns how to engage his hocks as quickly as possible. This is the basis upon which a course-builder will plan his course and what the rider must have in mind as he walks a course. A wide spread fence followed by an upright presents the problem discussed just now, for the horse who 'throws away' his back end over the spread fence, then having to re-engage his hocks in time to spring over the upright.

To teach a horse to pick up his rhythm and balance between fences is only basic flat work. The rider must drive the horse up to his hand having landed over a fence, immediately trying to establish the rhythm and adjust the balance by giving a series of half-halts, but by no means restricting the forward movement. When a horse has learnt to jump a fence out of a rhythm, and pick up this rhythm again once he has landed, he becomes easy to jump, and faults will be very few. As important as the horse staying in balance is the fact that the rider must also remain in balance, and this is where the rider's jumping position is so important. If the rider throws his weight forward in front of the horse over a fence, or worse still, throws the weight forward to one side, the horse's balance will be severely affected, particularly if the horse is young. An old horse which is more established will be less affected as he has probably learnt to adjust to his rider's foibles! The young horse who has problems enough adjusting his own balance will certainly find great difficulty in coping with a rider who is out of balance not only over the fence but on the landing too, which is the time when the horse most needs the rider to have an independent, balanced seat. The rider must have his weight firmly in the heel, his head and eyes up, a good bend at the hips, and he must allow the horse's head complete freedom. This position should be automatic for the rider as he jumps a fence; any alteration to it will cause the rider to lose balance which, in turn, will affect the horse's jump. For this reason, grid work is invaluable not only for the horse but also for the rider, as he can concentrate on his position throughout the grid, on the landing and the approach to the next fence. If the rider can only remember that the landing of one fence is the approach to another, it might help him to work more on the landing phase, instead of dismissing it in the excitement of having cleared a fence!

The rider would never dream of allowing the horse to perform poor transitions in the dressage arena, so there is no reason why he should slacken his standards when he is jumping. It is all too common to see a horse cantering disunited during a show-jumping round, with the rider either quite oblivious, or too busy thinking about where the next fence is to change from this unbalanced state. This same rider would never permit the horse to canter like this in the dressage arena, and would be quite shocked to think that the horse would actually canter like that anyway! The whole point of dressage is to be able to develop and adapt the schooling and obedience found there for different phases, and the horse should not lose all discipline as soon as a fence appears. All imperfections in the flat work will always be found out in jumping. It is not possible to cover up short-cuts!

The corner preceding an exercise or a fence is a crucial point in the preparation for the correct arrival at the fence. The horse must keep going forward on the corner, and the rider must ensure that he rides all the way round the corner, and does not restrict the horse with his inside hand as he tries to maintain the bend (*see* diagram 22). The all-important point is that the horse must arrive at the fence with his hocks well engaged in order for him to have the impulsion to jump the fence. Many people can jump a small fence quite easily, but have problems when they attempt something bigger because the bigger the fence, the more impulsion the horse will need, and if they restrict the bend, they will lose this impulsion. People worry far too much about their ability to see a stride too – with the same result. The all-too-common cry is that the cross-country is not a worry, but everything goes wrong in the show-jumping. The speed of the cross-country gives the horse the momentum to be able to stand further back at take-off, although this is not ideal, because there may come the day when the horse, having been asked to take off further and further away, says he cannot take off *that* far away. He will be so long in his stride that he has not room to put in a little one, and consequently he will hit the fence so hard that a fall is inevitable. The speed of the show-jumping does not give the horse the opportunity to stand off so far from the fences, because he lacks impetus, and this limits the take-off

**22 Riding the corner before a fence correctly**

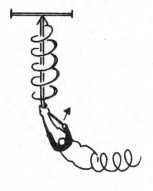

a *the use of the open hand allows the horse to go forward around the corner, maintaining balance and rhythm on the bend, and building up energy all the way into the fence*

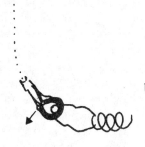

b *if the hand closes across the neck, the horse stops going forward around the corner, and runs out of energy during the approach to the fence*

area. If the horse is encouraged to go faster, he will inevitably jump flat and hit fences. The slow speed must be replaced by energy in the form of impulsion – precisely what the rider is aiming for in his work on the flat.

Although grids are invaluable in the preparation of horse and rider for jumping, they are only a means to an end and jumping fences from canter must be the goal. It is easy to fall into the trap of only jumping grids, where the horse is placed at the first element with a pole, and the rest just follows on automatically. Horse and rider must put all that work into practice over individual fences and then over a course. Many people tend to get into a panic when they move from the security of a grid to the single fence where there is no guide pole to place the horse for take-off. An eye for a stride is a natural gift which some riders are fortunate in possessing, but it can be enhanced by practice. Although many people know when they are wrong as they approach a fence, they are unable to take the necessary action: it is when the horse meets the fence at a take-off point from which he cannot jump the fence that a fault will be incurred – the horse will either stop or otherwise he will have the fence down. It is safe to say that the horse will meet a fence well provided that he is approaching the fence on a forward-going, medium-length stride, balanced and rhythmical. On a medium-length stride, with the horse propelling himself on his hocks with enough potential energy either to lengthen or shorten the stride without loss of balance or rhythm, there should always be scope for an adjustment of stride within the canter, in order to arrive at the take-off point necessary to clear the fence. If the horse is not working from behind, there will be no energy necessary to alter the stride, and he will be unable to adjust himself by either standing off a little or backing off as necessary. The golden rule of 'hold and drive' is required on the approach, the rider softening the hand a little towards the point of take off. This way the horse is given the chance to weigh up the fence himself and so help the rider. If the rider is 'hooking' and 'firing' into fences, the horse does not have a chance to analyse the situation and if the rider 'misses', a stop, knock-down or fall will usually result. It can be difficult to sit still on the approach, but unless the rider is in balance and rides rhythmically, the horse has no chance of maintaining his balance and rhythm.

In the old days, many people were taught to jump by the 'steady, steady, steady, one, two, three' method, by which the horse was almost bouncing on the spot while the rider looked for his last three strides and then fired the horse into the fence. With courses that are technically more difficult, rhythm and balance and a more forward-moving style have become more favoured, and for the average horse and rider, it is a more successful method. It is certainly a more economical way of jumping and, if this rhythm is maintained throughout a course (whether it be show-jumping or cross-country), it is far faster than the stop – go technique. It is all very well for the rider to alter the horse's stride to such an extent that he monopolises the approach and take-off, provided that he *never* misses his stride, but it is really far better to give the horse opportunity to help when necessary. A horse who is totally dominated by his rider will never learn to think for himself, and because one of the most vital attributes of the event horse is that he can help out in tricky moments, he must be given the opportunity during his training periods to do so.

The desire/need for correct basic flat work becomes even more apparent at this point as the horse cannot help if he is not going forward, is unbalanced, stiff, or unathletic. Moreover, if the horse is restricted in his flat work, then his jumping will suffer; provided that he is going forward strongly and is balanced, he will be able to adjust his own stride and jump the fences – particularly any show-jumping courses encountered in the event field, where the fences are not big, and certainly well within the capabilities of any schooled horse. If the rider tries to look for a stride, he may fall into the trap of not riding forward as he is doing so, and consequently the horse will not be going forward either (unless he totally disregards the rider). Unless luck is on hand and the horse is meeting the fence just right, he will not have the necessary impulsion to change his stride by lengthening or shortening it. So many people forget their flat work once it comes to jumping, and forget that within the confines of the dressage arena, they would most definitely use their legs very strongly to create impulsion before asking the horse for a lengthened stride, or a shortened one; once there is a fence in front of them, all this basic training seems to fly out of the window! Rhythm and balance in a forward-going manner is the key to successful jumping, whatever form that jumping might take, whether it be show-jumping, cross-country or steeplechasing.

In the Introduction, I stated that there are no rigid rules in the training of a horse, provided that there is an understanding between the horse and rider; also, that this could be illustrated by the existence of very varied styles of riding, particularly in this country, where we are steeped in a tradition of horsemanship originating in the hunting field. Jumping definitely brings out the natural riding ability in most people. There is no disputing that a good eye for a stride is a definite advantage, and separates the very good rider from the average, but it is possible too for the horse to be trained to help the rider, always supposing that the horse is ridden with this in mind – i.e. keeping the rhythm, balance and forward movement, and not interfering in an obstructive way. The very good rider has the ability not only to see his stride a long way out but also to maintain the rhythm as he makes very slight adjustments. This is wonderful to watch and the retirement of John Francome from racing has made Saturday afternoons very dull indeed, as he was absolute magic in this respect; he was always in perfect balance with his horse, and very seldom did you see him meet a fence wrong. Our top event riders are a delight to watch for the same reasons, and the top show-jumpers too are to be studied with great admiration, for they are jumping fences of enormous proportions, which require supreme accuracy. Note that a show-jumper is rarely seen going round his corners in a 'dressage bend' (most noticeably in a jump-off), but instead the horse's head is almost bent outwards. To understand the reasoning behind this requires careful consideration. It is because it is so important that the rider in no way restricts the forward movement around the corner preceding a fence with the inside hand. Also, a show-jumping class is generally won or lost against the clock and, in order to retain rhythm and forward movement with enough impulsion to jump very big fences off a turn, the horse's inside shoulder must be totally free, and in fact leading, being propelled very strongly from behind. Studying these horses, it is noticeable how the hocks are positively pounding up and down, with vast amounts of impulsion stored in the hindquarters, just waiting to be used. If the horse's shoulder should be lost on the corner, with this enormous amount of potential energy pushing from behind, it would provoke the same reaction as the loss of steering in a car on a corner – the car would skid . . . the horse would no longer be between hand and leg, his steering would go, and all precision would be lost. I am not suggesting that it is correct to go around corners with the wrong bend, but I merely point out that it is the natural way for a horse to balance himself on a corner. You will never see a loose horse in a field canter round a corner with a correct bend; he will always try to balance himself by keeping his inside shoulder underneath himself, and his head turned outwards. Should the ground be slippery, however, he will slip, as his weight is not evenly and correctly distributed. The racehorse is the same. He gallops along in a very natural way, with his jockey in perfect balance; with a head-on camera shot, he can be seen to be galloping slightly crooked – again in balance – and on the bends of a race-course, the horses can be seen to be balanced, on the correct lead, but again with the shoulder leading and the head bent outwards. If the bend is correctly established on the flat, of course, there is no reason why the horse should not bend around his corners before a fence, and still remain in a forward-going rhythm. I am simply pointing out the exaggerations/distortions of the horse's outline in a very specialised field, and emphasising the importance of not restricting with the inside hand on a corner.

When the horse is confidently jumping a small fence, is not weaving around in the approach to both parallel and upright, and is working well in his grid work, the time has come for him to be taken to a show to pop round the minimus class. A course of fences, particularly strange ones, makes the young horse easier to ride than a single fence. The strange fences will have the effect of making him 'back off' (i.e. shortening his stride voluntarily before the fence as he takes a look at it, helping him to find his point of take-off) so that the rider just has to keep pressing forward, and keep him balanced with as good a rhythm as possible in the circumstances. The horse is bound to be spooky, and the rider must resist the temptation of over-riding which will make the horse jump flat. He must allow the horse time to think what he is doing, just ensuring that he remains going forward, and jumps the fences quietly. The rider must, most importantly, be ready to anticipate the horse's reactions, being prepared at any time to get behind him and ride him forward if he shows any signs of trying to stop. If the horse's initiation to a show-jumping round at a show is unpleasant, it will take a long time for him to become relaxed about it all, and if he is tense, he will be back to stage 1 in his training, and as such, unable to progress beyond that point until he relaxes. Whatever the horse is asked to do, do not forget: rhythm and balance first and foremost . . . the rest follows. It is a good idea to try to do a couple of rounds at each show, rather than just one. The more the horse goes into the ring, the wider his experience, the better for him. He will probably knock a fence or two *en route* but, as he gains confidence and experience, he will learn to concentrate on his jumping and forget about all the distractions around the ring. An indoor jumping show is preferable for the first outing, as the horse is shut in the indoor school and cannot see other horses; this helps his concentration. It is the fact that he is on his own, away from all other horses, and doing something very different that can make him feel even more insecure and unable to think about what he is doing: the rider must be prepared to help. On no account, however tempting the idea of a rosette may be to the rider, should the young horse be asked to 'go against the clock'. This is the best way of ruining all the hours of patient training at one fell swoop. When the horse is sufficiently well balanced to cope with jumping off a turn, then he can be asked to 'turn up' to his fences, and indeed this will do him good as he will have to sharpen up his reactions to cope with the situation. Not until he has reached the stage of jumping regular clear rounds at Newcomer level will he be ready to turn in short at that standard. The best way to frighten a horse is to land him on the back pole of a spread fence, and turning in short before the horse is ready for it is an easy way of making that mistake. Confidence must be preserved at all costs.

The show-jumping phase is an important part of eventing. Five penalty points for a knock-down are difficult to make up in the hot competition of today. Many an event has been won or lost on the show-jumping, so it is paramount that both horse and rider obtain plenty of practice. The more difficult the rider finds show-jumping, the more he should practise. The principles for jumping any fence are the same, and to ride cross-country on some of the horses to be seen during the show-jumping phase at some events would fill me with a certain amount of apprehension! Discipline is so very important. It is quite commonly believed that too much show-jumping will detract from the horse's cross-country performance as the horse will not be allowed to stand off from his fences. This is not true, for, if the horse finds himself in a position where he needs to stand off a little further, as long as a rhythm is maintained, the increased speed will give him the impetus to do so. However, the art of good cross-country riding is not just to stand off a long way from the fences. Many of the courses today require a very nimble horse who can pop a fence and not just stand back and fly. If the only way of jumping a horse knows is jumping flat, he will get into far more trouble than the horse who knows how to jump from a deeper take-off point. In a three-day event, the extra effort entailed in standing off fences will take its toll, for it is obviously far more taxing for a horse to make a supreme effort at every fence, than just to pop over in a rhythmical way. This is why exercises at home are so helpful; they teach the horse to be able to do just that. It is far easier to encourage a horse to make up ground in a combination than to shorten him, hence the reason why all exercises should be built on the short side, so that the horse has to be quick and athletic. A long exercise will not make the horse use himself to the same extent and will actively encourage a rather sloppy jump.

Particularly with the young horses, regular jumping at home will be of benefit to both horse and rider. The number of times the horse is jumped per week is very much up to the individual horse. On average, when the horse is at Novice level, three or four times a week will be sufficient. This may happen to take the form of two or three consecutive days followed by several days without jumping, but again the individual requirements of each horse must be understood, and taken into account. If a problem is being encountered, for example, then it may be necessary to jump the horse every day until that problem is sorted out, and then have a complete rest from jumping for a while. Occasionally, it may be necessary to forget the jumping problem until the horse has progressed further in his flat work; then, when he is jumped again, the problem may seem to have been virtually solved. Jumping sessions for the young horse would be divided up between, say, grid work once or twice a week, then a single fence from canter on the other days, with some cross-country work interspersed now and again. Before jumping, a certain amount of flat work must be done in order to loosen the horse up, but not so much that the horse feels in any way tired; all his energy must be put into his jumping, and if the flat work has been overdone, then the horse will be unenthusiastic about his jumping and lose his spring. This spring which is so necessary in jumping may not be so apparent in the young horse at first. He may show a couple of springy jumps, and then start to 'step' or flop over his fences. This spring will return as his muscles strengthen and he learns how to jump properly off his hocks. Grid work will help tremendously in teaching the horse this spring, because the poles will mean that he is always in a perfect position to take off, and in a round shape with his hocks underneath him. The rider, by squeezing him through the grid, will be helping the horse to perfect this.

To introduce the fence into the jumping session, a trot-pole to a cross-pole is a good way to loosen the horse further and get him into the swing of jumping. This little exercise makes the horse pop over the fence in a round shape, and should he be feeling a little exuberant, it will prevent him from taking an enormous, wild leap over the fence, which will be of no benefit at all. The trot-pole will place him in the correct take-off spot, and if he feels the need to 'let off steam' over the first couple of fences, then he will just be able to go higher in the air, which is using his energy in the correct way. This is the same principle as using the horse's exuberance on the flat to do medium trot – that is, the potential energy is released, but channelled in such a way as to teach the horse something; he should not be punished. Once the horse has jumped the cross-pole quietly in trot, the pole can be put straight, and this jumped a couple of times. Then the trotting pole can be rolled in, and the fence jumped from canter. Alternatively, the pole can be rolled in, and the fence jumped from canter with a placing pole 2.75 metres (3 yards) in front of the fence. This is a very helpful exercise as it maintains rhythm into the fence, and ensures (same principle as the poles on the ground in the grid) that the horse's stride stays *round* prior to take-off. It also helps the horse adjust his stride before the fence and should the rider be feeling rather tense, this can give him confidence that he is going to arrive at the fence at the correct take-off point, confidence enough to prevent any temptation on the rider's part to take a pull, and hence stop forward movement. The rider can happily keep riding into the fence, knowing that the horse will sort himself out whereas, without a placing pole, he sometimes lacks the confidence to keep riding. This is where a good teacher is so vital. The rider MUST have total trust and faith in his teacher, so that he believes absolutely that he can jump that fence if the trainer says that he is to do so. As soon as the rider questions what the teacher has asked him to do, then he will never reap the benefit of the lesson. It may be, of course, that this teacher is the wrong one for him. Finding the correct person to help with any problem is a very personal thing, and the right teacher for one person may be the wrong one for another. The key word in learning from anyone is faith. The best rider does not necessarily make the best trainer, for often he is unaware of exactly what he has been doing on the horse. The best trainer is the person who can put into words precisely what he feels and can explain clearly the reasons behind what he thinks. As jumping is so closely connected with confidence, it is also vital that the trainer never gives his pupil cause for losing his confidence, either in the horse or in himself. The best teacher will be able to get the most out of his pupil without destroying any faith.

Many varied exercises can be carried out over a few small fences dotted around. Just popping over these fences on a very light contact from either trot or canter, allowing the horse to sort out the fence on his own is very beneficial; he has to think for himself. In the end, the horse must be able to help his rider, however good that rider may be: the best of riders will make mistakes, and unless the horse can think for himself a disaster may occur. It is not a good idea to dominate the horse completely in jumping, particularly in cross-country where it is impossible to meet every fence absolutely right, and the horse must be able to assist the rider as much as the rider assists the horse. So, practise jumping small fences, leaving the horse to his own devices, just keeping him balanced and rhythmical in whatever pace he is going. Jumping fences on an angle is good practice too: the horse should be conditioned to jumping whatever is put in front of him, whatever the angle and however short the notice is he is given. On a cross-country course, he will be surprised quite often by fences suddenly seeming to appear around a corner: although you have walked the course and know they are there, the horse does not, but he must not just grind to a halt whenever he is unprepared for what is in front of him. It is important to vary the speed of the approach, jumping a fence a little faster and then coming back to a very bouncy canter and popping over something from that pace, so that the horse learns to be obedient, and does not think that just because he jumps one fence fast, he will jump every fence fast. Doubles, combinations and bounces should all be jumped at home to give the horse practice over a variety of fences. Different sorts of jumps can be used within the doubles and combinations – a double of uprights, or parallel in and upright out, for example. Double bounces should be jumped occasionally too, as these do crop up on some courses and, even for a Novice horse, they do teach him to be alert and agile in his jumping. Provided that the going is good, jumping can never harm a fit and sound horse, and he is more likely to encounter problems from a lack of jumping than from an excess. Horses should love jumping . . . and practice makes perfect.

When it comes to cross-country schooling, the sort of fences which do need practice are the coffin, ditch and bank types of obstacles. A straightforward fence is easily negotiated, and although a couple or so are necessary for warming up, they are most unlikely to cause any problems. Most faults across-country are incurred at the fences which require the horse to be nimble and athletic but, assuming that the horse has had plenty of grid work, these should pose little problem for him. However, there are fences or hazards which do need practice – water, for instance. Large puddles make a good introduction and if a large expanse of shallow flood water can be found, that is best of all. The very shallow water will in no way frighten the horse, indeed he will probably thoroughly enjoy splashing around in it. A little fence built on the edge, or in the middle, soon introduces him to jumping into water. The horse must never have a fright in connection with water, or huge problems may occur as a result. But he must never get away with not going into water either, even if it means a lengthy argument!

Particular aspects of jumping and their associated problems and cures will be discussed in detail in the chapter on jumping problems. Basically our theories behind successful jumping, however, go hand in hand with our theories on flat work. Three things cannot be emphasised enough – free forward movement, rhythm and balance.

# THREE

# *Dressage*

The next four chapters concern dressage, show-jumping, cross-country, and steeplechase, and in each chapter are listed all the problems associated with each phase that I have encountered during the years I have spent schooling horses. They are listed in alphabetical order for ease of reference, although of course many problems are interrelated (but these are indicated in the appropriate places). Alphabetical order seems the most logical method of listing the various problems, as this avoids the need constantly to refer to the index. Each problem is discussed in terms of its symptoms, causes and treatment to make everything as clear as possible although sometimes, where appropriate, the symptoms and causes are discussed. The reader is then referred to the relevant stage in the blueprint so that he may continue with the correct pattern of training once the particular problem has been ironed out, or at least improved.

I am quite aware that this is a very personal view, that I may have missed out some problems experienced by other people, but which have as yet not come into my life with horses; but I am hoping that the comments on my experiences will still have a marked bearing on many of these, and that the reader will be helped in his understanding and consequent treatment of his particular situation. I am not laying down concrete rules, but merely providing ideas and methods which John and I have found to work for us over the years. We are always open to ideas and suggestions, because we know that every angle of thought is a help in schooling horses; often just a comment made by someone – not necessarily the best or most experienced person – can provide the key to a problem. This perhaps is the moment to mention how useful it is to do some teaching, as so often one can see something in others which is a fault in oneself, and having to explain this problem to the pupil often helps the trainer when he is reunited with his own horse. Even teaching people with much less experience than oneself is beneficial because, with them, the all-important basics are concentrated upon, and more often than not our basic faults are the cause of all our problems. Watch, and watch carefully, for it is possible to learn an immense amount – far more, in fact, than can ever be taught. Copying is one of the most important facets of a good rider; watching and understanding what you see, and feeling that you are doing the same when you are actually riding is a knack which cannot be taught, but has to be studied and practised. Application, therefore, is the secret of successful riding. It is not necessary to mould oneself completely on someone, but to copy them a little, provided one's individuality is maintained, is a great help in improving both oneself and the horse. Pinching other people's ideas is how we all learn, whether we have to pay for them, or just watch quietly and imitate.

Although the problem sections are divided up into headings of dressage, show-jumping, cross-country and steeplechase, any problem experienced in the dressage section is bound to affect the following three and, to a certain extent, vice versa. It is not a separate phase, and must go hand in hand with the other activities. I think it is always better to think of dressage as flat work, which eliminates that element of separation but, for ease of reference, it is simpler to classify it as dressage. Do not forget that if the horse cannot execute correctly his simple ABC in the dressage arena, there is no way he will be able to perform more difficult exercises, such as jumping, in the necessary controlled fashion.

## Problems encountered

### Above the bit

*Symptoms*: This is probably the most common evasion. The horse deviates from being on the bit by being either above it or behind it. These two basic evasions can incorporate a variety of additional problems, but all these can be condensed to one of the two fundamental incorrect forms. The horse is said to be above the bit when his nose comes beyond the perpendicular line of the arc (*see* diag. 24, p. 85), causing the arc to lose its roundness – i.e. the horse's back hollows and the hindlegs trail. This may happen only during a more difficult movement or a transition and be very slight, or may go to the other extreme, when the horse's shape is totally inverted and his head may become unsteady as well.

Being above the bit does not simply involve the horse becoming hollow, because once he is outside the rider's hand and leg he is free to do whatever he likes . . . the rider no longer has the complete control which can only be obtained when the horse is on the bit at all times. As a result the horse may well develop other bad habits and resistances which should disappear as the schooling progresses and once the horse is working from behind in a supple manner. These secondary resistances can range from a general stiffness or lack of rhythm on a circle, to fly-leaping into fences and loss of control on a cross-country course. So, the basic evasion of being above the bit can arise as a small resistance now and again, or as a major fundamental problem which has many related problems.

Bearing in mind that for the horse to be on the bit he must be straight, have his hocks underneath him and be relaxed in his jaw, it is clear that if one of these three requirements is absent, the horse is liable to come above the bit. Obviously the horse will not necessarily remain on the bit at all times once he has been on the bit once. The rider must ensure that, by correct riding, he maintains the energy from behind, and the suppleness throughout the body to enable the horse to keep soft in his mouth (*see* diagram 23).

One can tell from looking at a horse standing in hand how he has been working – by the shape of his neck and general muscle formation. If he has been working correctly, the muscles across his top line – i.e. neck, back and quarters – will be well formed and rounded. If the horse has been working in a hollow shape, these muscles will be underdeveloped, and there will probably be evidence

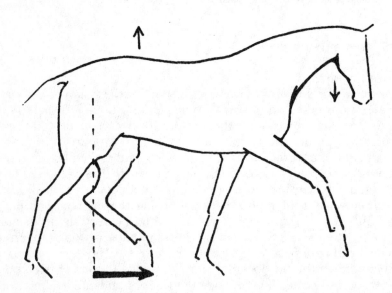

**23 The correct novice outline** — *with his back rounded and his forehand lightened the horse moves straight, with his hocks stepping well up underneath his body to produce plenty of impulsion; his nose is slightly in front of the vertical and his jaw is relaxed.*

24 **An incorrect outline — above the bit** — *with his hindlegs trailing rather than tracking up, and with his head high, the horse's back becomes hollow and his nose comes ahead of the vertical.*
Note: *The key to the horse's outline is the placing and the use of the hindlegs.*

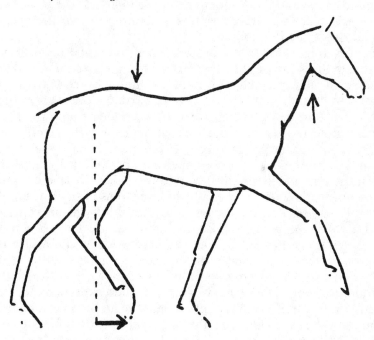

of a build-up of muscle underneath the neck, sometimes to the extent that the horse may even appear to have a ewe- or bull-neck (*see* diagram 24). If the horse is worked correctly, the muscle under the neck will gradually disappear to be replaced by the correctly formed muscle at the top, and the horse's conformation will improve dramatically. Many horses are built in such a way as to make it more comfortable for them to carry themselves in a hollow outline, and for these horses it is even more vital that the initial stages of training are well established; the horse must be encouraged to work in a long, low outline, in order to prevent the build-up of incorrect muscle, which would take a long time to remove, before correctly placed muscle could be developed.

The basic reasons for being above the bit remain largely the same while the degree of the fault can vary enormously. The rider will be well aware of a horse who is completely above the bit, but the slight coming above the bit is far more difficult to detect: this is where someone on the ground is so helpful as he is able to see what the rider sometimes cannot feel. The rider should notice some things though. From on top, the horse's neck should appear to be stretched in a round shape and there should be no wrinkles of skin at the base of the neck near the withers, as this is a sure sign that the neck is being carried tight and hollow.

It is very important to be aware of the difference between the horse being in a state of self-carriage and being above the bit. When the horse is being hacked out, for example, he should not be expected to be on the bit for two hours of road work. It is not fair to ask a horse to be on the bit when being ridden round the roads for the simple reason that the road surfaces are frequently very slippery. Quite naturally the horse is reluctant to bring his hocks well under him in case he slips (which he probably will and this is particularly noticeable in walk); consequently he will save himself a little by not striding out fully and by holding himself slightly tensely. If the rider insists that he 'comes onto the bit' the result will be a forced, tight shape, and of no benefit at all, so it is far better to let the horse find his own balance and reserve work on the bit for the appropriate place. However, even though he is not actually on the bit, the horse should be working from behind, up to the rider's hand, not slopping along. The racing world has a good expression for this, which is 'on the bridle'. (This conveys that the horse is pushing from behind, and that the rider has a contact without the horse leaning on the bit.) When the horse is on the bridle, he is between the rider's hand and leg, though not necessarily on the bit as we know it in dressage terms; it does mean, however, that the horse is working from behind, which is the all-important factor. When the horse comes off the bridle in a race, it means that he is no longer in the rider's hand, and has dropped contact either because he is tired or because he thinks he has done enough.

In fact, the shape assumed by the horse when he is above the bit is probably the most natural shape in which he can carry himself and, if you watch horses jumping, you will see that they do carry themselves like this, because it offers them more freedom in their head and neck both for the take-off and for the jump itself. However, from the dressage point of view, this is incorrect, and it is to this end that we are working at the moment; the 'jumping outline' will be discussed in the show-jumping section.

*Causes*: Bearing in mind that the horse is on the bit when he is straight, his hocks are underneath him and his jaw relaxed, any time the horse is above the bit, one can safely say that he has resisted and stiffened in his back, and/or his hind legs are not sufficiently active for the movement he is doing. With a horse who is working quite well, this will normally only happen when he is asked to perform a movement which requires increased use of the hindlegs, such as a 10-metre circle, a transition, shoulder-in or half-pass. If he does not have his hindlegs sufficiently well underneath him, he will not be able to perform the movement without using his head and neck to balance himself. The completely unschooled horse, who carries himself perpetually hollow, with a high head carriage, has exactly the same problem, but in an accentuated way; because his hindlegs are carrying neither his own weight nor that of the rider, he has to compensate the lack of balance by using his head and neck. The more he is allowed to carry himself in a hollow shape, the more difficult it will be to correct him, as the muscles will build up in such a way that will make it both extremely difficult and uncomfortable for the horse to round his outline when he is asked. A gradual process has to be undertaken to change his shape – remember how difficult it is to touch your toes if you are stiff in your back. When a horse is first broken, the weight of the rider upsets his balance and causes him to fall very much onto his forehand, and, until he adjusts this by bringing his hocks underneath him, he will be unable to carry himself efficiently. Certainly, with the weight so far forward, he will be unlikely to try to carry himself above the bit, but he will rather be on his forehand. This suggests that when the horse becomes above the bit it is rider induced: in fact, the change from being on the forehand to being above the bit is a gradual process, but it is a fairly natural progression for the horse who is shifting his balance to cope with the added weight of the rider. The rider *must* intervene with some basic schooling to teach the horse how to balance himself by using his hindlegs, rather than his head and neck, but if this schooling is not carried out correctly and, for instance, the rider tries to use more hand than leg (and in particular the inside hand), the horse will fight this restriction with some form of resistance – by coming above the bit, for instance, or crossing his jaw or throwing his head. The only way the horse can balance himself properly is by using his hocks and, unless he is taught how to do this, he will respond by resisting the bit and the rider's hand.

Inattention can also cause the horse to come above the bit. He may be working quite well, when something catches his attention in the distance, and he raises his head to have a look. I am sure you have all noticed how a horse will raise his head to look at a distant object, and lower his head to snort at something close by. This is because the horse focuses his eyes by raising and lowering his head:

the lens does not alter shape in the horse's eye, so the horse moves his head position to alter the focal distance. This explains why he will suddenly raise his head to watch something a long way away, and I always feel that the horse who has 'presence' is the horse with such acute eye-sight that he notices things far away, and of course raises his head to get them in focus.

Our veterinary surgeon, Peter Green, wrote the following regarding the horse's eye:

> The shape of the back of a horse's eye is not truly spherical. Instead it is shaped, in cross-section, more like an elipse. This is an aid to focusing, as the retina is not a standard distance from the lens. You and I focus our eyes by adjusting the shape and therefore the focal distance of our lenses; a horse, however, contributes to his focusing by varying the angle of his head and eyes to establish a clear image on the retina, which is at a variable distance from the lens.
>
> For focusing on distant objects he has to raise his head and look from an elevated position. In order to focus on closer objects he has to drop his head.
>
> This explains why there is a natural predisposition for horses to lower their heads as they approach a jump.
>
> Anatomically it is known as a 'Ramp Retina'.

*Treatment*  This depends on the severity of the situation, and so we will start with the horse who just hollows slightly on occasions, and then work on to the more serious cases. We have established that the horse will come above the bit when activity is lost from behind, and this is exposed in any movement where an increased activity is required. The most common case is the transition, when the horse must use his hindlegs to change pace and still remain in a round outline, while his hocks push him forward and also slow him down. Evasion at this point can happen with any horse, at whatever stage of training, and it is the most natural form of evading work. Preparation is the important part of a transition, for if the horse's hocks are not sufficiently engaged in the moment preceding the transition, then he will need his head and neck to enable himself to adjust his balance instead. So, to prepare the horse for a transition, it is necessary to perform one or two, or even a series of half-halts, each bringing the hocks a little further underneath the horse, and thereby adjusting his balance, so that he can make the transition from behind. With a horse who tends to try to come above the bit during a transition, these preparations are vital, and the rider needs to ask the horse to come a little rounder or deeper in his shape

before giving the transition aid – what I would term 'over-ask' – so
that if he does try to hollow a little he will still not come above the
bit.

It is important to ensure that the aids are very clear and that the
horse does not anticipate the change of pace; this is all a matter of
obedience and it is up to the rider to insist that the horse does not
change pace until the exact aids are given. Try to anticipate before
the horse does, and thus avoid the problems: it is obvious, for
instance, that one should not always make a transition in the same
place. A series of transitions will help enormously to teach the horse
that he must use his hocks during these movements: changing from
walk to trot and back again with only a few strides in walk is a very
useful exercise, as is canter – trot – canter with only a few trot
strides. In order to perform these transitions, the rider will be using
an increased leg aid, which has the effect of changing pace as well as
bringing the hocks further underneath the horse. These transitions
are best carried out on a circle, where the horse has to carry himself
on his inside hindleg; and by alternating the direction of the circle,
both hindlegs are activated equally. It is easier for the horse to make
a transition on a circle because, provided the horse is bent to the
shape of the circle and in a rhythm, the inside hindleg is well
underneath him and he is less likely to stiffen during the transition,
particularly as his head is slightly bent to the inside, and so he is
yielding to the rider's inside hand. Another way of increasing activity
in the hocks during the preparation for a transition on the circle is
to ask for a few strides of shoulder-in before asking for the transition,
but the rider must make sure the horse is back on one track during
the actual transition, otherwise he will actually be giving the horse
the opportunity to create another problem, which will then need
sorting out.

Transitions on a straight line are best avoided until those on a
circle have been executed correctly without loss of rhythm and
shape: if the horse still tries to come above the bit in these
transitions, and the rider feels that he is using as much leg as he can,
then further action must be taken. Obviously, if the rider increases
his leg, he must use an equal amount of hand, otherwise the horse
will merely increase his pace. This does not mean that the rider
pulls in any way in a downward transition, but instead he must block
with his hand. The difference between pulling and blocking is very
difficult to describe, and is in fact a feeling the rider will learn with
experience. I try to teach people that feeling by making them drop
their hands onto the horse's withers, and push downwards. Then I
make them close their legs in the dead squeeze of the downward

transition aid, and the more the horse tries to run through the rider's hand, the more I make them press downwards onto the neck, which makes pulling an impossibility. In this way, as the rider is blocking with the hand and not pulling, the horse will respond by using his hocks to balance instead of his head and neck, because he has nothing to fight but himself. Once the rider has felt the blocking action with the assistance of the horse's neck, then he can try with his hands in the normal position, avoiding any temptation to pull, for, as soon as the rider pulls, the horse will immediately retaliate by pulling back or, in this instance, by coming above the bit.

If the horse still attempts to come above the bit during a transition, and the rider feels that he is using sufficient leg, and is not pulling back or restricting in any way, then he must attempt to keep the horse in the correct shape by asking him to work a little lower a few strides before the transition. To ask a horse to work a little lower, the rider should ask him to flex a little more at the poll – by 'feeling' on the inside rein and then a little on the outside one, asking him to 'give' in his jaw. The rider can then drive the horse down onto the contact. On no account must the rider just wiggle the bit in the horse's mouth so that he is actually pulling his head in; the horse must always be ridden *from the leg*, and the hand must only ever assist it by containing energy. Another way of asking the horse to do this (without falling into the trap of restricting the forward movement) is to adopt the widened, or open, inside hand, in which he takes the inside hand on a line towards the centre of the circle which he is tracing – i.e. towards where someone would stand if they were lungeing the horse (*see* diag. 11, p. 32). If the inside hand is widened in this way, it is possible to retain the contact – even quite strongly if necessary, but feeling with the fingers at the same time – without pulling backwards; this, in conjunction with a strong driving leg, will have the effect of keeping the horse in a round shape. If the rider falls into the easy trap of trying to prevent the horse from coming above the bit by tightening the inside hand, the horse will fight all the more, in an attempt to come hollow because the forward movement will be restricted.

When the horse comes above the bit in an upward transition it is invariably the restriction from the rider's inside hand which starts the resistance in the first place. 'Inside leg up to the outside hand, with the inside hand merely the direction and asking rein' is the phrase which must be foremost in the rider's mind. In extreme cases of resistance in the upward transition, both hands may be widened to help keep the horse round, so avoiding any chance of a backward pull from the rider. Once the rider has corrected the problem he can then bring the outside hand back towards the neck and once the horse is consolidated in his transition work, the inside hand will also be able to return to the correct position.

In the trot to canter transition it is very common to find the horse coming above the bit simply because the rider is not following the movement sufficiently. In trot the horse's head is still, whereas in canter the head oscillates up and down with the pace, and the rider must be ready to follow this movement immediately the horse strikes into canter. If the rider is late moving his hand, the horse will automatically bring his head up against the restriction, and this will then become a habit which is difficult to break. To prevent this resistance, the rider must ensure that the horse is really working from behind in the trot, a few half-halts should precede the canter aid while the horse is asked to work a little lower, and, if necessary, the rider could slightly widen his hand in order to keep the contact. He must not increase this contact, or pull back, however, and he must be ready to follow the horse's head movement on the strike off. It is important not to increase or tighten the contact as the horse is given the canter aid as this will give him all the more reason to try to hollow in the strike-off.

Trot to canter on a long rein is very beneficial in giving the horse confidence that he will have no resistance in the transition, and it will encourage him to stretch his outline. Once this transition has been established the rider can gradually take up a light contact, but he must make sure that the horse is really engaged behind, otherwise he will immediately come hollow again. If the horse has been used to a restriction in the upward transition, the hollowing will become such a habit that, even if the rider loosens the contact completely before and during the transition, the horse is still likely to come above the bit and the resistance appears without the cause, this is where the half-halt (to engage the hocks) and the widened hand (to prevent loss of forward movement) are such useful schooling exercises; they make the rider help the horse rather than giving him something to resist. Once the horse understands that he must soften his outline, work on a long rein will help him not only to stretch the muscles along the horse's top line but also to bring his hocks underneath him (*see also* Long rein, page 144).

So, to recap, in dealing with the horse which comes above the bit in his transitions. . . . First prepare the transition with one or several half-halts, or ask for a few strides of shoulder-in. Then make several transitions on the 20-metre circle to make the horse use his hocks and adjust his balance. Make sure that the inside hand is not restricting the forward movement in any way, and use the widened or open hand (on the inside) to help keep the horse in the correct shape. However, be sure that it is the leg which is the main aid, and that the horse is not just being held in shape by the hand. Having the horse bent around the inside leg is ninety per cent of the answer: he then cannot stiffen his back and so come hollow and above the bit.

Now we move on to the horse who is permanently above the bit. This is a very basic problem and invariably one must retrace several stages of training to iron out the problem. As I have already mentioned, the horse whose natural way of going is incorrect has to change totally the way that he uses various muscles, and therefore the shape of these muscles (and probably his appearance) will alter considerably. So, it is important not to force the horse suddenly to go in a way to which he is unaccustomed: he must be given time to become supple, and this will not happen overnight.

It is a great temptation to use gadgets to speed up the process but, it must be realised that to *force* any physical movement can only result in stiff and even damaged muscles, and a gradual change is the only answer. A certain amount of lungeing is of great benefit as the horse can be stretched and suppled without the weight of a rider on his back and it is interesting to watch the horse working as many little problems can be seen by careful studying. We would use a Chambon (*see* Hollow, page 132) to help teach the horse that he must elongate his top line whilst using his hocks. The Chambon must be used very loosely at first to allow the horse to feel the action of the device. (With any form of restraint on a horse it is vitally important not to use it too tightly, particularly at first, because if the horse suddenly feels a restriction, he can react quite alarmingly, endangering both himself and his trainer, and frightening himself into the bargain by rearing and losing his balance. Any gadget must be introduced very slowly and carefully, allowing the horse time to understand its action and gain confidence in how he is expected to react to it.) Most horses learn to accept these lungeing aids quite happily, provided they are given time to adjust and become confident in them. Patience and care are the key words to prevent accidents. With a hollow horse which carries itself above the bit, we would recommend the use of a Chambon rather than side-reins, as the Chambon does not force the horse to hold his neck in a set position, but encourages him to stretch his top line – i.e. the muscles along his back, hindquarters and neck, which will be tight and unworked if the horse has been carrying himself in a contracted shape. The horse is free to stretch as long and low as he wishes, and indeed it is the trainer's aim to encourage the horse to work correctly in this stretched outline. Side-reins, on the other hand, do not permit the

**25 The different actions of the Chambon and side-reins**

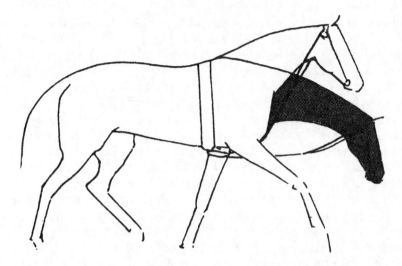

a *a Chambon encourages the horse to lower his head and stretch down, and to work unrestrictedly in a long low outline*

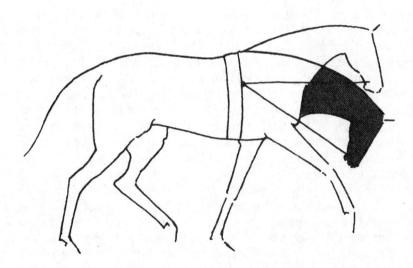

b *side-reins do not permit the horse to stretch when he tries to lower his head and, unless used carefully — so that the horse can be worked in a round but unrestricted shape — may cause the horse to become stiff in his neck, or to overbend.*

horse to stretch, and often they actually cause the unschooled horse to hold his neck in a stiff manner (*see* diag. 25, p. 93). This will affect all the dorsal muscles so, rather than dealing with the problem, they often exacerbate it. I am not condemning side-reins but merely emphasising that, as with every schooling aid, they must be used correctly to be of benefit. The length of the side-rein should be such that the horse can be driven forward with the lunge-whip to encourage him to work in a round but unrestricted shape; they are not intended to hold the horse in a set position, but merely to encourage him to seek the contact. The horse who has not yet learnt to come down onto the bit will often carry himself in a tight form and the wrinkles which may be seen at the base of his neck illustrate this. Once the horse has been loosened up with the Chambon, and has learnt to stretch himself, then side-reins may be used to advantage to teach the horse that he also has to respect the rider's hand and not merely run through the contact, particularly in the transitions. The horse must learn that he should not fight the hand, and with an unyielding, yet not pulling action of a side-rein, he will quickly realise that he cannot escape working with his hocks in his transitions. Lungeing, I must emphasise, is a great art. Anyone can 'whizz a horse round' on the lunge, but it takes expertise to make a horse work on the lunge.

There is such a considerable art to correct lungeing, while incorrect lungeing is of little or no benefit in the training of a horse, that it is worth while thinking about the method of lungeing, and taking care to do it correctly so that the horse is always improving, rather than just dashing or slopping round in an unbeneficial manner. The first thing to remember is that the trainer must remain absolutely on one spot so that the horse is made to trace a true circle. Unless the horse works on a true circle, he will be able to evade working properly, because if he comes off the track of the circle he will be able to swing either his quarters or his shoulders in or out, thus avoiding tracking up. The horse should work on the lunge as one would wish him to work when ridden – i.e. in a balanced rhythm, with a light contact and so he must be in a state of self-carriage, not hanging on the lunge-rein. The trainer must give and take with the lunge-rein until he obtains the required contact. If the horse has nothing to hang on, he cannot hang, and the same goes for when he is ridden: if the rider does not allow the horse to rely on his hand for balance, he will learn to use his hocks instead. It is up to the person lungeing the horse to ensure that he is going forward in a good rhythm, and this is easier than it sounds; he must always be one step ahead of the horse in thought, and either drive him forward a little, or say 'steady' before the rhythm is broken. In trot, the hoofmarks left by the hindlegs should fall exactly where the front hooves have been, and this is called tracking up. Invariably the horse will try to avoid tracking up by swinging his quarters or falling in as, in order to track up correctly, he must work hard, bending his hindlegs in all joints to keep the rhythm and remain on the one track. Keep the horse on a circle of a size which enables him to remain on the one track – i.e. 15 – 20 metres if possible – and only reduce the size of the circle when the horse is sufficiently suppled to be able to work correctly on the reduced size. Increasing and decreasing the circle is a useful exercise to make the horse work harder. Transitions on the lunge are also invaluable and make the horse use his back and hocks without the weight of the rider, and teach him to use himself to best advantage by adjusting his balance. Once the horse has mastered the knack of using his hocks to balance himself, to reduce pace and to propel himself forward on the lunge, then he will find it much easier to reproduce this when the rider is back on board. With the completely unschooled horse a total of fifteen minutes on the lunge is probably all he will be able to cope with initially, and then the time can gradually be built up until he can manage fifteen minutes or more on each rein. The length of time the horse will need on the lunge before the rider can work him from on top depends upon the individual horse, but we like to give a horse with a basic problem – such as being permanently hollow – nearly a week of lungeing before starting to ride him again. After one week of lungeing, the work should be fairly well consolidated, and the horse able to cope with being asked to work a little harder. We would then probably give him fifteen or twenty minutes ridden work, with ten or fifteen minutes lungeing prior to that. Lungeing the horse before he is ridden gives him a chance to loosen up, particularly over his back, so that the rider does not have the problem when he gets on of the horse being tight in his back. To continue the work done on the lunge, the rider should work the horse mainly on the circle, opening the inside rein as necessary and driving forward strongly with the inside leg to maintain impulsion. At the same time the rider must make sure that the outside leg is also working hard behind the girth to prevent the horse from swinging his quarters and evading work that way.

The rider should work the horse with the lungeing work in his mind, and should be aiming for the same results – i.e. rhythm, forward movement and suppleness, both laterally and directly. The same exercises which were carried out on the lunge may be used when the horse is ridden, as increasing and decreasing the size of the circle and changing the pace will all help make progress in the training. Eventually the horse will be quite happy to remain in a round outline in whatever he is being asked to perform.

With the horse whose first instinct is to come above the bit, the rider must remember that he only hollows because his hocks are not working, and he must not be tempted to pull the horse's head down. Although there are times when the rider's hand can force the horse into a lower shape, it is only a temporary state in which the rider is merely fooled into thinking that the horse is going well. Indeed it will lead to further problems as time goes by, as training can only progress when each stage· is *correctly* established. By pulling the horse into a shape, the rider is restricting the forward movement and this will undoubtedly cause all sorts of difficulties once the horse starts jumping, as a horse cannot jump with ease if he is not going forward.

Any work which helps to activate the hindlegs and supple the horse, both laterally and directly, will benefit the horse who comes above the bit. One must always remember the reasons why evasions occur and then work out ways of combating them. If the remedial work does not seem to be helping the situation, then think again why it is not working. Is the horse responding to the leg? Is he merely running through the hand as the leg is increased? Is the hand restricting in any way, particularly the inside hand in the upward transition? All these questions are relevant when considering how to stop a horse coming above the bit and, as can be seen, other sections about dressage problems may also need to be consulted. With reference to the Blueprint, provided that the horse has had a correct initial training, the problem should only be a slight one. If you are dealing with a horse who has had poor early education, however, then going back to square one is invariably the best method. Aim for rhythm, free forward movement and suppleness, and forget about the head carriage for the time being, and you will be surprised how the horse will gratefully respond to a soft contact, and will eventually start to seek down for the contact. Working on a long rein will, of course, continue this progress.

There are some horses who blatantly refuse to respond to the conventional methods discussed above. In the older horse with little or no sensitivity, a pair of spurs will make him pay more respect to the leg and a double bridle can be used to help remind him that he has to take notice of the rider's hand, although again one must be very careful not to fall into the trap of trying to pull the horse's head in, rather than driving him up from behind. As the double bridle helps contain the energy which the leg has created rather than allowing it all to flow away, the horse will then condense his form by bringing his hocks underneath him.

Many people resort to the use of running-reins, or draw-reins for the horse who is above the bit. This must seem a fairly logical approach to some people – the horse's head-carriage is too high, therefore the horse must be made to lower it. In the case of the older horse who is very stiff in his back, both laterally and directly, they can be of some use to the rider in his attempt to encourage the horse not to hollow. This is rather like saying that a dropped noseband is used to prevent the horse from opening his mouth, rather than keeping his mouth shut – i.e. the noseband is not so tight that the horse's mouth is clamped shut, but tight enough for it to be both uncomfortable if he tries to open his mouth and comfortable if his mouth is closed and relaxed. Running-reins used correctly should not be so tight that they are forcing the horse into an unnatural shape, but tight enough for them to come into action when the horse tries to come above the bit and hollow his back. The horse having been kept round in this way, he can then be made to engage his hocks further, which will consolidate the roundness of his shape and teach him at the same time how to use his hocks for balance and propulsion. The obvious danger of using running-reins is that the rider uses only the reins to 'create' the shape, rather than increasing the leg and using the reins merely to maintain it. If the horse's head is pulled down, a myriad of problems will ensue, from a basic lack of forward movement to a completely rigid, restricted horse with, inevitably, the loss of his natural paces. In this instance, once the running-reins are removed, the horse will immediately revert to his previous way of going, and the whole exercise will have been of no benefit whatsoever. It is only in conjunction with the rider's leg that running-reins can be of assistance in training and, in the majority of cases, they do not need to be employed at all. On the whole it is better to correct any problem without having to resort to them. On no account should they ever be used on a young horse, as physiologically it is unnecessary – a youngster being more naturally supple than the older horse – and anyway the progressive schooling of the young horse should make it totally unnecessary. The show-jumping world certainly do use running-reins a great deal, and evidently to great effect. It probably puzzles many people to see the horses in the practice arena of major show-jumping competitions being made to work with their heads almost between their knees. Actually, by doing this, the rider is exaggerating the roundness of the horse's outline and stretching his back as much as he can so that the horse is as supple and athletic as possible before he is asked to jump the enormous fences. By emphasising the shape required over a fence, the rider is preparing the horse as much as possible for the demands about to be made of him.

It is all too common to hear people sneer at the methods used by the top show-jumping riders, but far be it from us to criticise the masters at work, and what we must do is to try to analyse exactly why they are working their horses in a particular way, and realise that that method of training does indeed work for them. The bad rider, however, does tend to leave a poor impression, as does a bad example in any situation, and so it is very important to study the *top* riders. By all means compare their techniques with other people's, but do not take for a foundation the methods of a moderate rider and condemn others out of hand. As a final word on running-reins, I would like to point out that there are very few riders who are able to use running-reins to any long-lasting effect, and because of this I would not recommend their use.

With the horse who sets himself above the bit, a change of tack may help, and a certain amount of experimenting with different bits or nosebands may solve the problem. We are great advocates of the loose-ring snaffle as opposed to the eggbutt or any fixed-ring bit, except in special instances (*see* Behind the bit, page 101). With the loose-ring snaffle, by altering the position of the hand, the bit will move a little in the horse's mouth, and the horse will be unable to set himself on the bit. The eggbutt, on the other hand, and particularly the Fulmer snaffle with its fixed cheeks, remains in one position in the horse's mouth and does not move whatever the hand position. The horse is then able to set himself against the bit, making it far more difficult for the rider to keep a soft feeling in his hand, and he will instead have a dead sensation on the rein. These fixed-ring bits are invaluable in encouraging a horse to take a contact but, with a horse who is above the bit and needs to be coaxed into softening his mouth and yielding in his jaw, they can aggravate the situation.

The different actions of the various nosebands should be considered too, as the noseband is a very important part of the equipment. The dropped noseband, when fitted correctly, can help to lower the horse's head position, because the action is such that as the horse attempts to open his mouth, there is a specific pressure point on the nose, while pressure is also brought to bear on the poll, which encourages the horse to lower his head. It also acts on the chin groove, although on no account must the noseband be so tight that the horse is fighting it before he starts work. At all times the horse must be comfortable, otherwise he will not work for the rider . . . and quite rightly so. All too often, one sees nosebands so tight that the horse is trussed up like a chicken, and cannot even move his jaw; but, on the other hand, he must not be able to open his mouth so wide that he resists. I find the dropped noseband the most useful with the horse who comes above the bit, because of the specific pressure points it acts upon – nose, chin groove and poll – and because the double bridle is therefore its natural successor. The Grakle noseband with its cross-over action prevents the horse from crossing his jaw, and has a very specific pressure point where the two straps cross. However, there is no pressure on the poll, so for the horse who is hollow, it is probably not the best answer. The flash noseband prevents the horse from opening his mouth but has no particular pressure point so, for me again, it is not the answer to the hollow horse. It is important to give different bits or nosebands time for effect, and not immediately rule them out as useless just because they do not provoke an immediate response. The horse must be given time to adapt to the different actions and the rider must learn to assess how the horse is reacting to them. He must work out whether, in the long run, a particular combination of bit and noseband will be beneficial. And then, of course equipment can obviously be changed for various phases. The only very important consideration is the fitting of equipment, particularly the dropped noseband. This must on no account be too low as it can interfere with the horse's breathing, and obviously this is especially important should the rider choose to use it for the cross-country phase.

The treatment for a horse who carries himself above the bit seems to have been quite extensive, but this is because it encompasses such a wide range of problems, and these problems are fundamental ones. For the hollow horse, it is really a matter of retracing steps to stage 2 of the Blueprint, for a hollow horse is not truly pushing from behind . . . otherwise he would not be hollow. First, establish the forward movement of the horse with a good rhythm, using plenty of turns, circles and transitions, without pulling backwards or restricting him in any way, and then it is surprising how he will react by lengthening his outline, and eventually he will come down onto the bit in a correct way – from behind, with a supple back. Progress in schooling should be made automatically once the basic problems are ironed out.

### Anticipating

*Symptoms and Causes*: Since most dressage tests tend to follow much the same pattern, it is inevitable that horses will begin to learn the sequence of movements after they have performed the tests a number of times. As a result, the horse will think that he knows what is coming next in the test, and prepare himself in readiness. Unfortunately, this anticipation tends to make the horse rather tense in himself, and over-responsive to the rider's aids. When he becomes tense, his rhythm, forward movement and suppleness are all lost, and the general impression of calmness and harmony will also disappear (assuming that it existed in the first place of course!). The problem is that the horse stops going forward when he anticipates and, as the rider tries to push him forward, the horse (in his tense state) takes the aid to mean something different. One of the most common points of anticipation is the transition from long-rein walk to medium walk, and then either to trot or canter. Virtually every dressage test has a long-rein walk, or extended walk, so the horse quickly associates the finish of that movement with moving up a gear to another pace. Walk to canter is a movement which lends itself to anticipation, and then is difficult to correct, as the walk is the least easy pace in which to obtain forward movement. In the FEI test of 1975 (which is current at the time of writing) there are several movements which involve the centre line, such as a canter to halt transition, 10-metre circles, half-passes, and trot to canter transitions too. As a result, most horses – particularly as they become familiar with the test – start to anticipate something whenever they turn up the centre line, especially if they are in a rather 'well' frame of mind! As horses get older and wiser, depending on their character, this anticipation may get worse or better, but normally, if the horse is confident, happy and relaxed in his work, the amount of anticipation should be minimal and possible to control. It is really only a question of complete obedience which is, after all, the essence of training. But a horse can only be obedient if he is going correctly, for only then is he truly between the rider's hand and leg, and compliant with the rider's every demand.

*Treatment*: When a horse anticipates in a test, he will lose marks not only at the moment when he anticipates, because he will then be tense, possibly hollow, and lacking in forward movement, but also in the subsequent transition or movement, which will obviously take time to be properly established: the tenseness, caused by the anticipation, will cause stiffening in the back and a lack of drive from behind.

In this instance the rider must try to pit his brains against the horse's: we must try to beat the horse at his own game, by anticipating exactly what he is thinking before he has a chance to show it. When working at home, the horse should be made to perform the many transitions and movements which will be required in his dressage tests, but never in the same sequence. If the horse has some particular mental block about one movement following another, then the rider must work *through* that stage, not necessarily by confusing the horse, but by making him do as he is told when he is told and not before. If the horse does not always associate a long-rein walk with trotting or cantering at the end, but being walked on a shorter rein, he will become more relaxed and settled. It is a matter of keeping the horse in this frame of mind which is the fundamental objective, because unless the horse is calm, nothing else will be correct (*see* stage 1 of the Blueprint – Calmness, page 18). It is very important that the rider does not tense up himself as he prepares for a movement or transition. He must keep driving forward in a relaxed manner, shortening the reins from the long-rein walk almost so that the horse does not notice. It is a matter of creeping up the reins, rather than suddenly shortening them in a rush, as that is the perfect message to a horse that it is time for 'off'! At the end of a schooling session, or in the middle – it really does not matter which – the rider should practise giving the rein away in walk and then taking it up again, so that the horse becomes used to the movement of the hand on the rein. The same exercise may be done in trot and canter – everything should remain the same. Some horses become tense when the rider goes into sitting trot in preparation for canter: here the rider should alternate from sitting to rising trot until the horse accepts the sitting trot quite happily, without expecting a change of pace.

When at home, if the horse ever shows that he thinks he knows what is coming, always do something different, and avoid doing that particular movement – even for the whole of that session. Always be one step ahead.

## Behind the bit

Here is another of the most common evasions and, to my mind, one of the most difficult to combat. Once the horse has learnt how to evade working by dropping behind the bit in various ways, it is only extremely hard work coupled with perseverance which will cure the problem.

*Symptoms*: When the horse is behind the bit, he refuses to take a contact with the rider's hand and, with his nose coming behind the vertical, he does not go freely forward (*see* diag. 26, p. 102). Invariably he also loses his natural paces and stride. 'Overbent' is another term used to describe this, although when a horse is overbent, he may still have a contact with the rider's hand, having just come a little deep in his outline. With the horse who persists in dropping behind the bit, the rider will not be able to maintain a constant, steady contact,

**26 An incorrect outline — behind the bit** — *the horse is not going forward, his hocks are trailing and his neck is 'broken', so that his nose goes behind the vertical and he refuses to take up a contact* (see also *diagrams 23 and 24, pp. 84 and 85*).

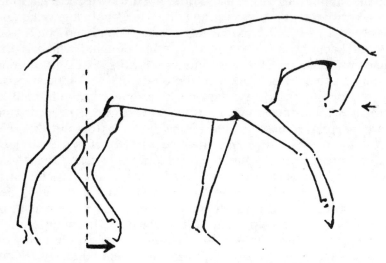

but will feel instead as if he has nothing at the other end of the reins – with the consequent lack of control. It is often the case that the horse will alternate between being behind the bit, so the rider has little or no contact in his hand, and being very strong, trying to run through the rider's hand (*see* pages 149 and 159). This situation stems from the horse's inability to carry himself on his hocks, and often he carries himself crooked as a result. The horse may drop the bit in various ways, but usually it is associated with a chomping of the bit, and combined often with a tipping head: most mouthy resistances, such as drawing the tongue back, sticking the tongue out, fussing with the bit (which can often be mistaken for head-shaking) and constant chewing are all instances where the horse is unwilling to take up a contact, and is therefore behind the bit.

*Causes*: The fundamental reason for a horse to get behind the bit is that he is not going forward and working from behind. Do not forget that any resistance in the mouth is directly connected with the back end: if the horse is not using himself properly behind, whether it be through idleness or a mechanical problem in his hocks, back or general 'motor', then this problem will manifest itself in his mouth. This resistance will take different forms in different horses, but one of the most common is for the horse to drop behind the rider's hand: a steady contact in the hand is only gained by the horse working steadily from behind.

Discomfort in his mouth can also have a bearing on the horse's resistance and so, if he is reluctant to take hold of the bit, and particularly in the case of the 'fussy-mouthed' horse, it is advisable to examine the horse's mouth carefully. Sharp teeth at the back will cause the horse to be uncomfortable with the bit, as they can lacerate his cheeks and make him sore. Wolf-teeth (shallow-rooted teeth found just in front of the upper molars, although lower ones can sometimes appear too) can cause the horse great discomfort, as they invariably make contact actually with the bit. They are particularly noticeable when the horse is asked to turn, as he is very likely to resist. Mouth ulcers or sores or any excuse of this sort is enough to give the horse reason for not accepting the rider's hand and showing his resistance by dropping behind the bit, or merely being fussy in his mouth.

Being behind the bit is not usually caused by rider error, while other resistances certainly can be: a horse who will not take a contact is often just like this, even if the rider is inexperienced, or even a little heavy-handed. A horse is more likely to resist by coming above the bit, or by leaning, or maybe by throwing his head, but if he drops behind the bit, it is usually of his own volition. A badly fitting bit, which may either be too high, or too low, or the wrong size, may cause a horse to be unwilling to take up a contact, but he will probably have a tendency to drop behind the bit in any case.

*Treatment*: Having decided that the horse drops behind the bit because he is not working from behind, the obvious answer to the problem is to make the horse motivate himself far more. However, if the rider is dealing with a horse whose basic paces are poor, he will probably only aggravate the situation if he asks too much. Trying to improve the horse's paces by very much stronger riding may well cause him to drop even further behind the bit as he is quite likely not to realise what is required of him and he may become tense as a result. Working on the basics is of course the answer, and improvement is achieved mostly by quiet persuasion and gentle riding, to encourage the horse to step out and so take the balance on his hocks and eventually take a contact. Long rein work will be of great assistance, coupled with work on the circle in trot, with many transitions, to supple the horse and make him engage his back end in any decrease and increase of pace. During this work, the rider must be very aware of the contact he has with the horse's mouth; he must ensure that he keeps this contact as even and as still as possible, so giving the horse the confidence to take up a contact. The rider must resist any temptation to move the bit in the horse's mouth as every time the bit moves, the horse is likely to drop the contact again. A horse which is dead in his mouth is asked to relax his jaw by the giving and taking of the inside hand, which moves the bit fractionally; a horse which is behind the bit requires the opposite treatment and must not be encouraged to drop the contact by movement from the hand. The bit to use on this type of horse requires consideration. The number one consideration is that the bit must be the correct size with a fairly thick mouthpiece. Because the horse needs to be encouraged to take hold of the bit, the bit best suited for this is a fixed type – either an eggbutt, a Fulmer with cheeks, a straight-bar (metal or rubber or synthetic fibre), or a snaffle with two joints and a flat connecting piece, known as a French-link. All these bits help to encourage the horse to take a steady contact by remaining still in the horse's mouth, thus giving him confidence in the bit. If the rider feels, after a time, that the horse has become heavy in his mouth with one of these bits, he can always change to something which is not quite so solid, such as the loose-ring snaffle. Once it is felt that the correct combination of tack has been found, and yet the horse still refuses to take a contact – however still the rider's hand, and despite all the suppling exercises and transitions which help to engage the hindquarters – then the rider must become a little more insistent that the horse remains on a contact, and learns not to evade work by dropping behind the bit. In order to maintain forward movement, but keeping the horse in the hand without pulling back, it is best to adopt the open hand. By opening both hands, not just the inside one this time, the horse can be driven strongly forward with the leg, yet kept on a contact which in no way restricts his forward movement. Do not forget that the horse is shirking work by resisting in this way, and that he must be taught that he has to work . . . and that life is far easier in the long run if he does. The more the horse tries to drop behind the bit, the wider the hand should be taken, so that the horse just cannot escape being between hand and leg, and so that the energy created by the legs is in fact contained in the hand, whereas before the horse was not producing any energy from behind. Gradually, and again this work is best done on the circle, which keeps the horse supple in his back at the same time, the outside hand can return to its normal position, provided that the horse does not immediately drop the contact. Working in shoulder-in on the circle for a few strides, and increasing and decreasing the size of the circle are exercises which help enormously in driving the horse up to the outside hand, as these are both exercises which emphasise 'inside leg up to the outside hand'. The more the horse is driven up to the outside hand, the more constant the contact will be, and the less chance the horse will have to drop behind the bit.

Being behind the bit is invariably linked with a crooked horse – i.e. a horse who is either permanently or occasionally on two tracks (*see* Crookedness, page 110). While there is a lack of drive from behind and a reluctance on the horse's part to take any contact, the horse is not between the rider's hand and leg, and consequently the rider is not in control. The parallel may be drawn here with a car going round a corner at speed, with the driver whose foot is off the accelerator; the driver is not controlling the car, which becomes a free agent, likely to slip and skid. Instead the driver must keep his foot on the accelerator (as the rider must have the horse working from behind) and his hands firmly on the wheel (maintaining a steady contact in the rider's hand) in order to prevent the car from skidding on the corner (to keep the horse on one track). If the horse persists in carrying himself crooked, the rider must refer back to stage 2 of his training before he can make progress. If the horse is not straight, then he will not be going freely forward; indeed, until such time as he is going forward, it will be impossible to keep him straight. Any exercises which will motivate the horse into 'thinking forward' are the answer here, whether it be jolly hacks to cheer him up and make him think 'positive' before starting on a schooling campaign, or perseverance actually during the schooling sessions – working on stronger paces out of circles and general vigorous work. (Before trying to find a way to keep the crooked horse straight, it is important to realise how a horse does, in fact, manage to carry himself crooked. It is commonly believed that it is the horse's quarters which the horse moves off the one track but it is very often the shoulder which the horse uses to avoid staying straight. By falling either in or out with his shoulder, he is easily able to avoid the correct straight form he must assume in order to work properly.)

The majority of horses are more crooked one way than the other, and the rider must try to understand exactly why the horse finds working correctly (straight) so very difficult. If the horse found the work easy, then he would not need to find ways to evade it, so any horse who is crooked is bound to have some problem somewhere behind the saddle. This may be a general muscular weakness through lack of schooling, or a malfunction of one of his joints behind, or a problem in his back. As soon as a horse starts to go crooked, the rider knows that he is finding whatever he is doing difficult, and rather than create a problem which then has to be ironed out, it is always best to try to avoid that problem in the first place. Once the horse has learnt how to evade working in this way, he will become more difficult to cure. If the rider feels the horse come off the true track, then he must relax the hand (without throwing away the contact of course), and drive him forward strongly. Then he must give him some exercises which will re-engage his hindquarters before asking him to repeat the exercise he was doing. Having ascertained that the horse is as likely to swing his shoulders out as he is his quarters, the rider will discover that it is easier to try to re-align the shoulders with the quarters, rather than the other way round. If the rider spends too much time trying to move the quarters to match the forehand with his leg, the horse may respond too much to the aid by moving his quarters across, while not moving forwards from the leg. This creates yet another problem in itself – where the horse rocks his hindquarters from side to side as soon as the rider applies the leg strongly, rather than engaging his hocks and lowering his croup. The crooked horse will be only too willing to swing his quarters, as working with his hocks is what he is evading in the first instance! Moving the horse up to the outside hand must be the aim, because, if the rider achieves this, the horse is working from behind, and then the outside hand helps to control the forehand. These two problems – being behind the bit and crookedness – are so interrelated that I have discussed them at length together, although there are further comments on crookedness in the section under that title.

Once the horse has been persuaded to take up a contact, he should then be asked to work long and low, stretching his top line; there must still be a contact though, so that he realises that even when he is on a long rein, he must still work from behind. When the rider works the horse, by driving strongly with the leg, and keeping a contact, he is encouraging the horse to lengthen his frame. This stretching work is of benefit to the horse because it supples the muscles along the top line and frees the back. I would like to mention at this point the use of sitting and rising trot. In my view, the horse who is reluctant to go forward and resists by going behind the bit, or by going crooked, is more likely to feel encouraged to work more freely from behind when working in rising trot than if he is encumbered with the rider's weight, which may give him further cause for resenting work! If the horse is not going correctly, then it means that something somewhere is not functioning as it should, and far better to give the horse the benefit of the doubt by relieving him of extra weight, and, after all, it is the rider's legs which are the main aids for bending and for forward movement, and not the seat. This is an important fact to remember in the jumping phase, because it is not as easy to use the seat in the jumping position in the same way as it is in dressage. Indeed, one would not want to because, with a shorter stirrup, the rider's seat would be much further back in the saddle and this would give the horse reason to hollow rather than maintain the round shape necessary for jumping. The event horse must learn to be responsive to both the seat and the legs as, in the more advanced dressage phase, he must be ridden in sitting trot and therefore must accept the rider's seat, while in all the jumping phases it is the rider's legs which form the basis of any aids for acceleration and deceleration. The seat will not come into action as much, so the horse must move from the leg at all times.

## Chewing the bit

*Symptoms*: This is fairly self-explanatory, occurring when the horse is unwilling to take a steady contact with the bit; he persists in chewing or chomping on the bit all or some of the time that he is being ridden or lunged. The horse will often tip his head at this point too; the two evasions tend to go hand in hand. The rider will have an unstable contact with the horse's mouth and, as the horse refuses to go up to the bit, it will be impossible to have the horse truly between hand and leg. In other words, the horse will be behind the bit, which is his way of evading work.

*Causes*: The horse may champ the bit for a variety of subsidiary reasons but, in the end, it is really because the horse will not go up to the bit, is not going forward from behind nor willingly engaging his hocks, and is therefore not between the rider's hand and leg, where he would be under complete control. This may be rider induced when the horse is shortened in front and not given time to find his own balance. If the horse was totally between hand and leg, he would have to do as he was told, and would not be able to avoid work with these secondary evasions. When horses are excited or on edge, they will invariably chew on the bit. Watching racehorses on the television at the start of a race when they are really keyed up, you can see that they are all champing at the bit – hence the expression. However, during dressage the horse is required to be totally relaxed and settled, so constantly chewing on the bit is not acceptable, because it is a sign that the horse is rather tense and worried about his work.

Another reason for chewing the bit may be discomfort in the mouth, either from ill-fitting bits, sharp molars, ulcers or wolf-teeth. Some horses are broken with bits with keys on them: these are designed to encourage the horse to play with his bit, so creating a wet mouth, which is supposedly soft. A soft mouth is actually totally dependent upon the balance of the horse, and his natural manoeuvrability. A dry mouth or hard mouth is created by a badly balanced horse and poor schooling. If a rider hangs onto a horse's mouth, he will soon create a wooden-mouthed horse, but this is indirectly caused by the hocks not carrying the horse. A horse who is capable of working correctly, with his hocks underneath him, will have a very good mouth, regardless of how he has been ridden in the past. An example of this is a horse belonging to John's father, called River Boy (see plate 3b), whom John and I both point-to-pointed. He was a lovely horse, and John and I both won races on him, but in a race, or galloping at home, he was very strong. I certainly couldn't hold him in a race, but I started eventing him when he was twelve when his legs showed signs of not standing up to further racing. He did six events and won four of them, doing the best dressage test on each of those occasions. When he had learnt how to work within the confines of a dressage arena, he had the lightest mouth that you could ever wish for, and that was after seven years of hunting and racing. So here is proof that it is rubbish that a horse's mouth is 'spoilt': provided that he learns how to balance himself and be sufficiently supple, his mouth will be similarly responsive. Because of this I believe that keys are not only unnecessary in making a horse accept the bit in his mouth, but can also result in the horse perpetually champing the bit. A low bit will certainly encourage a horse to champ as he has to catch the bit continually to prevent it dropping onto his teeth, whereas a bit which is too high in his mouth is more likely to cause the horse to cross his jaw to avoid the action of the joint or mouthpiece.

*Treatment*: For the horse who champs the bit, is obviously behind the bit and refuses to go forward up to the rider's hand, read the advice given in the section on Behind the bit (page 101) again: see also Shortened stride, Overbent and Not going forward (pages 161, 153 and 149). To encourage the horse to take a steadier contact, and accept the bit in his mouth a little more, a straight-bar snaffle – either rubber or metal – or otherwise an eggbutt or fixed-mouth bit (such as a Fulmer) can help. Because these bits remain still in the horse's mouth, they give the horse confidence to take hold of them a little more than the bit which moves in the mouth, such as the loose-ring snaffle. A snugly fitting cavesson noseband, which restricts the jaw higher up rather than interfering with the mouth area, can make it uncomfortable for the horse to keep chewing the bit; this too may help to discourage him.

It is worth noting that horses do not as a rule chew the bit when they are galloping, and this is because they are normally up to the bridle when they are moving at that fast pace. From this it can be seen that the problem is that of getting the horse sufficiently motivated to be up to the bit in the slower paces. This is only achieved by him working from behind, up to the rider's hand. Chewing the bit is not an easy habit to cure; the horse must be driven strongly forward, but kept in a balanced form with the rider keeping a very still, light contact with the horse's mouth. When the horse accepts the bit, the rider must reward the horse by just maintaining that very light contact, which will only grow firmer and more constant when the horse works consistently through from behind. The rider *must* be patient and be content with small amounts of progress, otherwise no progress at all will be seen. As soon as the horse drops the contact, and starts to chew the bit, the rider must offer him the hand, and drive the horse forward before gently taking up the rein again. Once the horse has been encouraged to stretch down onto the bit, he can then be coaxed into taking more of a constant contact (*see* Long rein, page 144). The ultimate aim in this case is for the horse to accept the bit and the contact from the rider, and, when the horse does take the bit, he must be rewarded immediately; the rider should remain very still and almost passive, not asking for any more until the horse is fairly constant in his work, and is confident about what he is being asked to do. Until the horse takes a light contact, it is impossible to progress beyond the stage of rhythm and bend, but it is usually because these stages were not properly established correctly that the problems arise in the first place.

Working a horse with this type of problem, one normally finds that the horse will trot round the outside of the school on a very light contact but, as soon as he is asked to circle or alter pace, he will immediately drop the bit. To eliminate the problem with the circle, it is vital that the inside hand does not move the bit in the mouth as the rider asks the horse to turn. The aid must be a very gentle feel, encouraging the horse to keep hold of the bit, even though he is yielding to it. If he should drop the bit, the rider should offer the inside hand forward, driving the horse onwards and keeping a still outside hand; then, once the horse has accepted the contact with the outside hand with an open inside hand, the rider should take up the rein again. This may have to be repeated many times, and the essence is to drive the horse immediately forward with a relaxed, offering hand, so that he is urged to seek the contact for himself.

Use an exercise such as shoulder-in for half a dozen or so strides out of the corner, circle, and then repeat, to make the horse really use his back and his hocks; follow that with several transitions; and then back to the circle and shoulder-in pattern, to get the horse working properly. This should be followed by some rewarding work – trotting round the outside of the school, being content with a rhythm and a very light contact – with the rider sitting very quietly, so that the horse understands what he is expected to do. After all, he does not know that it is wrong to chew his bit, and there is no way that we as riders and trainers can explain to him other than by corrective schooling.

In a transition, the rider must be positive that he is not pulling back with his hand and that the contact does not alter. The horse must respond to the rider's leg aid throughout, and so use his hocks; if he drops the contact during the transition, the rider should immediately offer him both hands and make him find his own balance, merely repeating the exercise until the horse learns his lesson. It may be necessary initially to block firmly with the hand a couple of times in the downward transition, to prevent the horse running through the hand, but once that has been done, the hand must be very light and on no account should it pull back.

As with the horse who is behind the bit, this evasion is a painstakingly slow one to overcome, because the horse knows just how to avoid working from behind . . . but patience and hard work will be rewarded in the end.

## Crookedness

This evasion really goes hand in hand with the horse not going forward, and being behind the bit (*see* pages 149 and 101).

*Symptoms*: The horse will not be on one track, but will trace a different track with his hindfeet from the one which his front feet are tracing. This may vary depending on which rein the horse is on, but the quarters will be consistent in the way they swing to avoid remaining on the one track. The rider will be aware of the crooked feeling the horse gives him, and will feel that the horse is not truly between hand and leg – with either the shoulders or the quarters swinging one way or the other and the horse perpetually edging one way. It is this crookedness which makes it impossible to have the horse absolutely between hand and leg, and this will be all the more apparent when the horse is asked to perform more demanding exercises. Because he is not pushing in a balanced way from behind, he will not be equally in the rider's hand; this will show, especially in medium work where the horse is expected to drive forward even more strongly from behind, maintaining rhythm and impulsion. There is nearly always an interrelationship between crookedness and a tipping head – a horse not going forward and being behind the bit.

*Causes*: The horse deviates from the straight line because he is not pushing forward evenly from behind. Lack of impulsion in a horse is similar to lack of pedalling on a bicycle – the bicycle is difficult to keep straight and, unless the rider has excellent balance, wobbling off a straight line is almost inevitable. The horse finds himself in the same situation when he lacks drive from behind; he will either swing his shoulders or his quarters to compensate for lack of balance and will give a wobbly feel to the rider. This is particularly common in the young horse who has not yet learnt to use his hocks to adjust his balance. If a horse has a physical problem behind – whether it stems from the back, or from stiffness – he will be unable to stay on the one track, and will avoid working correctly by stepping sideways as opposed to bringing the hocks underneath him. Most horses are one-sided to a certain extent anyway, and so, from an early stage in training, it must be impressed upon the horse that he must always go straight, so that there is no chance of him getting into the bad habit of going crooked. Some horses may only go crooked at times. This is particularly noticeable in medium or extended trot, for example, where the horse is required to push more from behind and, because of inactivity in that quarter, there is an involuntary deviation from the one track. The canter is a pace where crookedness often manifests itself, with the horse bringing his quarters to the inside in order to balance himself when he is neither carrying himself evenly on his hocks nor working from behind. It is interesting to watch a head-on shot of a flat race, for it is easy to see how racehorses balance themselves by galloping with their quarters to the inside and their head bent slightly away from the direction in which they are going; this is their natural way of going but for dressage we have to alter that by making them use their hocks.

*Treatment*: One of the most basic corrective measures to be taken in order to straighten the horse up is one which is equally applicable to the bicycle wobble: the horse must be driven forward strongly, even increasing the speed a little if necessary. This is certainly the best way to straighten up a wobble on the centre line; by increasing the speed a fraction, the horse will straighten up, and then the rider should take a half-halt to retain the necessary balance and speed within that pace. On the whole, it is easier to correct crookedness by aligning the shoulders with the hindquarters than the other way around. This invariably means a stronger control with the outside rein to prevent the shoulders from swinging, making the horse push forward without losing the impulsion sideways. If the rider tries to straighten the horse too much by using the leg, the horse will begin to associate leg movement with moving the quarters independently rather than with moving forwards, thereby creating a problem in itself. Although the horse must be prepared, of course, to move away from the leg – in the shoulder-in, half-pass, etc. – the leg should ostensibly mean move forwards, and the aid given for these movements must be specific. If the rider has his leg perpetually working towards keeping the horse straight, it will then present him with difficulties of differentiation when he comes to ask for these two-track movements. Plenty of circles and suppling movements and changes of bend, such as serpentines, where the horse must change direction, are very helpful in containing the shoulders and quarters. If, for example, the horse falls out with his shoulder on one rein on a circle, by changing the rein the shoulder is then captured on the next circle, and similarly when the original rein is taken up again. Swinging quarters can be dealt with in the same way. The horse must be made more supple in his back so that he is able to trace the correct shape of the circle required of him, and increasing and decreasing the circle, shoulder-in and other suppling exercises will assist this. Shoulder-out along the long side of the school helps to contain the shoulder and activates the hocks at the same time, and it may also be carried out for a few strides on the circle. This exercise is particularly beneficial if the horse is heavy in the outside hand.

It is worth watching to find out whether the horse carries himself crooked when he is without a rider as, if this is the case, there is evidently something mechanical which is affecting him, and it is important to ascertain exactly what and where the problem is. It is necessary to have a good veterinary surgeon who specialises in horses and who will be able to help in such cases. The vet must understand precisely the demands put on competition horses in order to be able to recognise the more intricate problems. Crookedness in a horse can often stem from a back problem – whether it be muscular or skeletal – and it is wise to have a back specialist check the horse, so that either the horse can be treated, or back trouble can be ruled out as a cause.

Backs are a fashionable subject, so I asked our veterinary surgeon, Peter Green, to give an expert opinion:

With regard to the old chestnut of 'vertebrae out', the most reasonable theory is that the problem is a muscular one which results in an uneven lateral pull on the dorsal spinous processes of the vertebra concerned (*see* diagrams 27 – 29).

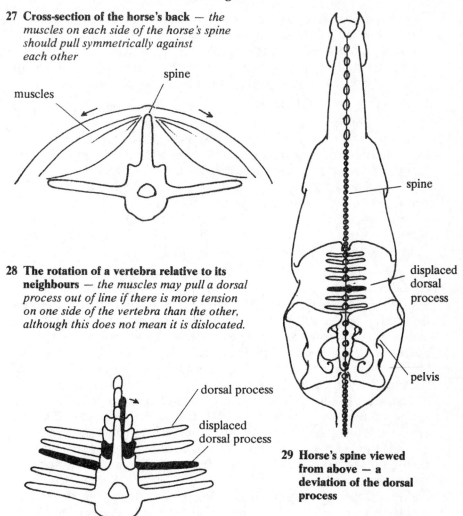

**27 Cross-section of the horse's back** — *the muscles on each side of the horse's spine should pull symmetrically against each other*

muscles

spine

**28 The rotation of a vertebra relative to its neighbours** — *the muscles may pull a dorsal process out of line if there is more tension on one side of the vertebra than the other, although this does not mean it is dislocated.*

dorsal process

displaced dorsal process

spine

displaced dorsal process

pelvis

**29 Horse's spine viewed from above — a deviation of the dorsal process**

If you can imagine several vertebrae in line – like doughnuts threaded onto a pole – each with their dorsal processes in line, this represents the optimum spinal conformation. Each vertebra has its own unit of muscles either side and it is quite conceivable that, should one side be pulling more than the other, an individual vertebra may rotate relative to its neighbours. This does not affect the longitudinal alignment of the vertebrae – they can in no way be said to be dislocated, but it *will* result in a deviation of the dorsal spinous process.

It seems that manipulative procedures sometimes succeed in relieving the muscular spasm which is pulling the vertebra sideways, and therefore restore normal alignment. We certainly regularly see horses which have one process out of line, some of which can be restored to alignment by manipulation.

It does seem, therefore, that the horse can be given some muscular relief by physiotherapy sessions, so by all means have the horse's back checked by a reputable back expert. Do not expect a miracle cure, though, and be prepared to have the treatment repeated quite regularly. Of course, the fact that the horse is crooked may have nothing to do with his back whatsoever, and it could be stifle, hock, or even fetlock behind which is causing the stiffness and reluctance to work. Again, the vet can help you with this, as the horse will carry himself crooked for a reason, and this reason must be discovered before a cure can be found.

### Crossing the jaw

*Symptoms*: In this evasion, the horse opens his mouth, and moves his bottom jaw to one side or the other, or moves it from side to side in an attempt to avoid the direct action of the bit on the various parts of the lower jaw. A plain snaffle acts on the tongue, the lips, the bars, the corners and, with the addition of a dropped noseband, the poll. With a curb, viz. the double bridle, the additional points of action are the roof of the mouth and the chin groove. In order to evade taking the action of the bit, the horse will cross his jaw, relieving his mouth both of the direct pressure from the bit and, of course, the rider's hand. The rider will experience a strong dead feeling in his hand as the horse crosses his jaw, and a subsequent lack of control.

*Causes*: Bearing in mind that resistance in the mouth is directly connected to the weight-bearing ability of the hindlegs, it becomes apparent that when the horse crosses his jaw, it is merely his way of saying that he cannot respond to the rider's demands because of a lack of balance and inactivity in the hindquarters. The horse will normally only cross his jaw when the rider takes a firmer contact on the rein – if there is no contact, the horse has nothing to resist, and therefore no reason to cross his jaw. This is proof in itself that the horse is unable to carry himself in a specific shape because his hocks are not carrying his weight, and that of the rider, in such a way that he can obey his rider's aids. In order for him to remain soft in his mouth during turns and transitions, he must use his hocks to propel himself and adjust his balance and pace. If he does not engage his hocks during these movements, he will have to use his head and neck as his balancing pole, and if he finds restriction from the rider's hand then he will resist by, in this case, crossing his jaw. When he does cross his jaw, he is saying, 'give me freedom to use my front end, I need it for my balance', and the rider must realise that, because of the inactivity of the hocks, the horse is unable at that moment to carry out his requests correctly.

If a horse is uncomfortable in his mouth generally, this will cause him to cross his jaw. The difference between the horse who crosses his jaw as a resistance against the rider's hand, and the horse who crosses his jaw against the bit itself can be seen as soon as the horse is tacked up, as the horse who resists the bit will immediately cross his jaw when the bit is merely put into his mouth, and before a contact is taken up by the rider. It is important to be aware of the reasons behind the resistance before it can be remedied.

*Treatment*: Careful note should be made of exactly when and why the horse actually does cross his jaw before deciding how best to deal with the problem. With the horse who crosses his jaw as soon as the bridle is put on, the first thing to ensure is that the bridle is fitted correctly, that the bit is the correct size and not too high (for a horse is more likely to cross his jaw against a bit that is too high in his mouth than one that is too low). The bit that is fitted too low can create other problems: the horse can get his tongue over the bit, for example, or develop a fussy mouth because of the bit banging on his teeth. Another question to ask oneself is whether the bit you are using is the right bit for that horse. If the horse appears to be uncomfortable, ask yourself why that might be so. Some horses have rather large tongues, for instance, and the nutcracker action of the snaffle is very uncomfortable for them, in which case a French-link snaffle, with two joints and a flat plate in the centre could be the answer. There is no concrete answer to bitting horses, and really finding the correct bit for different horses is a matter of trial and error. It is obviously better to stick to bits approved for dressage, otherwise the horse may go beautifully in a bit which is not allowed, and it will be a matter of having to start all over again to find the key to the horse's mouth when it comes to a competition. There are a great variety of different bits which are 'legal' and which cope with most horses' requirements. Most saddlery shops of good repute will be quite helpful, and horsy friends are quite happy to lend bits, which are one of the few things which rarely get damaged (apart from rubber snaffles which do not seem to last two minutes)! Before changing the bit, however, it is best to have a look in the horse's mouth and check that it is not sore in any way, from ulcers, lacerations caused by sharp teeth, or by aggravation from wolf-teeth. The vet will deal with the teeth, and it is advisable to have a horse's teeth checked at least twice a year. It is well known that most mouth injuries are quick to heal, and a few days without a bit in the mouth should see a recovery. Continuing to use a bit while the horse has a sore mouth will only give the horse further grounds for fighting the bit. It is worthwhile being patient, because once the mouth has healed the horse no longer has an excuse. He will take time to forget the discomfort caused by mouth problems, however, and the rider must remember this mental state when riding him again.

Usually the first reaction to a horse who crosses his jaw is to slap on some form of restraintive noseband, either dropped, flash or Grakle. Although I agree with this principle to a certain extent, bearing out the age-old saying of 'Horses are like women, shut their mouths and you can take them anywhere!' (what a chauvinist attitude!), it does not cure the actual problem, which is that the horse is not sufficiently on his hocks. However, once the horse has got into the habit of immediately crossing his jaw as soon as he feels a contact on his mouth, it is then very difficult to drive him up from behind: he will merely run through the rider's hand by crossing his jaw, making it impossible for the rider to contain the energy his legs are creating. By employing a noseband which discourages the horse from crossing his jaw, it will then be possible to teach the horse to use his hocks to greater advantage, instead of creating a vicious circle in which the horse is driven up but no benefit is reaped; although his hocks are coming further underneath him, the horse is too strong in the hand of the rider. On no account should the noseband be so tight that the horse is unable to flex his jaw as this will make the horse even more uncomfortable in his mouth, giving him more reason to resist, and causing him perhaps to be even deader in his mouth than before. The noseband should only be a deterrent – i.e. it should be there to prevent the horse from opening his mouth and crossing his jaw, not to keep his mouth shut – there is a subtle difference. It depends on the individual horse as to which type of noseband is preferable. Different nosebands suit different horses, and there is no rule by which to decide. Which noseband to use is a personal thing, and some people prefer one to another, but really it does not matter which is chosen as long as it suits the rider and his horse.

As the horse only crosses his jaw when working on a contact and it has been ascertained that this is because he is not working sufficiently from behind, all exercises which increase the activity in the hocks, and supple the back and other joints behind are means to improve the horse. The rider must find out at what point the horse starts to resist; he must, in a schooling session, be meticulous about the order of working the horse (*see* Chapter Two) and then it will become obvious at what stage the horse starts to find his work difficult. For example, if the horse starts to cross his jaw as soon as the rider asks him to turn to make a circle, it indicates that the horse cannot balance himself on a circle of that size, either because he is too stiff to trace the circle with his body, or because his hocks are not coming far enough underneath to carry him. Either way, the rider will have to increase the use of his inside leg to make the horse bend and bring the inside hock further underneath him, so driving the horse up to the balance rein of the outside hand. He will have to give and take with the inside hand. It takes two to pull and so, if the rider immediately gives with the inside hand as soon as he feels resistance from the horse, and then asks again with an increased inside leg, the horse will realise that he is not being restricted with the inside rein and that there is nothing for him to fight. If, when the horse resists, the rider immediately goes tight in his inside hand, the horse will merely resist more by crossing his jaw . . . and so begins the vicious circle. Give and take, ask and reward are the key words to overcoming the problem of a constantly crossing jaw: give the horse nothing to resist and he cannot resist, but at the same time, of course, he must be asked to work a little harder to improve his way of going. The rider has to ask the horse to come up to a contact, which must itself be gained from driving with the inside leg up to the outside hand, in order to allow the horse to move freely forward.

Crossing of the jaw is not a natural thing for a horse to do and is rider-induced – by a restricting hand combined with a lack of balance on the part of the horse. The horse must therefore be taught how to balance himself, in order to carry himself and his rider without having to resort to the rider's hand for support. Aim for self-carriage and a crossing jaw will then be avoided. Go back to the basics of rhythm, straightness and free forward movement; forget about asking the horse to come onto the bit; it is amazing how the horse automatically starts to work in a rounder shape with no resistance.

**Counter-canter, problems with**
*Symptoms*: The horse may shorten his stride and lose his rhythm, lose the bend, or change legs, either with a flying change, or just in front.
*Causes*: Counter-canter demands strength and suppleness from the

horse, and should not be performed until the horse's basic training is well consolidated and he is able to carry his weight well on his hocks. Any loss of rhythm or stride-length occurs because the horse is not using his hocks sufficiently – either because he is weak, or because he lacks training, or because the rider is not driving the horse through enough from behind to maintain his impulsion.

*Treatment*: To prevent any change of lead, the rider must keep his weight evenly distributed, and not slip to the outside, as this will encourage the horse to change legs to keep his balance. It is also vital that the rider keeps the bend, as any change of bend will automatically unbalance the horse so that he changes lead. It is up to the rider to use enough leg to maintain the necessary impulsion during the counter canter to ensure that the horse remains in rhythm and does not alter his length of stride or lose the bend.

Some horses find counter-canter easier than others, but it is an exercise which improves with training and maturity or strength. Counter-canter forces the horse to engage his hindlegs, and in particular the outside hind, which is then on the inside and must flex more in all joints to enable the horse to retain his rhythm, balance and shape. The naturally stiff-gaited horse will find counter-canter demanding and will require extra help from the rider to enable him to perform it correctly. However, with all horses it must be introduced gradually by the use of the demi-volte (i.e. changing the rein by riding a half-circle, normally 10–15 metres in diameter, followed by a return to the track, so that a tear-shaped loop is executed). The number of strides of counter-canter on the return to the track should be slowly increased until the horse can eventually remain in counter-canter as long as required. Another method of introducing the exercise is to ask the horse to make shallow loops between the quarter-markers on the long side of the school. The horse must remain the same throughout the loop, maintaining his rhythm, shape, and length of stride, and the rider must prepare the horse by ensuring that he is going well forward in the canter before the loop, and must then ride him strongly during the movement to avoid any loss of impulsion. The importance of introducing the movement gradually cannot be stressed strongly enough: if the horse once learns that he can change legs during this movement, it will lead to problems in the future. As he tenses, his back stiffens, his hocks trail slightly and, because he is then off balance, he has to change legs. Very soon, of course, he will change legs whenever he feels any tension in a test, and the rider will find this problem increasingly difficult to correct as it becomes a habit.

Once the horse has become strong enough to perform this

movement he should then accept being asked to canter anywhere on a named lead – provided the turns are within his capabilities – without losing his rhythm or forward movement. He will then have happily accepted counter-canter as part of his schooling curriculum, and this confidence will be apparent when he performs the movements in the arena without problems.

## Disunited canter

*Symptoms*: Rather than cantering with the correct sequence of legs – viz. outside hind, inside hind and outside fore together, and then finally the inside fore as the leading leg – the horse changes behind, or in front, so that the sequence becomes inside hind, outside hind and outside fore together, and then inside fore. In other words, whereas, in true canter the two legs which hit the ground at the same time are diagonals, when the horse is disunited, these two legs are on the same side. This unbalances the horse, and is extremely uncomfortable for the rider. The horse cannot push from a disunited gait, as is proved by the fact that a horse always changes from a disunited canter to a united canter just before the take-off of a fence; he cannot jump from disunited pace, because he is unbalanced and lacking in propulsion.

*Causes*: The horse will only canter disunited if he is unbalanced and his hocks are not underneath him. He is unlikely to strike off into a disunited canter, but will change either in front or behind depending on the situation, so that he is then disunited. The horse will change behind either when he fails to bring his outside hind sufficiently far forward to balance himself, or when he swings his quarters to such an extent that he *has* to change leads behind. A change in front normally happens during a change of direction when the horse does not use his hocks, and so only changes in front: during a movement in counter-canter this is quite a common form of evasion, when the horse is not driving quite enough with his hocks and falls in with his shoulder.

*Treatment*: When a horse does change legs behind, the quarters must be controlled more effectively with a firmer outside leg behind the girth. The horse cannot change leads behind if the hocks are engaged, the horse is going forward and the hindquarters are in line with the forehand. If a horse finds canter one way more difficult than the other, he may try to avoid cantering for any length of time by changing: the rider must strengthen the horse in this case by gradually increasing the length of time spent on canter work, until the horse is capable of carrying the necessary weight on the outside hind.

If the horse does change, the rider must take the horse back to trot, immediately canter again, and then ask for a trot transition once a united canter has been established. A horse will often try to take one disunited stride in the canter to trot transition and, in doing this, he is avoiding engaging his hocks properly during the actual transition. The rider must prepare for the downward transition correctly with a series of half-halts to get the horse's hocks as far underneath him as his stage of training permits; but he must ensure that the quarters do not swing out, as this would allow the horse to go disunited in the transition. The horse must then be driven forward into trot, so that the hocks are kept working throughout the movement, and the rider must not be tempted to let the horse draw back into trot, and so lose the forward movement. The horse will not go disunited if he is working from behind, so the forward movement must be maintained at all times.

## Excitability

*Symptoms and Causes*: A self-explanatory state of affairs, with the horse finding life a little too much for him to cope with at a particular time. This excitement can manifest itself in many different ways: the horse may leap around, bucking, rearing and generally being a menace, but he may merely sweat profusely, shake, becoming very tense and nervous. If we cast our minds back to the horse's natural state, the moment of greatest excitement for him in the wild would have been when he was pursued by an enemy, or during a fight for supremacy in the herd. We have domesticated the horse, turning him originally into a work animal and a war-horse, and then into an object for our amusement. This statement may not appeal to many people, but it is true, as any form of competition involving horses is really only for our own self-glory and fun – the poor horse has little choice as to whether he wants to do it or not. It is unfortunate that those horses who decide that they do not want to race, jump or obey our wishes are termed 'dogs' and ungenuine, when really they are not as stupid as we like to make out. However, they are the horses it is generally best to avoid if you want a happy relationship with a horse! Anyway, we pack our horses' relatively small brains with an awful lot of data and excitement, introducing them to aspects of life which they were not originally bred to endure, and it should be remembered that they must be allowed time as youngsters to learn about life and what is has to offer them. There is a very fine line between the horse being excited by, and being nervous of what is about to come. Many times people do misinterpret the horse's reactions to exciting things, and assume that, because they themselves feel a certain way, the horse must too. They do not, perhaps, appreciate that because the horse is unable to reason, he has more cause for concern than the rider has: the sweating, dancing-around-with-ears-firmly-pricked state does not necessarily mean that the horse 'cannot wait to get on with it', and indeed may mean he is suffering from stress and nerves. It is absolutely necessary to understand the horse, and to interpret his reactions to every situation. For instance, a fresh horse will find something very exciting which will not stimulate him at all when he is tired. For this reason, it is always best not to take a young horse to an event or show when he is underworked, because any excuse – even tiny things – will give him ample opportunity to find life agitating and behave abnormally. Having been very excited, the horse will have been overstimulated and is likely to behave the same way the next time he goes out, instead of taking things in his stride. *Treatment*: I have discussed excitability under the cloak of calmness in the Blueprint and that section should be studied when trying to *prevent* a horse becoming overstimulated and, therefore, excited in his work. It is normally at a competition that a horse tends to become excitable because of the other horses around him, especially when they are cantering and jumping. The best introduction for the young horse to a show would be a dressage show, where (normally!) the other horses are working quietly and there are no galloping ponies and undisciplined animals leaping around: horses are influenced by other horses and, given this quiet introduction a horse will react accordingly. The only way to cope with excitement is to discipline the horse, so that he is influenced more by the rider's aids than by his own emotions (Ha!), even when he does find his surroundings conducive to behaving in an excitable manner – i.e. he remains sufficiently controlled still to be manageable. Every horse is entitled to feel excited before hunting or cross-country but, as they become conversant with what is expected of them (knowing that, in fact, it is not frightening, but merely exhilarating), with any luck they are then able to cope with the excitement in a quieter way. However, the older and more experienced horse will know only too well what is coming next, and may be over-exuberant in his anxiety to set off! An overexcited horse is a danger not only to his rider but also to bystanders or fellow competitors, and it is therefore important that he is kept under control and not allowed to follow his instincts should they be a little wild! If you feel that your horse might find certain circumstances exciting, it is wise to make sure that he has had plenty of work leading up to the occasion, so that he is not feeling over-fresh. If possible, have the horse out for a time at home before going to the show or, alternatively, lunge him before getting onto him, provided that you are confident about his not getting away from you. So that the horse can be lunged with a greater degree of control – which is desirable when you are lungeing in an open space – the lunge-line can be attached to the bit on the far side, then passed over the top of the head, and through the bit ring on the side nearest the trainer. It is not an ideal way of lungeing, but sometimes the horse is so strong on the lunge when he is excited that it is the safest method, provided that there is someone experienced on the end of the lunge-line. It is important to remember, too, that this is not allowed before a dressage test as it is considered to be a 'running-rein'.

It is always best to hack the horse to his first meet, or at least give yourself a good distance from the horsebox so that the horse is almost a little weary when he arrives. This will give him less chance to find it all too exciting, and even if he is then a little tired, it will not matter, as he should not be kept out too long on his first few times in any case. If a young horse is kept out hunting all day he will certainly get very tired, both physically and mentally, and a very tired young horse will often appear to be getting more and more excited; he is, in fact, reacting rather like an overtired child who becomes overexcited as a result of fatigue. He will remember the unpleasant aspect of feeling exhausted, and will associate hunting with something exciting yet rather uncomfortable; this impression will remain in his brain, and the next time he is likely to be even more wound up about it all. On the other hand, it may make him even more excitable if he is only exposed to a very short time out hunting, as he will not have been given time to settle down and realise that, in fact, it is not all excitement after all, and that he is there to perform a task. Deciding how long you should stay out is a matter of knowing your horse's character. Most horses do need several 'days' out hunting to make them settle, and the more shows and events they have participated in the better. There are not many horses who do not quickly become accustomed to the life they are given to lead, and, once they understand the routine, they do generally accept whatever they are asked to do. It is normally the first event of the season which provokes the biggest response from the horse, as he is out of the routine of event life. That is the time, therefore, to make sure that he is not under-worked and that he is given a little longer in his warm-up time to relax. If time allows, the older horse often benefits from being ridden twice before the dressage.

Even if the horse is finding life rather jolly, it is up to the rider to ensure that he is still obedient, and he must be firmer in his treatment of the horse. Stronger riding is the answer, not chastisement. If the horse is tense about his surroundings, he needs the quiet insistence from the rider to settle him down, rather than any additional worry; he does not want to have to be wary of having a kick or a smack or a sharp reminder from the rider's hand. If the horse is allowed to play around every time he first comes out of the box at an event or show, this will become a habit to be cured, and it is therefore up to the rider to make sure that the horse's exuberance is used profitably, not wasted in unnecessary misbehaviour. Once the warm-up period is over, the rider must be determined that the horse should concentrate and, even if something interesting is going on in the far corner of the field, the horse must not be allowed to put his head in the air to watch what is happening. When the horse is working, he must be expected to concentrate fully: if he is permitted to let his attention wander outside the dressage arena, it is unreasonable to expect him suddenly to concentrate one hundred per cent merely because he is within the confines of the white boards. It is important not to overwork a horse before a dressage test, otherwise he will appear listless; a little contained exuberance, on the other hand, can be used to advantage, to give elevation and presence.

However, even if all precautions are taken, a young horse may still behave in a quite dramatic fashion on his first encounter with a show. The rider must be ready for such an occurrence by having adequate help on the ground to hold the horse and give a good leg-up. It is never wise to try to mount an excited horse, because if the horse tries to move off quickly, an accident can easily happen. A leg-up is far safer, but the person who gives the leg-up *must* be experienced – a bad leg-up is hopeless on a restive horse (and awful at other times!) and can only cause further problems. The person holding the horse must also be experienced, and must know exactly when to let go of the horse, because if a horse tries to move forwards and is prevented from doing so at the crucial moment, he can often rear, and any lack of balance at that stage will make him go over backwards. As soon as the rider is aboard, the horse must be allowed to go forwards, and it is up to the rider to get his stirrups as quickly as he can (these of course should be of the correct length, and the girths sufficiently tight that they will not need tightening straight away). A firm contact (with one hand in the neck strap) and a strong driving leg are vital, so that the horse is driven forwards and is not given the opportunity to either buck or whip round. Provided that the rider keeps driving him forwards, even if the horse does try to buck, it should not be of the unseating variety, as it is only when the horse is able to twist sideways that the rider has little chance of staying on board. A buck which is driven forwards will be more like a jump, and these are not difficult to sit on. The buck-and-whip-round is very difficult, and those horses who try to rear and follow it with a buck are the most tricky of all, and so it is very important that the horse is sent forward into a good strong trot if he shows any sign of misbehaving, and this should be continued until the horse has really settled down properly. The sooner the horse is then taken to another show the better, so that he learns that shows and events are just a continuation of his general work and training, and nothing to get worried and excited about at all. By all means allow the horse to enjoy himself, but keep it within disciplined limits, and when it is time for the horse to settle and work, then he must work constantly without a lapse of concentration until he is allowed a long rein. He should then be walked around the showground for a while to see the sights and to allow him thoroughly to relax in his surroundings, so that the next time he goes to a show, he knows precisely what to expect.

### Falling in

*Symptoms*: Instead of tracking true (the hind feet treading in the tracks traced by the front feet), the horse does not bend around the rider's inside leg on the circle, and the hind feet will move off the one track, either to the inside or the outside (*see* diag. 8, p. 27). The horse's body will appear to be bent in the opposite direction to that in which he is going and his head will be turned to the outside, which will undoubtedly cause a loss of rhythm.

*Causes*: Lack of training and lack of obedience, particularly to the inside leg aid, but to the aid to bend in general. Both these are, in turn, caused by stiffness. Falling in can also be caused by a horse shying at something too because, in attempting to move away suddenly, his balance is lost and to fall in is inevitable.

*Treatment*: The rider must work on the suppleness of the horse and his response to the inside leg (*see* Stiffness, page 165, and Shying, page 162), and any exercises which increase the general suppleness of the horse will help correct the problem. (*see* stage 4 of the Blueprint – Straightness, page 26). In a difficult case where the horse really does refuse to take any notice of the inside leg, an open hand can be used. Approaching a corner, the rider takes the outside hand out towards the wall of the school; he asks for a bend with the inside hand and inside leg, but guides the horse into the corner with the outside hand, so that he cannot fall in on the turn. The rider must make sure that he uses enough inside leg to maintain the rhythm, and also to teach the horse that he is to bend around that leg, and not merely to rely on the hand. This exercise may be used on a circle, so that the horse moves away from the inside leg, but the quarters must be contained by the outside leg so that the horse does not merely avoid bending by swinging away from the inside leg. The rider must always try to work towards closing the outside hand and opening the inside, or the problem of crossing the inside hand and 'holding' the bend will ensue – and these two are possibly the worst and most difficult habits to cure in a rider (*see* diag. 11c, p. 32).

### Falling into trot from canter

*Symptoms*: Instead of using his hocks to slow down, the horse places all his weight on his forehand; his centre of balance is so far forward that a trip will often be the result, and undoubtedly there will be a loss of rhythm in trot. The trot will take time to become established while the horse adjusts his balance, and takes some weight back onto his hocks and, until he does, the trot will be heavy, with the horse running on his forehand with a hurried stride.

*Causes*: Any gaps in the horse's training will become more apparent in transitions, where the horse must use his hocks to change efficiently from pace to pace, and canter–trot requires more hock action than trot–walk. For this reason any faults in the way the horse is working will be emphasised in the canter to trot transition. If the horse falls into trot it is because he is not using his hocks to make the transition, which means that he will lack balance which, in turn, will make him run through the rider's hand (*see* page 159): all these combine to make a moderate transition. This may all be caused by lack of basic training, or by lack of preparation from the rider for one particular transition. Unless the rider drives the hocks up under the horse in canter by using the half-halt, the horse will have no chance of suddenly engaging his hocks whilst actually making the downward transition; he will have to rely on the rider's hand to maintain his balance, or otherwise lose his balance altogether and run onto his forehand. If a rider should actually pull at the horse to make him trot, instead of closing the leg and blocking with the hand in the transition, this may cause the horse to fight the bit, therefore losing his hocks and his balance, and resulting in a shambling transition. All these problems and their causes are very much interrelated, and invariably, if the root cause is cured, not only will the canter to trot transition improve, but many other movements which rely on the engagement of the hock, on balance and on the resulting rhythm.

*Treatment*: Whatever the cause of the horse falling into trot may be, the treatment is the same: basically the horse must be taught to use his hocks, and also the correct use of the aids must be ensured. The rider must make a series of strong half-halts in the canter, and drive the hocks further under the horse, so that the horse is then in a position to take the weight on his hocks to make the transition into trot. The rider should aim to make the horse canter in as condensed a form as possible for the half-dozen or so strides preceding the transition, giving a strong aid into trot and driving forward at the same time, yet not allowing the horse to run through the hand. It is important that the rider does not fall into the trap of not allowing the horse to go forward in his transition; the horse must carry his weight on his hocks but move strongly forward at the same time. These transitions should be practised several times during a training session, as the horse has to use his hocks to a certain extent in any transition even if it is not perfectly executed; if the transition is well prepared, and even reasonably well done, it will be of benefit to the general training of the horse. The transition will improve in time, once the horse has learnt how to use his hocks to best advantage, and is strong enough in himself to be able to use them at all times. Invariably, it is the horse who falls into trot who will try to run into canter or come hollow in the transition; these are all signs that he is not pushing from behind, so the practice in the upward and downward transitions will help each other. Similarly, correcting faults in transitions will help the way the horse goes in general, as making him use his hocks more in transitions will help him to use them more at other times.

**Falling out**
*Symptoms*: The horse drifts outwards with his shoulder, particularly on the turn, consequently losing the rhythm and the true one-track movement. The rider will feel that the horse is heavy to turn, and hangs away from the direction he is being asked to go.
*Causes*: The rider is not containing the outside shoulder on the bend, and so the horse is heavy in his steering. A horse which is hanging towards home or the other horses will behave in this manner (or in the opposite way – i.e. fall in). The horse is avoiding working properly between the rider's hand and leg, and is not bending correctly around the corners.
*Treatment*: The horse must be straightened by an increased outside hand and outside leg aid. If the horse is swinging out, he must be firmly corrected by aligning the shoulder with the quarters, which is a matter of leading the horse over with an opened inside rein and being a little stronger with the outside hand. If necessary, move the outside leg forward to help the outside hand until the horse is

straight, and then move it back to the normal position behind the girth.

This is a case for prevention rather than cure. The horse must not be allowed to fall out with his shoulder in the first place; the rider should not allow the shoulder to swing, and then have to correct it. This is a relatively simple problem to solve, and the situation can be improved by plenty of turns and changes of direction, which will teach the horse to keep his shoulders in line with his quarters. If, changing direction within a circle or using the serpentine shape, the shoulder has fallen out on one rein, it will immediately be captured on the other rein, as it will now be on the inside. Other helpful exercises include shoulder-out (for a few strides) on a circle, or simply bending the horse to the outside on a circle. If the horse is being worked from the inside leg up to the outside hand, the fact that he is trying to fall out with his shoulder does at least show that he is in the outside hand, and merely needs containing.

### Four-time canter

*Symptoms*: Instead of working in a three-time canter, the horse creates a four-time beat by splitting the diagonal and hitting the ground with the outside foreleg fractionally ahead of the inside hind. (In gallop the four-time beat occurs again but the diagonal beat is split the other way around.) The horse will have lost the smooth rocking motion of the canter, and will be stiff in his back, uncomfortable to ride, and will appear stilted to the onlooker. The horse shortens his stride in front and not behind so he loses impulsion within the pace as there is a lack of engagement from behind.

*Causes*: The four-time canter is the result of a horse's not going forward and not working from behind: this is invariably caused by the rider shortening the horse from the front while just not driving him up from behind. He is being asked to canter in a more collected form but this means that not only is he being asked to do something difficult (*too* advanced), he is also being asked incorrectly; the stride pattern inevitably suffers and the four-time canter is the result.

*Treatment*: Since the horse is not going forward and is inactive behind, the first stage of correction must be to drive the horse strongly forward, perhaps even increasing the quickness of the pace in order to maintain a three-time beat. The horse has to be encouraged to push more and carry more of his weight on his hocks. The canter itself must become more elastic and positive in its action, and I find that one of the best ways of obtaining this is to canter strongly in a forward position. The horse can be driven up strongly from behind and this way, without the rider's weight on his back, he is encouraged to loosen his back and bring his hocks underneath him. Once the horse has been made to produce a true canter in this strong canter, the rider can gradually ask for decreases and increases of pace within canter and work on transitions in order to make the horse work as much as possible from behind: should the horse drop into the four-time beat, he must immediately be driven forward again. It will take time to eradicate a four-time canter, depending, obviously, on how set the horse is in the habit. If the young horse should lose his true rhythm, the rider must react quickly and ride him forward strongly with a relaxed hand, in the knowledge that the only reason the horse drops into four-time is because the stride is shortening from the front – which indicates restriction from the rider.

In some cases of four-time canter, counter-canter may be of benefit. By increasing the suppleness of the horse, it also makes him engage his hocks. Alternatively it may exacerbate the problem, because the horse tends to fall into a four-time canter whenever he finds the canter work difficult; because counter-canter is a demanding exercise, it may only serve to encourage this.

### Halt, problems with

*Symptoms*: In a correct halt, the horse should move smoothly forward – without losing his shape or rhythm, without resistance, and with his hocks underneath him – into a state of immobility, with his four feet standing square. The horse may halt not square, crooked, or wide behind; he may fall onto his forehand, which may cause him to trip; he may resist in his mouth; he may wander into halt; or finally, he may not remain still once he has halted.

*Causes*: All the above faults are symptomatic of a transition in which the horse is not using his hocks. In order to execute a halt correctly, the horse must lower his croup and bend his hocks: an inability to do this can stem either from a lack of general training, or from weakness. Problems with immobility – ranging from inattention, to fidgeting, excitement, or tension – may originate in the horse's general temperament, although they can also be put down to youth, bad training, or pain, especially in the back or mouth. It may be that the rider is asking the horse to halt too abruptly (rather than progressively) for his stage of training.

*Treatment*: It is important to stress at this point that the halt will only improve as the horse's basic training progresses. If attempts to correct the halt are made before he has learnt how to use his hocks in an easier transition – from trot to walk, for instance – he will find it almost impossible to halt properly. The rider should work towards his halts 'generally', because if he makes a big issue of them, the horse will soon become tense, and any problems will be aggravated.

Whilst perfecting other transitions, and teaching the horse to respond obediently to the closed leg and blocking hand, the rider will be laying the foundations for a correct halt transition. When the rider does come to ask for halt, even in the early stages of training, it is important that he asks the horse gently and quietly to stand as square as he can, even if the transition is not perfect. He should also try to remain stationary for a while, so that the horse does not anticipate moving off immediately. As soon as the horse has halted, the rider should soften his hand and leg, and relax the horse, if necessary, by patting him – not only on his neck, but also behind the saddle. This will serve a secondary purpose, because the horse will become accustomed to the removal of the hand from the rein, and this will prepare him for the salute of a future dressage test.

To obtain a good halt, the rider must prepare for the movement in whatever gait he is in, by giving a couple of half-halts and asking the horse to flex a little more at the poll if he shows any sign of resisting. Then he must drive him into halt, by closing the leg strongly up to a blocking hand. If the rider pulls backwards, the horse will immediately resist in his mouth, which will cause a chain reaction – a stiff back, and inactive hocks – and all of these will lead to a poor halt. Eventually, however, with training and perseverance, the horse will come automatically to a square halt, provided that the correct preparations are made and the correct aids given.

Straightness in this transition is of the utmost importance – as it is in all transitions – because any deviation from the straight line will indicate that the hocks are not engaged and, therefore, that there is a lack of balance. If the horse wavers off the straight line during the transition, the rider must make sure that he rides forward strongly in order to engage the hocks further. The rider may also use his legs – while he is doing this – to straighten the horse, by holding his quarters, as long as he makes sure (at the same time) that the shoulder does not escape.

In the horse's early stages of training he may be allowed to move progressively into halt, and it is only as he becomes more advanced in his work that he can be expected to halt directly from his previous gait, be it trot or canter.

It is important that the rider is consistent in his training. He should always insist upon square halts in his schooling sessions, remembering never to allow the horse to halt 'any old how' at any time. The horse will gradually learn to halt square at all times, and then the rider's task will be much easier.

Since the horse will only be able to perform a good transition to halt once his basic flat work is correct, I think it is sufficient to explain why things go wrong, rather than going into lengthy correction procedures: there is little one can do if the preparatory work is incorrect.

### Head unsteady

*Symptoms*: This may vary from an occasional toss of the head, to a perpetual tipping, tossing or shaking. The rider will be unable to maintain a steady contact as it will be broken every time the horse throws his head or dips it downwards.

*Causes*: By changing the position of his head or nose, the horse is evading the direct contact with the bit and thereby basic work. The unsteady head carriage may also be the result of problems in the neck region of the horse, or discomfort in the mouth, face or ears, or even outside influences, such as irritating flies. The horse will dip his nose to avoid flies crashing into his face . . . sometimes it is the very small flies which cause most annoyance: they are difficult to see, and it is puzzling why the horse objects to them so violently. Any muscular spasms in the neck will make it awkward for a horse to maintain a steady head-carriage, and by moving his head up and down, he is trying to ease any tightness there. A badly fitting bit, or the wrong bit for that particular horse, or sores in the mouth will obviously make the horse uncomfortable, and therefore give him reason enough not to accept the bit. Horses can suffer from mites in their ears too, which can make them shake their head, and sometimes this problem can become so bad that the horse is virtually unrideable.

*Treatment*: The cause must be ascertained before a treatment can be effected. Obviously the outside influences must be investigated first, viz. is the bit the key to that horse's mouth, has the horse any sores, ulcers or lacerations in his mouth which could give him cause to evade the bit with an unsteady head? Is he sensitive to flies? Can the vet find any sign of problems with his ears or any signs of damage in the neck area? All these questions have fairly obvious answers, but this does not mean that the problem itself is necessarily easy to solve. Until the horse is comfortable in his mouth, he will not keep his head still, and even when he is more comfortable, the habit he has acquired of constantly moving his head may take a while to break, as he will have soon realised that he can also avoid working in this way. Fly repellent may help to combat the fly problem, or, in a chronic case, a fly net on the end of the horse's nose can be very successful. Remember, though, that this would not be permitted in the dressage arena. Ideally, one should be able to work a horse into such a concentrated state of mind that he does not notice the flies, but that is easier said than done! It is worth checking when buying a new horse whether it is a head shaker, or allergic to flies, or pollen because although research is being carried out in this field, no cure has yet been discovered. Any irritation in the horse's ears will give rise to a shaking of the head to relieve it, but this will only bring him immediate and temporary relief; but with regard to curing the root problem permanently, a vet may be able to help.

If the horse is merely dropping the contact every so often, and coming either above or behind the bit (particularly in transitions or more difficult movements), the rider can actively work the horse a little harder from behind to try to keep his hocks working more, and thereby encouraging him to keep a steadier contact. The horse will soon have learnt that by tossing his head, albeit gently, he can avoid working correctly, and the rider must teach him that any avoidance of hard work is unacceptable. An increased use of leg pushing up to a steady contact with a widened hand shows the horse that even if he tries to toss his head, he does not escape the contact. When he finds that he cannot escape the contact, he will realise what is required of him. The rider must be careful, however, not to restrict the forward movement or he will exacerbate the head throwing. If, however, the horse is unsteady in his head but deliberately drops the contact, he is coming behind the bit (*see* page 101).

**Hocks trailing**
*Symptoms*: The horse is reluctant to bring his hocks underneath him and take the weight off his forehand. The hindlegs will be inactive, and the hocks unbending, rigid and stiff. Directly affected by this inactivity will be the contact in the rider's hand, and the horse will resist the bit in a variety of ways – by being on his forehand, leaning, being above the bit, being hollow, crossing his jaw and so on.
*Causes*: Conformation will have a great bearing on how much the horse is able to engage his hocks. If the horse is built with his hock out behind him, he will naturally find it far more difficult to bring his hock and hindleg far enough under him to carry the weight most efficiently: a short, upright hindleg will lack the leverage to allow it to flex sufficiently to come right underneath the body; but a long, weak hindleg will also err on the inactive side. The horse will have

to make far more effort in order to bend a long hindleg at the hock and generally this horse will have a rather sloppy, toe-dragging action – even if it is meant to have a big jump! Obviously, any physical injury or ailment in the hindleg, hip or back area will have an immediate effect on the horse's athletic ability to bring his hocks underneath him and use them correctly.

*Treatment*: Before the rider concentrates on the carrying capacity of the hocks, he must be sure that all the earlier stages of the horse's training have been correctly established. The placement of the hindleg is integral to stage 5 in the training programme, and can only be worked upon when the previous four stages have been consolidated. Suppleness in the horse is vital as unyielding muscles will make it very uncomfortable for the horse to work in the necessary athletic manner to be able to bring his hocks underneath him. (*See* stages 1–5 in the Blueprint but, for any problems encountered *en route* refer to the sections discussing them individually in this chapter.)

Trotting poles – firstly on the ground, and then raised to about 30 centimetres (1 foot) off the ground – will make a horse who does not bend his hocks or fetlocks flex all his joints and will help to supple him generally. The poles will teach the horse that he *can* bend all his joints and, although this will not bring about an immediate improvement, it will help the horse to learn how to use his hocks. Eventually, having been taken through other exercises such as transitions, shoulder-in, enlarging and decreasing circles and counter-canter, the horse will improve by degrees.

If, whatever exercises are performed, the horse still does not seem able to bring his hindlegs underneath him, and the situation seems stagnant, then it may be time for a vet's examination, to see whether there is some deep-rooted physical problem which is causing this block against work. Obviously, it is impossible to force a horse to use his hocks, but he can be taught how he can use them to the best of his ability, adapting his natural way of going so that he can perform the work required of him . . . but it all takes time!

### Hollow

*Symptoms*: This is one of the most common problems in the untrained horse, who is said to be hollow when, instead of the hocks being under the horse, the back soft and relaxed, and the neck completing the round shape, the back is hollow and tight, and the hocks inactive and trailing. The horse appears high and restricted in his outline, and is therefore above the bit. A horse who has been working in a hollow shape will be incorrectly muscled, with a distinct lack of muscle on his top line – i.e. along the crest of his neck, across his back, loins and hindquarters – but with a bulge of muscle on the under-side of his neck, which has developed as a result of his high, tight head-carriage. A hollow horse will appear to be long backed and short necked, but will improve in shape quite dramatically with corrective training.

*Causes*: A hollow horse has developed the way of carrying himself in an inverted shape with a stiff back and high head-carriage as a result of a lack of correct training from the outset. A horse with a naturally high head-carriage from the point of view of his conformation will be predisposed to being hollow, as it is more natural for him to carry himself in that way, and probably more comfortable too; he must be taught how to work in a rounder shape from the outset, so that his muscles, particularly those across his back, develop in the correct way.

*Treatment*: A horse who has been ridden with a hollow outline for any length of time will be slow to redevelop the correct muscles needed for working in a rounder outline: the top muscles along his neck, back and hindquarters will have become contracted over this time, and they must be gradually stretched and eased. This will enable the horse to bring his hocks further underneath him, so that he can carry himself and the rider more easily. Work on a long rein will be of immense benefit as a suppling exercise. Work on the lunge with a Chambon will be of great benefit in this instance too, as the horse can be worked long and low without the weight of the rider: some muscle will be built up in the correct places which will enable him to carry the weight on his hocks, plus the weight of the rider.

The Chambon is an attachment which is used only with the horse on the lunge. It consists of a headpiece, with two straps either side, to which are attached two rings. A strap from the girth comes up between the front legs, and then divides into two; these two smaller straps pass through these rings on the headpiece, and attach to the bit (*see* diag. 30, p. 134). As the horse tries to raise his head, there is pressure on the mouth and the top of the head, but this is relieved, of course, by the horse lowering his head and neck. In no way is the head pulled in, and the horse is free to put his head on the floor if he wishes. The Chambon must be introduced very carefully, and the horse must learn precisely what is expected of him before any degree of tightness is introduced; if it is put on too tightly too soon, before the horse understands how to cope with it, there is every possibility that he might panic, and rear, with a chance of being sufficiently unbalanced to go over backwards. In all the years that we have been using a Chambon with real success, we have never

**30 The Chambon**

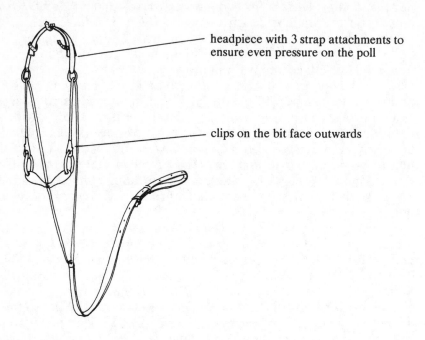

headpiece with 3 strap attachments to
ensure even pressure on the poll

clips on the bit face outwards

had an accident, but we have always been very careful and patient
in our use of it. (I hope I have not spoken too soon!) To introduce a
horse to the Chambon for the first time, we do not attach the long
straps to the bit, but only to the top rings (*see* diagram 31a), so that
the horse learns about poll pressure, and how to lower his head and
neck without any pressure on his mouth. Once the horse is working
quite happily like this, then the Chambon may be attached – quite
loosely – to the bit (*see* diagram 31b). It must be quite loose so that
if the horse raises his head beyond a certain point, he has to work
with a very slight contact. The point beyond which this contact is
established obviously varies from horse to horse, so it is far better –
if in doubt – to ask a more experienced person to start the horse off
on his Chambon work. This way the horse is introduced to the
Chambon correctly with no risk of an accident. Avoiding these
possible pitfalls is really a case of common sense, and patience – as
in any form of training – is the key word. The horse should be
driven forward on the lunge, so that he learns not only to carry
himself in a long, round frame, but also that, by rounding his top
line, he is able to bring his hocks right underneath him. The horse

**31 The correct fitting of the Chambon — in conjunction with a snaffle bridle, surcingle and breastplate**

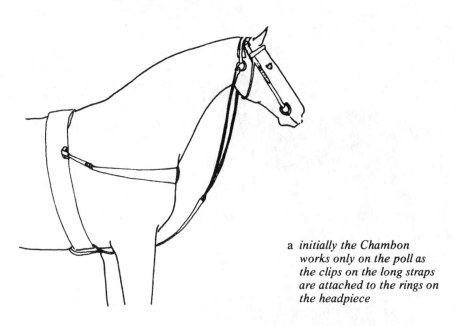

a *initially the Chambon works only on the poll as the clips on the long straps are attached to the rings on the headpiece*

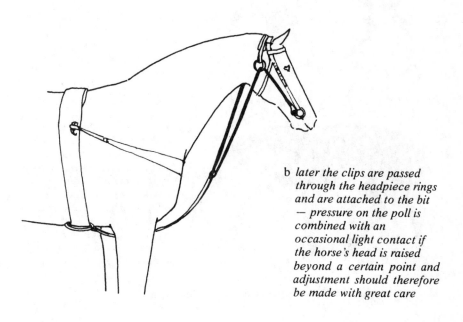

b *later the clips are passed through the headpiece rings and are attached to the bit — pressure on the poll is combined with an occasional light contact if the horse's head is raised beyond a certain point and adjustment should therefore be made with great care*

will eventually swing along with a loose back in a round outline with driving hocks . . . and when he has learned how to do that on the lunge, he will find it far easier to reproduce the shape once the rider gets back on board (*see* diagram 32).

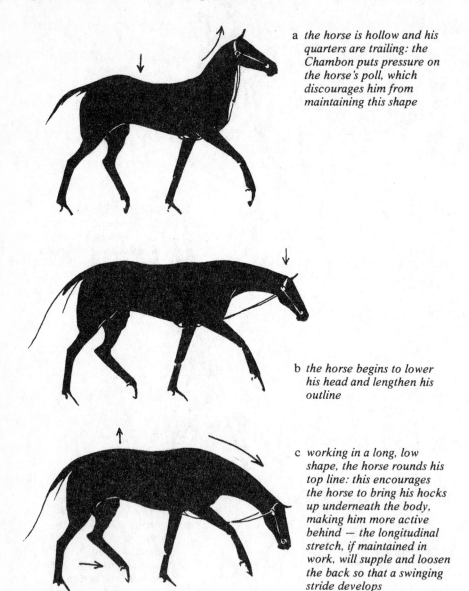

a *the horse is hollow and his quarters are trailing: the Chambon puts pressure on the horse's poll, which discourages him from maintaining this shape*

b *the horse begins to lower his head and lengthen his outline*

c *working in a long, low shape, the horse rounds his top line: this encourages the horse to bring his hocks up underneath the body, making him more active behind — the longitudinal stretch, if maintained in work, will supple and loosen the back so that a swinging stride develops*

**32 How the Chambon can affect the horse's outline**

Lungeing and riding can generally be interchanged in the re-training, although I find that the most benefit is derived from Chambon work if it is really consolidated by being used every day for a week, if not longer, depending again on the horse – how weak he is and how quickly he learns. It will take more than a week for the muscles to develop properly, as that will take months, but they will have had a chance to stretch a little and become more supple. When the horse is ridden again, the rider should continue the stretching work, not only directly reproducing the Chambon work but also making the horse stretch laterally by bending around the corners: he must be suppled in both ways in his back for him to become truly supple. The horse is an athlete, and we should try to reproduce in him the exercises undertaken by the human athlete. When warming up, the human athlete bends and touches his toes (direct flexion) and bends from side to side (the lateral bend of the horse) (*see* diags 3 and 4, pp. 7 and 14). The more supple the person or horse, the further he will be able to flex either way, but bear in mind the training involved before a stiff person is able to touch his toes and that if asked to do those sorts of exercises too early, quite severe damage could possibly ensue. The horse cannot say that his muscles are hurting, but may show it in different ways – by becoming upset, for instance – and we, as riders, must understand the horse and give him every chance to become supple without damaging him in any way by asking too much too soon.

**Hopping into trot**

*Symptoms*: In the walk to trot transition, the horse does a little hop on the first stride instead of moving smoothly from one pace to the other.

*Causes*: The horse is not going forward in the transition because he is not pushing from behind. It is also possible that the rider is restricting the forward movement of a transition with his hands.

*Treatment*: Study the section on not going forward (*see* page 149), and read the Blueprint on free forward movement (*see* page 19). Because the horse is not driving forward with his hocks in the transition, the rider must be far more positive in his forward aid to force the horse to work from behind. The rider should ask the horse to come a little lower in his outline, by driving him strongly forward with the leg, and then he should give the aid for trot – making sure that the horse does not drop behind the contact as he moves into the lower gait. He must be absolutely sure that he is not restricting the forward movement, particularly with the inside hand, and must allow the horse to step forward freely into trot. If he does restrict the horse with his hand, the horse will resist either by coming above the bit (*see* page 83), or by hopping into trot (similarly trot to canter – *see* Strike-off into canter, page 166).

## Jogging

*Symptoms*: The horse jogs instead of walking forward properly.

*Causes*: A horse may jog for various reasons, of which excitability is one of the most common. The horse, eager to be getting on with things, jogs almost on the spot, and his energy, instead of being used to generate forward movement, merely makes the horse go up and down. Another reason is anticipation (*see* page 99): the horse tries to trot before the aid is given. The horse may also interpret the aid for an extended walk as an aid for trot, trying to break into trot as a result. Otherwise he may jog simply because he is not going forward properly. Whatever energy he does generate is used up going up and down instead of freely forward, as it is – to a greater degree – when the horse is excited.

*Treatment*: Walk is four-time, and it is the last pace to become established in the horse's training. Trot, being two-time, is the pace at which most work is done, as it is the easiest in which to establish both a rhythm and a forward movement, whereas walk is a pace which is easily spoilt by being hurried or restricted (by a rider who is over-trying in his schooling), and must be kept as natural as possible. It is important that the horse is worked in walk, so that he becomes accustomed to doing movements in a forward manner in that pace. He must learn to accept the leg in walk without automatically breaking into trot, and provided this is established in the early stages, jogging should not be a problem. If a horse jogs from excitement, it is probably best to drive him forward in a strong trot until he has settled down, trying again afterwards to establish the walk. The rider may have to tell the horse that he is not allowed to jog, by closing his leg, and blocking with his hand until the horse walks, then relaxing the aids and repeating them again as necessary until the horse understands. The rider must never lose patience on these occasions, as a jab in the mouth will be of no benefit whatsoever and will merely make the horse even more 'up tight', as he becomes apprehensive about the rider's hand as well as being excited. Once the rider has established the walk, he must try to drive the horse forward as much as possible to make him really stride out and work. If he tries to jog, the rider must half-halt, and then drive him forward again. The horse jogging in anticipation is covered in the separate section on general anticipation (*see* page 99), and the treatment is discussed there.

The horse who jogs in his extended walk is perhaps jogging because the rider is asking a little too much in a particular situation. The aid for an extended walk must be very clear. As each foreleg moves forward a leg aid on the same side helps to drive the horse into a longer gait, and, being an alternating aid, it is quite different from the aid to trot. It is important that the horse is given no reason for misinterpretation, so that if he does jog, it is from him trying a little too hard, rather than from being confused. To know how much one can ask in the walk is a matter of feel, and the rider must just practise, both at home and at an event, so that the horse is as perfectly happy on a contact in walk as he is in other paces. The walk does tend to be neglected as a pace and, after the trot and canter work in a session, the horse should be made to walk on a contact before being allowed a long rein: he must learn to work on a contact in walk as in any other pace, and he must be able to perform upward and downward transitions from and to walk with no change of contact because practice in transitions will make him conversant with the various aids and obedient.

One of the best places to improve the walk is out and about around the roads, when the horse has a real purpose to his walk, and this can then be reproduced in the dressage arena. He can learn to remain on a contact, and yet maintain a natural free-going walk with no inclination to jog, and provided every time he tries to take one step of jog in his career, he is corrected immediately, he will not, one hopes, pick up this bad and irritating habit.

### Lazy

*Symptoms*: A total lack of enthusiasm from the horse to partake in any work, and a reluctance to move forward from the leg. The rider will feel that he has to nag at the horse constantly with his leg just to keep him moving, and even then there will be a lack of response. The horse will probably appear to be slopping along at a slovenly pace, with the hocks only slightly engaged – if at all. The general impression will be one of hard work, heaviness and a distinct lack of harmony between horse and rider.

*Causes*: We will start with the young horse who will show signs of laziness when he is very first broken. This is due to the fact that the young horse is completely ignorant of the meaning of the leg aid. He does not understand what the rider means when he applies his leg, and of course, why should he? All he understands at the backing stage are the voice commands, or the flick of the lunge-whip; legs mean nothing at all to him.

An older horse may display the same lazy characteristics as the young horse, although he is not really lazy. He might just not know what the aids in a more subtle form actually indicate; he may be used to a hefty kick in the ribs as a sort of go forward, faster aid, and a good heave on the reins meaning stop.

However, there are some horses (as there are people!) who are basically bone idle. They pretend not to understand the aids – rather like turning a deaf-ear to what they do not want to hear!

The horse might, of course, be showing the signs of laziness because he is in fact ill. A horse cannot say that he feels terrible so he can only show this by displaying total lethargy, while we are often mistakingly berating him for being idle.

*Treatment*: The young horse has to be taught exactly what the legs mean. From the lungeing stage, where he responds to the voice and the lunge-whip, he must progress first to accepting the rider's weight, and then to the pressure of his legs on his own sides. The change from being on the lunge to being ridden loose is, of course, a very crucial stage and if the horse has been long-reined, the steering should be no particular problem, but the introduction of the leg aid must be done with tact. The voice is very important at this stage, and must be used in conjunction with the leg, until the horse realises that the leg does in fact mean move forward, or slow down, depending on the specific aid used – either the slight vibration for an upward transition, or a dead squeeze for a downward one. A young horse is very hard work, for not only does he not understand what legs are, but he also has no particular reason for wanting to go anywhere anyway. He sees little point in trotting around a school, and certainly sees no virtue in going round the corners when it is so much easier and quicker to cut them! Explaining to the horse that you want him to do all this takes time and patience, and very vigorous riding. Riding a young horse which is immediately over-responsive to the leg might be easier initially but he will probably end up a rather neurotic, very highly-strung animal with a far from easy temperament: I prefer, personally, to be able to really kick a youngster round the school, so that he becomes used to the legs, and accepts them with no resentment. Once a horse associates the voice command with the leg, the leg aid will be able to become more and more subtle, and the horse will seem more and more responsive. It is very rewarding teaching young horses these early lessons, and, if the teaching has been correct here, there should be no problem encountered later on with transitions either up or down.

The older horse who is rather unresponsive to the leg because he is ignorant and not because he is disobedient has to be re-taught the meaning of the aids and will benefit from the nudge – click – smack routine (*see* Not going forward, page 149). The lazy horse will not be going forward, so read the advice given in that section where applicable too.

The horse who is just plain idle has to be stirred up! He must learn that when the rider wishes him to work, then work he will. How often do we hear, 'Oh, he wakes up as soon as he sees a fence'? – laziness shown on the flat invariably stems from boredom . . . boredom from routine and from endless rather motiveless flat work in the form of circles and yet more circles, for hours on end. This is why schooling must have a purpose in each session, so that both horse and rider feel that they have achieved something. Assuming that the horse has become reluctant to work, and therefore rather lazy, the rider might have to resort to a pair of spurs to wake up the horse, or to a schooling whip. These artificial aids must, however, be used to advantage. The horse ignores the leg rather in the same way as one ignores a nagging voice – a short, sharp reminder is far more effective than a long tirade. It is the same with the horse in his reaction to the aids: if the horse does not move forward from a nudge or squeeze, then he must be given a sharp 'dig' with the spurs, or a flick with the schooling whip to send him on, but on no account must the rider restrict the horse at that moment. The horse must feel total freedom to go forward, because if he encounters any restriction from the rider's hand, he will be receiving a muddled aid and he might not truly understand what is required. If the rider constantly niggles at the horse with his leg, or is forever flicking him with the whip, not only will the horse become immune to this new permanent 'irritation' but the rider will become tired and totally ineffective. The horse must know that the rider means business, but that does not mean that he needs to be punished, or made to become worried or upset; he must merely respect the rider's aids, and be aware that if he does not, then he will receive a reminder which gives him a little shock, rather than pain or fright. Try to make the schooling sessions interesting for the horse by giving him plenty of exercises to do, and lots of variety, even introducing some more difficult movements to keep him on his toes, getting him to work from behind because he needs to, rather than just because you are trying to force him – figures 8–10 metres in diameter, for instance, or, coming up the centre line, circling outwards one way then the other, or shoulder-in, or leg-yield – any exercises which activate the hocks, and work the horse without his realising.

I would far rather have a horse who tends towards being lazy than one who is perpetually on the point of boiling, as the lazy horse is far easier to work with; at least one can do something positive about it.

**Leaning**

*Symptoms*: When a horse leans, he is relying on the rider's hand to keep his balance. This may either be a constant problem or just an occasional one, occurring when the horse should engage his hocks to a greater extent to adjust his balance, and, in failing to do so, uses the rider's hand as a support. The rider will experience a very heavy feeling in his hand, and the horse gives him the impression that he will fall flat on his face if the rider does not hold him up (*see* diagram 33)! The horse is like a see-saw – until the back end lowers, the front end cannot be light.

*Causes*: Conformation plays quite a big part in this problem because, if a horse is built with a poor shoulder and front, and a back end which he finds difficult to lower and bring underneath him, he will also find balancing himself quite a challenge. It is his inability to carry himself on his hocks that makes him rely on the rider's hand to correct his balance and to enable himself to perform the tasks required of him. Youth and weakness are certainly the other main causes initially, and once the horse learns that he can

33 **An incorrect outline — leaning on the rider's hand** — *the horse is relying on the rider for support when his hocks are not sufficiently engaged* (see also *diagrams 23, 24 and 26, pp. 84, 85 and 102*).

gain support for himself from the reins without having to use his hocks, he will not bother to learn how to engage his hocks to adjust his balance unless he is specifically taught otherwise.

*Treatment*: The horse's centre of balance must be moved back, so that the weight is removed from the forehand and carried on the hocks. In order for the horse to learn how to adjust his balance in this way, the rider must remove the strong contact – hitherto a balancing aid – and make the horse carry himself on a light contact. In the same way as pulling, where it is said that 'it takes two to pull', the horse cannot lean if he has nothing on which to lean. The type of bit used on a horse which leans should be carefully considered. The family of bits which remain set in the horse's mouth, such as the eggbutt or Fulmer, is best avoided, as the horse can just fix his mouth on this type of bit, and however the rider adjusts the position of his hand, he cannot affect the action of the bit. Until the horse is more responsive in his mouth, the rider will be unable to drive the hocks underneath the horse, and will consequently be fighting a losing battle. The best type of bit is the loose-ring snaffle, or maybe even a snaffle with rollers, which does not allow the horse to 'set himself' in his mouth. A bit which positively discourages the horse from leaning on it is the one to use to start with, but once the training progresses, a milder bit may be used.

Any movements which increase the engagement of the hocks will help in improving the horse's balance, so plenty of transitions, both up and especially down, for example, will be of great benefit, provided that the rider does not allow the horse to rely on his hand during them. The rider must precede the movement by a series of strong half-halts to make the horse engage his hocks prior to the transitions, and then engage them further during the transitions themselves. If the horse tries to lean on the hand, the rider should give and take with his hand, perhaps moving the bit a little in the horse's mouth to shake the horse off the heavy contact, while at the same time using as much leg as he can to ask the horse to activate his hocks and to carry his weight on them. Circles, trotting poles, and any other exercise which will improve the carrying ability of the hocks (*see* stage 5 of the Blueprint, page 33) will help adjust the horse's balance. Leaning comes under the same category as 'on forehand': although it does suggest more of a heaviness in the rider's hand (whereas 'on forehand' implies that the horse's whole centre of gravity is too far forward), the horse is not necessarily like a ton weight on the end of the reins but is just rather low in front.

**Long rein, problems with working on a**
*Symptoms and Causes*: In order to work correctly on a long rein, the horse must seek down onto the contact in a longer frame; this way, he is stretching his muscles and exercising them in a way which is beneficial to him, allowing him to bring his hocks underneath him and work in a round shape. In a free walk on a long rein, the horse should lengthen and stretch his outline, and walk forward in a loose and purposeful manner. When he fails to stretch downwards, his frame will be hollow, and the walk strides will be restricted. The same may be said for both trot and canter too, although long rein work in these is not actually required in a dressage test. As a schooling exercise however, it is invaluable, as the muscles are stretched and worked in the correct way, loosening up the horse before he is asked to work harder. It is a way of going that every horse should learn to accept as, with the back stretched and therefore elastic, and with the hocks being driven under him, he learns to balance himself in a longer outline. A horse who refuses to work long and low is obviously stiff in his back and unused to being asked to work in this way; his back muscles will be contracted and unable to stretch which means he cannot work on the long rein. He is therefore unable to round his back, which means he will be unable to bring his hocks underneath him. Whatever resistance a horse shows, whether it is merely in being hollow and above the bit, or in being unsteady in his rhythm, or in being tense and excited, work on a long rein will relax and supple the horse as no other way can succeed, and it is a must for all training, whether it be for dressage or jumping.
*Treatment*: To ask a horse to lower his head without coming behind the bit, but keeping on a contact in a round, longer shape, the rider must ask with the hand and drive with the leg. The hand should be an open hand, either with just the inside hand brought in on a line towards the centre of the school, or with both hands taken away from the horse's neck, asking the horse to lower his head and, at the same time, immediately allowing him to stretch down and forward if he wishes to do so. If the horse is driven forward with the leg at the same time, he will soon realise what is expected of him. As soon as he tries to bring his head higher, the rider must respond by asking him to lower his head and neck before he has a chance to raise it.

The rider should be aiming to have the horse's head almost on the ground, while still maintaining a contact, a good rhythm and, of course, a correct bend on the corners. In this way, the horse is being suppled and stretched in the same way as an athlete: he bends to touch his toes (the horse's long rein work) and bends from side to side (as the horse bends around the corners) (*see* diags 3 and 4, pp. 7 and 14). Until he has gone through all his suppling exercises, he is unable to perform, and the horse is precisely the same. However, it is up to the rider to know when the horse is ready to work and obviously some horses may need more suppling up than others.

The long rein walk is a part of the actual work of a training session, and must be practised as such. It must be a separate exercise, and not just a shamble at the end of the session, when the horse saunters around on a loose rein, with the rider half-asleep! The rider must pit his brain against that of the horse to teach him that he is not going to canter every time at the end of his long rein walk, and he should intersperse a walk on a long rein with a walk on a contact, so that the horse does not anticipate the gathering of the shorter reins with an immediate increase in pace. However tedious this work may be at home, it is vital to the end result of a truly obedient horse. (If the horse tries to jog, *see* Jogging, page 138).

Chambon work on the lunge will of course help the horse to work in a round outline (*see* Hollow, page 132) and will strengthen the muscles without the weight of the rider.

### Medium trot/canter, problems with

*Symptoms*: Instead of the horse lengthening his stride and maintaining his rhythm, he either quickens or loses his rhythm and achieves no medium work as a result. Sometimes a horse may lengthen his stride and stay in a rhythm in medium trot but he moves 'wide behind' in the movement.

*Causes*: In order to lengthen his stride, the horse must have the potential energy in his hocks ready to be released as needed (*see* diags 12 and 13, pp. 38 and 39). If he is lacking impulsion (potential energy) he will not be able to produce a longer stride and maintain his balance (and so rhythm too). Instead he will fall onto his forehand and merely quicken. When a horse goes wide behind during medium work, the indications are that his hocks are not engaged and although he may have had the potential energy needed to produce some longer steps, he has failed to keep his hocks underneath him within the pace itself. (An interesting observation we have made is that horses which go wide behind in medium trot are bad travellers, because they try to balance themselves by widening the hindlegs – when there is little room in a horsebox – instead of bringing their hocks underneath them.)

*Treatment*: Some horses find medium trot naturally easier than others and they can 'change gear' without losing rhythm or balance with no difficulty at all; others take longer to be able to increase the length of their stride and they try to hurry along on their forehands. Every horse is capable of producing some medium work although it may take a long time to extract it, and the importance of correct training up to this point becomes obvious when asking for medium work, because to perform medium trot and canter the horse must work from behind and be able to make transitions without resistance. It is up to the rider to prepare for medium trot or canter by making sure that the horse has plenty of impulsion. He should make a series of half-halts and set the horse up on the corner, whilst driving the horse very strongly from behind to make him engage his hocks to the maximum (according to his stage of training). He should ensure that the horse is completely straight before releasing and driving him forward, and he must also make sure that he has an even contact in both hands and is not restricting any forward movement with his inside hand. He must *allow* with the hand so that the horse can increase his length of stride, but he must not throw the contact away, otherwise the horse will fall onto his forehand. It is important that the horse remains soft in his back, and if the rider sits throughout his efforts to obtain medium trot, he might make the horse tight and *unable* to work: he will become tense in his back, which means he will not be free in his movement, and his stride will become shortened and hurried. It is often far easier to start with rising trot. In a dressage test, the corner preceding a change of rein across the diagonal, which is when medium work is normally required, should be used to maximum advantage to engage the horse's hindlegs, creating as much energy as possible – which can then be released as medium trot or canter.

A good exercise for teaching a horse how to push with his hocks and release his forehand is to ask for medium trot on a line from, for example, E to C. The rider is driving the horse almost into the school wall (this must be a high wall, preferably in an indoor school), but the horse will be backing off the approaching wall and this has the effect of bringing his hocks underneath him, and lightening his forehand. This, taken in conjunction with the power produced by the rider driving the horse forward, will encourage the horse to loosen up his shoulder movement and engage his hocks. This may sound a strange method, but it teaches the horse not only that he is able to move more freely with his shoulder but also how to use his hocks. This exercise may be turned into a diamond shape in the school (*see* diagram 34) where the horse's hocks are forced even further underneath him on the sharp corners, in order to enable him to push more in the medium pace. The rider drives the hocks

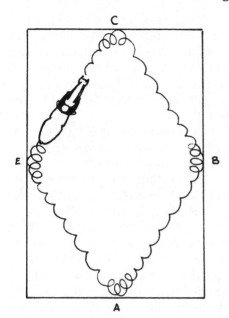

**34 The diamond shaped exercise —**
*using the corners and walls of the
school to develop medium trot*

underneath the horse in the transition back to working trot on
nearing the end of the school and again on the corner and the horse
is then in a position to produce a more pronounced medium pace
upon demand. This is a strenuous exercise of increase and decrease
of pace enforcing the engagement of the hindleg and should be used
in moderation, bearing in mind the fitness of the horse. Once the
horse has learnt the idea of the motions involved in medium trot, he
can then be asked to perform it along the long side. At first the rider
should only ask for a few strides, maintaining rhythm and balance,
and then he can gradually increase the number of steps. Later,
another exercise which helps keep the hocks under the horse is to
make several transitions from working to medium trot along the
long side: each time the horse comes back into working trot, the
rider should drive him strongly forward to engage the hocks and
should then insist that the horse goes immediately into medium trot
again without any grey areas of shuffle or hurried strides as he
makes the transition. Medium trot on a circle is a very difficult
exercise: great demands are placed on the horse not only to increase
his length of stride but also to maintain his bend and his balance. He
should be asked to take just a few steps initially, and then it should
be gradually built up until the horse is able to carry himself for
longer.

Asking the horse to move from half-pass to medium trot will improve an established medium trot because the horse is in a very concentrated form before being asked for the more extended pace. In the half-pass the horse will be working hard on his hocks and this energy can then be utilised in a medium trot. The horse will realise what he is capable of producing, and this will then help when the movement is executed in the usual place across the diagonal. It is just another way of engaging the hocks before asking for medium or extended work. In canter an exercise with the same idea behind it can be used; it helps the horse who loses his hocks, drops onto his forehand and quickens his stride in the medium canter. The horse is asked to work in counter-canter around the corner, and then the rider changes the rein across the diagonal. The horse will have to work very hard with his outside hind (in fact the leg on the inside in counter-canter) around the corner but it will then be able to push the horse up and forward into a good medium canter, maintaining rhythm and balance. All these exercises concentrate on obtaining total rhythm and balance, and on achieving and storing maximum energy in the hocks, which can then be put to use in the medium work. However, the rider must always make sure that the horse is perfectly straight in these exercises before he asks for a change from working to medium pace, otherwise he will have restricted the amount the horse can produce.

A horse may produce a very good medium trot if he is fresh or excited. The rider may not feel totally in control at the time, but at least he knows that the horse will be capable – with training – of reproducing the elevation and scope of movement in time. It is a good moment to encourage the horse to produce as much medium pace as he can because it teaches the horse how he must use his shoulders and hocks in a free, loose manner to perform medium or extended work. When out on a hack a horse is often more willing to 'free off' in his movement than in the confines of a school, and again, if the horse is persuaded to use himself then, he will find it easier to reproduce the same results in the school.

The horse who tries to come hollow in his medium pace is not working properly from behind and will not be able to produce any true medium work – his back will be stiff and therefore he will be unable to push from behind. The rider should ask the horse to come a little lower before the medium – flexing at the poll – and then he should drive him strongly forward . . . or he could work with his hands wider apart (to stop him pulling back and halting the forward movement): this will prevent the horse from losing his correct outline. Obviously correct training up to this point should mean that these problems will not arise!

### Not going forward

*Symptoms*: The horse does not move forward with a purpose, and is not pushing from behind. He will not go straight (in the correct way), and will be able to deviate from the one track whenever he feels like doing so. The rider will feel that he has neither petrol in the engine, nor acceleration when required – there is no feeling of positive action.

*Causes*: This may be a root problem which is probably the case with all newly broken horses, or it may occur as a result of the rider trying to 'collect' the horse incorrectly – i.e. from the front: restricting the forward movement with the hand, rather than by driving up from behind. 'Too much hand and not enough leg' is such a common cry, but already a lack of forward movement has ensued. In the less obvious cases, the rider who is being restrictive with the inside hand is the one who stops the horse going forward; invariably this rider is working back to front, trying to hold the bend and the shape with the inside hand, rather than working the inside leg up to the outside hand.

*Treatment*: With the green horse who does not understand that he must go forward, strong encouraging riding is the answer, with plenty of hacking out in company to give him enthusiasm and reason for his work. He must learn that when the rider applies a forward aid – i.e. a slight vibration of the leg rather than the squeeze of the downward transition – he must move forward immediately. The nudge–click–smack routine comes into play here. If the horse does not respond to a gentle nudge, then he must have a firmer nudge. If there is still no response, the rider gives a firmer nudge and clicks with his tongue at the same time, and if that does not work, he gives the horse a flick with a schooling whip, whilst nudging with his leg and clicking. The horse will learn to connect a slight punishment with not taking any notice of the initial leg aid – all this must be done without upsetting the horse needless to say – and this is how obedience is learnt. The flick of the schooling whip should not hurt, but should be used to reinforce the leg as an extra aid, in much the same way that spurs are used. The horse must know that the leg means forward – but remember that forward is not fast. When the leg is applied, the horse should not try to increase speed, but merely increase activity – potential energy which can be used when the rider needs impulsion. A horse that runs from the leg is not correctly trained, although many horses do try to respond in this way (*see* Running through the hand, page 159).

It is up to the rider to test whether he is supporting the bend and the shape with his inside hand, and he must realise that if he is, he will be restricting the forward movement, and therefore that his training of the horse is incorrect. If the horse remains in the same shape when the rider offers his inside hand forward, then all is well. If, however, the horse immediately comes above the bit, or falls in on the corner, then it is the inside hand which is protecting the shape and bend . . . the horse is not working correctly from behind in a forward-going manner. This is a fundamental problem, all too commonly seen, which creates endless trouble in the future, both on the flat and particularly over fences, and it is a trap which can be avoided.

Going forward is, of course, the essence of horsemanship, as one rides horses to get from A to B and what we do in the process is secondary!

### One-sided

*Symptoms*: The horse is more willing to bend one way than another, and is less responsive in its mouth on one side. As a result, the horse will find certain movements far easier to perform on one rein, shoulder-in, for example, circles, transitions and half-pass, to name a few.

*Causes*: Ninety-nine per cent of any resistance in the mouth is connected with the carrying capacity of the hocks, so that it can safely be said that if one hock is not doing its share of the work, the horse will be one-sided in his mouth, and stiff to bend on that side. A horse's bend around a corner is affected by how much the inside hindleg can be brought forward under the horse, and not just how supple he is laterally. This is more noticeable in trot than walk, as it is in trot that the inside hindleg has to move forward the most in order for the horse to track up. The direct effect of a 'lazy' hindleg can be noticed in any horse who has been injured on a hind limb: a horse who has hitherto gone easily to either hand suddenly becomes very one-sided so that he is much stiffer on the rein where the injured leg is the inside hind. Most horses are slightly stiffer to one way than the other, and it is more common for horses to be less supple to the right than to the left. I asked our vet about the theory which suggests that the way the foal lies in the mare's uterus affects his natural flexibility later in life, and his comments were:

The position which a foal assumes in utero has been thought to influence his natural lateral flexibility later in life. From about the sixth month of gestation the foal assumes an upside-down position with limbs flexed and the head towards the mare's pelvis. It is inevitable that there will be some twisting and lateral bending of the trunk of the foal depending upon which horn of the uterus has accommodated the pregnancy, and the displacement of the uterus by the abdominal viscera. The majority of mares carry the uterus more to the right than the left and this results in the foal being upside-down with a flexion to the foal's left – i.e. towards the midline and pelvis of the mare. This may well give an animal a predisposition to bend better to the left than the right, although I am unable to find any sensible investigation of this theory.

The other possible explanation is that everything is done to a horse from the near-side – he is led on that side from an early age, he is tacked up on that side etc., and it may be that this has made him more able to flex to the left than to the right?

The other possible cause of a horse being one-sided is a problem in his mouth. Sharp molars, or wolf-teeth, for instance, can affect the action of the bit because it does actually come into contact with these small, shallow-rooted teeth (generally located directly in front of the upper, and occasionally lower, molars).

*Treatment*: Sharp teeth can be remedied very quickly by rasping. Wolf-teeth are normally very easily removed by the vet, and, because of their shallow roots, this can be done with or without some local anaesthetic. The horse will not be able to have a bit in his mouth for a few days, but mouth wounds are particularly quick to heal. Do not expect the horse to be radically improved immediately the tooth or teeth have been dealt with, as he will imagine that the discomfort is still there for quite a long time.

Apart from working through the general suppling exercises, and concentrating more on the stiff rein than the good rein, there is no miracle cure for making a horse use his weak leg as much as his good one. In order to lessen the problem the rider must not hang on the horse's dead side with his hand. So that the horse has nothing to be dead against, he must give and take with the inside hand on the stiff side, so that the problem, although not removed, does not become chronic. Once the horse realises that he can lean on the rider's hand on the inside on his bad rein, he will continue to do so, and will rely more and more upon that hand to balance himself, rather than trying to use his hocks. It will be noticeable that it will be no problem, on the horse's good rein, getting the feeling of inside leg up to the outside hand, whereas, on the bad rein, the horse will not work up to the outside hand, but tries instead to take the contact on the inside one. To help the situation as much as possible, the rider must persevere, working the horse through shoulder-in, spiralling circles, shoulder-out or bending for a few strides to the outside on a circle, leg-yield, serpentines and so on, to help engage that inside hindleg, and shake the horse off the inside contact.

It is interesting to note that when a horse is stiff to the right in trot, in canter he is better to the right than to the left. This is because the inside hindleg on the right rein in trot becomes the outside hind in the left canter, and it is the outside hind which has to do the carrying in canter. It alone supports the horse's weight on the first beat, and if that leg cannot come well under the horse, the whole canter pace is affected. The outside leg can be made to work harder in canter if the horse is worked on a circle and the rider uses a strong outside leg. He should try to make the horse canter a smaller circle with his hindquarters than with his forehand. This will help activate the hock on the outside, and make the horse use the leg more to carry the weight. Counter-canter will also improve the outside hind's weight carrying capacity. All these exercises must be carried out in small doses initially, otherwise the unaccustomed work may aggravate an already weak side, because the horse will tend to turn towards his easier side to avoid the discomfort of difficult work. It will take time to build up strength and suppleness which will lead the horse to become less one-sided, and on no account should the rider spend over long trying to improve the weakness. Short spaces of time will be far more effective, and will also minimise the risk of doing any damage to the muscles or ligaments. Before any of these exercises are used, of course, the rider must make sure that the horse is fully warmed up, otherwise the horse cannot be expected to work to the best of his ability.

## On forehand

*Symptoms and Causes*: The horse is not carrying his weight far enough back, because his hocks are not engaged sufficiently to carry himself and his rider in balance (*see* diags 14 and 16, pp. 51 and 52). As a consequence, the forehand is heavy and low, and the hocks are trailing and inactive (*see* diag. 33, p. 142). A horse on his forehand does not always carry his head very low; it is possible for a horse to be on his forehand with his head in a high position as well, because by holding his head high, the horse is falling heavily onto his shoulders. The stride may be short and choppy as a result (*see* Shortened stride, page 161). The rider will feel as if he is riding a horse who is bearing down in front, with a lack of manoeuvrability, particularly in the faster paces. The faster a horse goes, the further forward his centre of balance moves, so if a horse is on his forehand to start with, this will be more accentuated as he goes faster. In order to remain balanced at a fast gait, a horse must first learn the basics of balance in the slow paces, and it is not until he can balance himself by bringing his hocks underneath him that he will be a pleasant and obedient ride at all paces.

A young horse will automatically be on his forehand, as his balance will have been drastically upset by the added weight of his new rider. He will find the necessary adjustment of balance very difficult at first, and it is only by progressive training that he will learn how to cope with it, eventually using his hocks as a fulcrum. As soon as the rider gets on the young horse, his weight will have the effect of pushing the centre of balance further forward, similar to the feeling we have if we carry an unaccustomed heavy load on our shoulders or back. Our balance is immediately altered, and it takes us time to adjust to it, and normally *we* do that by altering the position of the load. A horse cannot do that, for the rider is relatively still, and although we alter our weight distribution by leaning forward in the gallop and to jump, we really only do that more to keep in balance with the horse's movements than to help the horse adjust his weight.

*Treatment*: The training procedure for the horse who is on his forehand, whether he be old or young, is to follow the basic training programme, and teach him how to adjust his balance and use his hocks. There is no short-cut and, in some ways, the older the horse the more patient one must be. Although he is more mature than the young horse, it may be a case of re-training muscles to work in a different way from the one in which they have been working previously. Start from the beginning of the Blueprint, concentrating particularly on the exercises in stage 5 which improve the carrying capacity of the hocks.

### Overbent

*Symptoms*: In profile the horse's nose drops behind the vertical; the rider subsequently loses control, finding either that he is without a contact in his hand or that the horse is very strong. A horse may also go behind the vertical under the influence of a rider who desires the horse to be exaggeratedly deep in his outline to stretch the muscles to the maximum.

*Causes*: When a horse is overbent he may simply be behind the bit or he may be pulling hard, which causes him to tuck his nose into his chest. Both these situations are due to the horse not carrying himself on his hocks and not working from behind, causing a lack of balance and rhythm and a fluctuating contact in the rider's hand. Sometimes the horse is forced into a deep shape by a rider who is using more hand than leg, or by one who has a heavy unsympathetic hand.

A rider may ask the horse to work in a deeper outline to loosen and stretch the horse's muscles as much as possible, encouraging him to round his outline to the full. This requires expert riding to be used to advantage and since it is a situation intentionally induced by the rider, it does not come under the category of a problem.

*Treatment*: In the case of the horse who is behind the bit or pulling, the sections under these headings should be studied, and also the sections in Chapter Two on the general pattern of training. The rider must soften the hand to allow the horse to adopt the correct shape (*see* diag. 23, p. 84). 'If in doubt, always relax the hand' is a motto I follow in training and riding horses and I find it effective in almost every instance. A horse who tucks his nose in behind the vertical must be encouraged to stretch down and forward to a contact, so work on a long rein (*see* page 144) will be of benefit, relaxing the tight form which the horse adopts when overbent. Knowing that the horse must carry his weight on his hocks before the rider can take a positive contact in his hand, the horse must be worked towards increasing the activity from behind; indeed being overbent could have been the result of a lack of activity in the hocks.

### Pulling

*Symptoms*: Reluctant to remain in the pace specified by the rider, the horse wants to go faster. The degree of pulling can obviously vary – so that the rider can feel quite comfortable with the horse keen to get on with his business (this is better described as being 'well up to the rider's hand'.) He can, on the other hand, sometimes feel as if he is having his arms pulled out. An inexperienced rider might mistake the first feeling for a horse pulling. Ultimately, the aim is to have the horse well up to the hand, almost to the point of taking a good hold, particularly when jumping, but this must not be confused with the horse actively pulling, which is a fault in training. Pulling must not be confused with leaning, when the horse is heavy in the rider's hands by being on his forehand (*see* Leaning, page 142 and On forehand, page 152).

*Causes*: The horse may pull for a variety of reasons. First, it may be in eager anticipation of what is to come, although this is unlikely in basic flat work! A fresh horse will pull from exuberance, and will settle down once the fizz has gone out of him (*see also* Excitability, page 120). A more sinister reason is that the horse is in fact running away from pain, and this is one of the most common reasons for a horse pulling. It is difficult for us to understand why it is that a horse will try to run away from a pain caused by a bit or a rough hand, but it is the case. It is quite within our comprehension to realise that a horse will run from a stick, spurs or fear of the rider, but that he will try to pull harder on the bit if that very action increases the pain is very hard to accept. However, a horse will pull all the more against a bit which causes him pain, or if his mouth is split in the corner, even though pulling makes it worse. Pain in the back will also make a horse try to run away. Normally, the horse who pulls with his ears back is running away from pain, whereas the horse who pulls with his ears pricked is just 'eager'.

*Treatment*: This depends on the cause. To settle the horse which pulls out of excitement or eagerness, follow Stage 1 of the Blueprint, and also read the section on Excitability. With the horse who has always been allowed to pull, and is therefore just rather undisciplined, bear in mind that 'it takes two to pull' (*see* Leaning, page 142) and that by pushing the hocks further under the horse and lightening the hand, the horse will learn that he is not to hang on the rider's hand. The number one lesson to learn is that a horse cannot be prevented from pulling by merely pulling back at him. The only way to lighten the heavy forehand, which is basically the trouble, is by using a strong leg up to a giving-and-taking hand, thereby giving the horse nothing to pull against. A series of half-halts and plenty of transitions, and a firm but quiet insistence that the horse should not pull against the hand is the correct approach. A yank will merely aggravate the situation and give the horse reason to be upset, which will be an added complication to cope with. During the half-halts, mentally say 'NO' with a very strong leg and blocking hand, then relax, sit quietly with a light contact, and keep repeating the half-halts until the penny drops. This may take some time, but patience will be rewarded far more than a loss of temper, and because correct schooling is being undertaken, it will also prove more helpful in the future. Always remember that the horse probably does not understand that he should not pull, and that the rider must teach him.

A polo pony we were once sent to get fit for the coming polo season is a good example of a horse running away from a pain in his mouth. We were presented with his bridle, which we were told he had to wear otherwise he was much too strong, and would gallop off. This was a very long-cheeked twisted mouthpiece double bridle, with a flash noseband, and the pony was a nervous 14.2hh. To cut a long story short, we used to ride him in a straight-bar rubber snaffle with a cavesson noseband and he had a very sensitive mouth. The only time he would get strong was when his rider took too strong a hold on him, and he would immediately start to worry that something was going to hurt him. In the double bridle he perpetually tried to gallop off, which all rather speaks for itself. In many cases, a more severe bit only makes the horse pull all the more, and so a change of bit, if the horse does become too strong, must be very carefully considered. For flat work, there is no reason why a horse should not learn to work well in a straightforward snaffle with either one or two joints. If the horse pulls out of anxiety, try a milder bit – in an enclosed space, he will hardly gallop off very far. This pulling out of pain is closely associated with tenseness (*see* page 172) and often if the basic cause is discovered to lie within this general problem, many of the more specific difficulties can be sorted out.

Running away from pain in the back, or from the weight of the rider, is a problem which can only be handled with understanding and, in the former case, with the help of a vet, as he may be able to suggest some treatment to ease the tight muscles causing the pain. Check too that the saddle is not down on the withers or spine, and use a couple of numnahs to spread the pressure. Some horses are naturally more sensitive than others, and the rider's weight causes them sufficient discomfort to upset them. With these types of horses, it is best to sit very lightly, to see if that makes any difference, and it is always interesting to note how these horses behave on the lunge without the weight of the rider. One horse we once had behaved impeccably on the lunge; he was quiet, rhythmical and non-resisting through his paces, but, as soon as the rider was on board, he became tense, trying to run away, grinding his teeth and was generally very difficult. Eventually we had to have him put down, as x-rays showed that the spinous processes in the wither region were severely damaged – evidently due to a fall sometime in his distant past – and the weight of the rider was more than he could tolerate. If only horses could talk, how much easier our task would be.

### Quarters swinging

*Symptoms*: The horse does not remain on one track, particularly on a corner or circle, and avoids bending around the rider's inside leg by swinging the quarters out. In much the same way as a driver who loses the back end of a car on a sharp bend, the rider is not in control of the horse.

*Causes*: The quarters swing because of stiffness in the back and a fundamental lack of training. It shows an unwillingness on the horse's behalf to track up on the circle, and it is a resistance to bending around the rider's inside leg aid. If not enough outside leg is used behind the girth, the horse will be able to swing outwards so that he can evade working correctly on the circle.

*Treatment*: Plenty of suppling exercises will help the horse to keep his hindquarters on the same track, with the rider ensuring that he is using sufficient outside leg in the correct position – i.e. behind the girth (*see* stage 4 of Blueprint – Straightness, page 26). A good exercise to help correct chronic cases of swinging quarters is to work on a 20-metre circle, asking the horse to track a slightly smaller circle with his hind feet, but retaining the bend. By stretching the muscles on the outside of the horse, which are the ones which allow him to bend, this exercise makes them work a little harder. If the rider tries to stretch these muscles by riding smaller circles, the horse will merely respond by swinging his quarters all the more as, finding a larger circle difficult enough, a smaller one seems virtually impossible. His muscles must be worked and exercised to enable him to be supple enough to bend, and there is no point trying to do exercises in which the horse can wriggle out of working properly. The horse cannot swing his quarters if the rider is just asking the quarters to move over without allowing the size of the circle to diminish, and consequently the necessary muscles are exercised in the right way (*see* Stiffness, page 165).

**Rein-back, problems with**

*Symptoms*: The horse refuses to move backwards, rears, resists by opening his mouth and/or throwing up his head, steps back out of rhythm, rushes back, or fails to stay straight.

*Causes*: There are two main causes of an incorrect rein-back. The horse may not understand what he is required to do, either because his training is not sufficiently advanced or correct, or because the rider has failed to give the correct aids: these two are interrelated, because if the rider's aid for rein-back is incorrect, the indications are that he does not fully understand the aids and their uses in general, and so the horse's basic work might well have suffered. The other main cause is discomfort and this can be further sub-divided into pain and stiffness. The rein-back should be considered a means to an end rather than an end in itself, in that it should be used to increase the engagement of the hocks. In order to do this the horse must be supple and athletic, so it is understandable that some stiff horses will find this movement difficult. For the same reason, a horse which is experiencing pain in any region from the withers backwards, including any part of the hindleg, is likely to resist the request to rein back, as the added strain will only exacerbate his problem.

*Treatment*: The horse must use his hocks in the rein-back to maintain his rhythm and balance and in order to be able to move forward again immediately he is asked. He also has to understand the fundamentals of training – meaning that he must know the leg aids and also respect the contact from the hand. Unless he has this knowledge, the horse will fight the aid to rein back; the rider, having established a square halt, drives the horse forward into a blocking hand, so that the energy, instead of being allowed to flow forwards, moves the horse the requisite number of steps backwards. The rider must be satisfied with one or two steps initially, and the horse must then be driven forwards.

This movement should not be practised too often, otherwise the horse will start to associate halting with stepping backwards and yet another problem will arise! It may be necessary for the rider to seek assistance from someone on the ground, who will push the horse backwards as the rider gives the aids, saying 'back' at the same time. Gradually this person's help can be dispensed with once the horse understands what is required of him. As long as this movement is correctly and patiently introduced, the horse should accept it quite happily as part of his training, but it is a movement which can cause tension in the horse if he misinterprets the aids or if he starts anticipating.

On no account should the rider pull to ask the horse for rein-back, and the more the horse refuses to go back, the more the rider must increase the leg. If the horse rushes backwards, the rider can correct this by asking for only one or two steps of rein-back and then driving the horse forward before he can start rushing back. Once the horse reins back from an aid, rather than of his own volition, the problem will be solved. Someone on the ground may also help in this instance by giving the horse some reassurance when he is asked to rein back.

The horse who throws his head during the movement has probably been taught the rein-back by a rider who used more hand than leg, causing him to hollow his back and raise his head. The rider's hand aid must only be sufficient to prevent the horse from stepping forward and the contact – from the preceding movement through to halt and on to the rein-back and then forward again – should alter only as much as is required to allow the horse to move forward or to block his movement. The difference between an allowing hand and a blocking hand is a matter of feel which comes with experience, and the inexperienced rider can help himself and his horse by always remembering that he must never pull, and that the horse should be prevented from moving forward, rather than made to slow down, stop or go backwards.

One important aspect to consider when asking a reluctant horse to step backwards is the danger that he might resist by rearing. If the horse should rear, the rider must immediately relax the contact and keep his own weight well forward to lessen the chance of the horse going over backwards. If the horse is threatening to behave violently in this way, he can still be taught to go backwards: the rider should dismount and ask him from the ground, by standing at his shoulder and pushing him backwards, repeating the word 'back'. Once the horse responds, the rider can then remount and try again – with someone on the ground, until the horse associates the aids with the movement. This lesson should not be practised for long each day, and, even when the horse learns how to rein back, he should be asked to perform it regularly, although not necessarily every day, and it must be interspersed with some simple halts without a rein-back.

### Resisting

*Symptoms*: The horse is said to resist when he disobeys his rider's demands. This may manifest itself in many different ways, all of which are dealt with under the separate headings in this chapter. Resisting is a word which occurs with monotonous regularity on dressage sheets!
*Causes*: These are covered under the separate headings discussing the different ways the horse has of resisting, but the fundamental cause is a lack of training. The horse has not been taught well enough to carry himself on his hocks and to be able to work in the balanced, rhythmical and supple way which indicates that he is on the bit.
*Treatment*: Basic thorough schooling and training should be under-taken where the horse is given time to strengthen and develop the necessary muscles for working at the required level. A horse will resist something that he does not understand or he finds difficult, and the rider's task is to educate him both mentally and physically to be able to comply with the rider's demands.

### Running through the rider's hand

*Symptoms*: When the rider applies the leg to drive the horse up together, it has rather a different effect: the hocks are not engaged, and the horse tries instead to go faster and becomes very strong; his shape remains the same rather than condensing. The horse will feel as if he is bearing down on the rider's hand, and the more the rider tries to drive the horse together, the stronger he becomes.

*Causes*: There is a lack of understanding by the horse; he does not recognise that leg aids do not necessarily mean 'increase pace', but mean 'come together, bring your hocks underneath and lighten your forehand' too. A horse who finds it difficult to adjust his balance and to take the weight on his hocks will be more prone to being heavy on his forehand, and so predisposed to running through the rider's hand. Conformation plays quite a part in this problem, as it does in the horse who is on his forehand (*see* page 152) because a horse with a heavy front and without a 'back end' to match it will find difficulty in carrying the weight in his hocks. This differs from basic pulling in as much as the horse does not necessarily want to go any faster; because his hocks are not carrying him sufficiently, he just cannot keep his balance, particularly in the transitions, and he feels he has to go faster.

Incorrect schooling is in all cases the real reason, even if some horses are more likely to try this form of resistance than others. Those horses will obviously take a little longer to learn how to balance themselves but, provided the correct steps are taken in training, the end product should be a pleasant, obedient ride. This is why it is so important to teach a horse *from the very beginning* that legs mean stop as well as go forward or faster. Downward and upward transitions should be practised repeatedly in the horse's early stages, and indeed used as suppling exercises throughout his whole career.

*Treatment*: Riding transitions *ad infinitum* are the answer, until the horse learns to adjust his balance without either using the rider's hand as a balancing aid, or ignoring it altogether. The rider must be strong in his legs and seat to combat the horse's strong resistance but must, on no account, pull back. A giving-and-taking rein will give the horse nothing to set himself against, and, if necessary, the rider could move the bit a little in the horse's mouth (but very gently) in order to keep the horse soft and non-resistant during the transition. The horse can try to run through the hand when the pace is established and not just during a transition, so try using repeated half-halts – a strong leg with a positive blocking hand – followed by a light hand as a reward, so that the horse learns that if he carries himself, life will be comfortable. As soon as he tries to run on again, repeat the half-halts until he understands. This is the same procedure as that to be followed if the horse pulls (*see* page 154) or leans (*see* page 142), and of course the three problems tend to have the same root causes.

If the horse is an older but rather ignorant animal, one may sometimes have to resort to changing the bit in order to make any impression upon him at all. A horse who has run through the bit all his life is going to resent being made to work from behind and will probably use all his strength to resist doing so. If that is the case, a stronger bit may be used to great advantage. A move from a snaffle and dropped or crossed nosebands to a double bridle is the 'purest' change, provided that the horse accepts the bit in a non-fussy way. A dead mouth will often become quite responsive in a double bridle, but remember that this is only the case because he is backing off the bit a little, and using his hocks instead.

If the energy created by the leg cannot be contained, then the horse will never come together at all, but will remain strung out with his hocks trailing. For a horse to bring his hocks underneath him, the rider has to drive him up with the legs and seat, and contain the energy created in the outside hand, otherwise the horse will only go faster. If the horse ignores this outside hand, he will not bring his hocks underneath him or lighten his forehand; the further the hocks are under the horse, however, the lighter the controls will need to be (*see* stage 5 of the Blueprint, page 33).

### Shortened stride

*Symptoms*: The horse does not stride out in his natural pace when he is ridden, but takes shorter, usually rather hurried steps and lacks rhythm. On the lunge or loose, the horse has a much longer stride.

*Causes*: This may be caused by interference at some earlier stages of training: the rider may have tried to 'collect' the horse before he was ready, and so, instead of bringing the hocks under in order to shorten from behind, the horse shortens from the front. He may also be running along, out of balance, and unable to keep a longer stride pattern because of this lack of balance. His hocks will be trailing, and he will be pulling himself along on his forehand with no propulsion from behind, and therefore there will be a lack of rhythm (*see* On forehand, page 152). Alternatively, he may not be going forward at all; indeed he may be behind the bit to such an extent that his paces are affected. Tenseness can also cause the horse to take shortened, hurried steps . . . as can excitement. A problem in the back region may have the effect of making the horse unwilling to take long, level strides too, as this is likely to cause the horse discomfort. A horse who is unhappy in his mouth will not move forward well, as he will be reluctant to come up to the bit, and short strides will be the result. The problem should be viewed from the veterinary angle too, as 'poddling' movement in front may well be an indication of the initial stages of a problem in the feet, such as navicular or pedalostitis, or maybe jarring in the shoulder or wither region, or sore shins (an inflammation in the tendon sheath which lies along the front of the cannon, caused by concussion).

*Treatment*: Whatever the cause, the answer is to go back to the basic stages of training. First of all, is the horse relaxed and going freely forward? Once that is established, then the rhythm and the suppleness of the horse must be worked on. The more supple the horse is both laterally and directly (the bend around the corner, and the roundness of the outline), the looser his movement will become. Unless a horse is naturally a very good mover, his paces will be directly affected if he is basically stiff; even if he is an excellent mover, the paces will become even better once he is more supple. So, the method of working the horse is set out in the Blueprint, and further details about excitability, tenseness (on forehand, not going forward), and stiffness, all come under their separate headings. This is a perfect example of one problem being very closely connected with another more basic one, and how, once the basic one is ironed out, the subsidiary troubles subside. A problem in the back is a case for the vet to advise upon, as are sore shins, jarring and foot trouble; he should be called upon whenever it is felt that the shortened stride may be health-related. Although it is good for one's morale to try to interpret these problems oneself, a veterinary surgeon will, or at least should, be able to identify precisely where the problem lies and to give correct treatment. It is very important to discover exactly what the horse's work programme can be – whether he can continue working or whether he must rest – so that further damage cannot be done. The danger of interpreting the symptoms oneself is that one may reach the wrong diagnosis, give the wrong treatment, and cause permanent damage as a result. I strongly feel that we owe it to the horse, who cannot explain what hurts, to consult an expert when we feel that something is amiss, rather than just muddling on. Anyway, as horses are so costly, a little more expense when it really matters is neither here nor there.

## Shying

*Symptoms*: The horse sees something that frightens him and he either refuses to go past it, tries to take a wide sweep away from it, or whips round. This object may be something which he sees in the distance, and the shy will be well anticipated by the rider, or, alternatively, he may suddenly see something out of the corner of his eye, and jump sideways very quickly, taking the rider by surprise.

*Causes*: Some horses are naturally more 'spooky' than others, and infuriatingly will spook at some seemingly insignificant object, but will walk calmly past the most frightening looking lorry, or jump the most enormous fence when asked, without an idea of what might be the other side. There does not seem to be any concrete rule about why horses differ so, except perhaps that as they grow older and more mature they do learn to cope with things which, as a youngster, they found terrifying. Having said that, some old horses are just plain silly about some things, but it is mostly a bit of a game to them and, if ignored, they soon behave themselves!

*Treatment*: This depends very much on the character of the horse. I have found, without exception, that if the shying is ignored to a certain extent, the horse will not bother so much and vice versa. For example, we have all come across the horse who shies every day at the same pole lying in the corner of the school. If this horse is kicked or flicked with the whip every time he moves to shy, the situation will become worse: he will automatically become tense as he approaches the area as he will associate shying not only with the spooky object in the corner, but also with a reprimand from the rider. As soon as he becomes tense, everything will be lost – the suppleness, rhythm, free forward movement and so on – until the whole issue is blown out of all proportion . . . just for the sake of going past a pole on the ground. It is far better to cut the corner slightly, maintaining the rhythm and shape, and then gradually to work deeper, edging towards the fearsome object once the horse is working sensibly. Shying, don't forget, is an indication that the horse has his priorities wrong, as really he should be more responsive to the rider's aid asking him to move over than he is frightened of the pole or whatever he is shying at. So, rather than worrying about the shying problem, the rider should concern himself with making the horse more obedient to the leg; he should concentrate on doing exercises which make the horse move away from the inside leg, such as enlarging the circle, shoulder-in and leg-yield. The strongly applied, increased aid will correct the shying, without upsetting the horse.

There are some horses who are really just avoiding working by shying at everything and anything, and who might need firm handling but I still find that although this shying is an excuse, it is connected with a lack of confidence. If the rider is patient and builds on the discipline, the horse will develop more confidence in himself and his rider, and the shying will virtually disappear. I firmly believe that a pat is often the answer rather than a kick, and would rather ride very strongly and firmly than have to chastise a horse.

If a horse is very spooky, and really does not ever settle down, then the fact that he might have defective eye-sight must be considered. This is particularly likely of the horse who shies suddenly, as he might catch the glimpse of something out of the corner of his eye which he cannot identify, and which therefore alarms him. (The vet will put one's mind at rest by having a look.) The horse's history as a species has made him very susceptible to fright, as in the wild he had many natural enemies, and being a herd animal, he does feel insecure on his own. Shying is all part of this insecurity, as is napping, and we as riders and trainers must try to understand this; it is very irritating, but still more irritating is the combination of shying and tenseness one has to deal with as a result of one's own shortcomings in dealing with the initial problem.

## Slipping

*Symptoms*: The horse slips either in front or behind, not only on a corner, but also on the straight. An unbalanced horse is more likely to slip than a horse who is carrying his weight on his hocks. The surface in dressage or show-jumping arenas is invariably grass which tends to give little purchase unless the going is perfect – i.e. when the horse makes definite indentations with his feet, without any possibility of sliding in any direction.

*Causes*: Any surface, apart from perhaps sand, can be slippery, and the harder the surface the worse it becomes – take a road surface for example. It is sometimes thought that a horse will not need studs unless the ground is wet, but it can be just as difficult to grip on dry ground, probably more so, as the horse cannot make an impression on the surface.

A horse hates to feel the ground move under his feet, and quickly loses confidence if he does so. The horse can slip in all directions, not just sideways, and even the smallest slip will affect the manner in which he carries himself. When walking on icy ground, a person will hold himself slightly rigid and take shorter strides to avoid slipping. A horse will behave in the same way and, once his muscles become tense, he will lose all ability to work correctly: he will be stiff in his back, unable to bring his hocks underneath him, and unrelaxed in his jaw. The horse will not reason that if his hocks are under him, he will not slip, and so the situation turns into a vicious circle: once he slips, it will be more difficult to make him bring his hocks under him, and hence the more he will slip. Studs are therefore as important for flat work as they are for jumping.

*Treatment*: Some horses, who have learnt to associate dressage arenas with performing on a surface similar to an ice-rink – when either the ground is dry and slippery or wet and greasy – need their confidence boosted and to be extra certain that they will not slip, two studs can be used in each shoe. One stud is in the normal position on the outside, and the other on the inside quarter. On no account should two studs in each shoe be used while jumping in case the horse should strike himself on landing, but there is minimal risk of damage occurring on the flat.

Once the horse has gained confidence in the working surface, he will start to relax and be supple and responsive, whereas if he is rigid for fear of slipping, the rider will be stuck in Stage 1 of the Blueprint.

**Stiffness**
*Symptoms*: Stiffness is associated with a lack of suppleness in the horse's back. In order for the horse to be able to bend around his corners, or bring his hocks underneath him, he must be supple and elastic, especially in the muscles along his back that allow him to stretch one way or another. Obviously, the horse can be stiff anywhere but normally, when one reads 'stiff' on a dressage sheet, it is in connection with the back. If the horse is stiff in his back, he will try to evade the rider's request to bend, by being hollow in his outline with inactive hocks, and either by falling in or by swinging his quarters out on the corner.
*Causes*: Either a lack of training, or a problem somewhere in the back region, or discomfort encountered when the hocks are brought underneath the horse will cause stiffness. The length of the horse's back will affect his suppleness: the short-backed horse will find bending around his corners far more difficult as he will be naturally more rigid in his spine than a slightly longer horse. A parallel here may be drawn between two pieces of stick – a short length and a longer length. The short stick is far less flexible than the longer stick, but a very long stick will be fragile and rather weak.
*Treatment*: As suppleness is such an important feature of the athletic horse, any stiffness must be corrected as much as possible. Whatever the cause, the treatment is much the same, increasing the elasticity and flexibility by using and stretching the muscles in a variety of exercises. In any cases of stiffness, there is one very important factor to bear in mind: the horse must be given sufficient time to warm up before the muscles are asked to work harder. Forcing the muscles to stretch before they are loosened up will only result in damage: the fibres of the muscles may be torn, and the horse will be even stiffer as a result.

A stiff horse will have many interrelated problems, for he will be unable to establish a true rhythm, particularly on the smaller circles and, of course, in the more difficult movements, such as shoulder-in or half-pass. He will be unable to bring his hocks far enough underneath him to gain true self-carriage, and so the whole process of training will come to a halt (*see* stage 4 in the Blueprint – Straightness, page 26). There is no magic treatment for making a horse more supple, just a progressive training plan of bending and stretching exercises, all of which include circles, changes of bend, enlarging and decreasing circles, transitions, shoulder-in, leg-yield and trotting poles. All these exercises use the muscles which need to be worked and, if a little more is asked each day after the warm-up period, they will become more supple. Some suppling work should be done at walk. Simply bending the horse around the leg in small circles and turning his head right round to the inside will really stretch the lateral muscles, and working the horse long and low will stretch the muscles along the top. Lungeing work in a Chambon (*see* Hollow, page 132) will also stretch these muscles, and having no weight on the horse's back is an advantage. Indeed, with a horse who is very stiff in his back, the less weight on it the better and, until the horse can carry the weight on a *relaxed* back, it is important not to aggravate a stiff back with too much sitting trot, or heavy seat in canter. A supple-backed horse will accept the rider in sitting trot without tensing, but the more the rider attempts to make the stiff back supple by driving hard with the seat, the worse the situation will become. One must be aware that the horse may try to remove the weight of the rider by automatically tensing as soon as the rider goes into sitting trot, and sometimes one must work through this stage by persisting in sitting trot, but making sure, at the same time, that one does not tense up in one's own back, which will create a vicious circle. There must always be a give-and-take situation, and no two horses are ever alike. It is a matter of trial and error with each horse, working out what is best for which horse. If one method fails, then try another, trying to analyse the reason behind the horse's reaction.

It goes without saying that the saddle should fit correctly, and that a numnah should be used to spread the pressure and make the saddle more comfortable for the horse to wear. Any discomfort in the saddle region will cause the horse immediately to stiffen against it, so check that the tack is right for the horse.

### Strike-off into canter, difficulties with

*Symptoms*: These can vary enormously. The horse can run into canter, by coming above the bit in the transition – sometimes to the extent that he actually jumps into canter. Alternatively the horse may persistently refuse to canter on a specific lead.

*Causes*: The first problem is associated with a lack of training: the horse falls onto his forehand and does not engage his hocks in the strike-off. A resistance in the transition invariably originates with the rider who is restrictive with his hand as the horse goes into canter. When the horse jumps into canter, it is an exaggeration of this situation: the horse wants to go forward into canter but is restricted to such an extent by the rider that he has to jump into the first stride. Blame for an incorrect strike-off may also be placed on the rider. The aids may have been unclear, or the rider may have been sitting to the outside – which affects the horse's balance, and all but forces him to strike off incorrectly. If the rider has trained the horse poorly from the start, of course, he may not understand what is expected of him anyway.

A horse may be worse on one lead than another, and sometimes it may be very difficult indeed to get canter on one rein. This is either because the horse is not bringing his outside leg (which is the first beat of the canter) underneath him or because he is swinging his outside shoulder, which then allows him to lead with his outside foreleg.

*Treatment*: In order to ask a horse to move from trot to canter the rider should take a half-halt in trot just before a corner, ensure that there is a correct bend, and then, with the outside leg behind the girth (which is where it will be anyway to control the bend), he should ask the horse to strike off into canter with the inside leg – positioned a little further forward than it would be to ask for a bend. The rider's weight should be placed, very definitely, on the inside seat-bone in order to aid the horse's balance. Obviously the whole aid should be positive, rather than being a vague message which will merely encourage the horse to shamble into canter. If the horse falls onto his forehand into canter, the rider must make a series of strong half-halts to drive the hocks under the horse, before asking for a transition, because he will most definitely be on his forehand in canter if he is on his forehand in trot. The rider must not allow the horse to increase the speed of his trot, pulling himself along on his forehand, but must make the horse canter from his hocks. Plenty of trot–canter transitions will help the horse to use himself properly, and improving the basic trot will automatically improve the canter.

Although the rider must not let the horse run into canter, he must also be very careful not to restrict him: coming above the bit or jumping into the transition to evade this restriction will soon develop into a habit. In this instance the horse is fighting for the freedom to use his head and neck, rather than propelling with his hocks. The horse must remain on the same contact throughout the transition and the rider, in order to obtain this, must have the horse prepared sufficiently well (with half-halts), so that his hocks are underneath, and there is enough potential energy stored for positive forward action. If, when the rider maintains the faintest of contacts, the horse still comes above the bit as he goes into canter, the rider should execute the transition in one of two ways. Either he should lower the outline before the transition by asking the horse the flex at the poll, or he should make the transition on a long rein, taking the hand wide, so that the horse cannot evade a contact but at the same time is not restricted at all. Once the horse has learnt that he will be driven forward into canter, that he will meet with no restriction as he moves from trot to canter, and yet that must still remain on a contact, the rider can then start to move his hands back to their normal position, opening the inside hand whenever necessary until the problem is solved.

The rider must always think that he is driving the horse forward into canter, and must not draw back during the transition. Although this is always true, it has to be even more emphasised if the horse tends to jump into canter. Driving the horse forward too much may lead to a very fast trot, but this speed must be replaced by impulsion, created by half-halts. A strong forward canter aid from a positive trot with no restriction from the hand will effect the cure.

An incorrect strike-off should be remedied merely by giving the correct aid, but sometimes this is not enough: the horse sometimes refuses point-blank to canter on one lead, and if he really does not want to canter that way, he will have learnt all the tricks to avoid doing so. If, for instance, the horse will not lead with his near-fore (the left rein), try to obtain the lead using some of these methods: they are really exercises to outwit him, and they are arranged according to the severity of the problem!

(a) Trot a circle on the right rein and then, as you change out of the circle onto the left rein, ask for a left strike-off. This defeats the horse who swings his quarters out and falls in with his shoulder, because what was the outside/inside on the right rein, will be the opposite once the rein is changed, and this may be sufficient just to capture the shoulder or quarters, and result in a left strike-off.

(b) If the horse merely falls out with his shoulder, maintain a very firm contact on the outside rein, almost to the extent that the horse is bent to the opposite direction with his head and neck. This will stop the wrong strike-off which has been caused by the outside shoulder escaping to the outside.

(c) If the quarters fall out, use a very strong outside leg, trying to push the quarters inwards slightly just before the strike-off, containing the shoulder at the same time.

These are fairly simple methods to deal with the less tricky cases, although there are some horses who still manage to disobey. If, however, the rider concentrates on getting the horse to be completely obedient to the leg in his trot work – moving away from the leg, and bending correctly around the corners – the horse's canter transition should improve; his refusal to strike off on a particular lead is merely one more form of disobedience to the leg.

It seems that some horses really do develop a mental block about leading on a particular leg, and the more one tries, the worse the situation becomes. I have found that trotting poles arranged in specific ways can be of great help, as the horse will find himself striking off correctly without any fuss or upset. One pole should be laid on the ground three-quarters of the way across the diagonal and the rider should ask for a strike-off into canter just before the horse takes off to jump the pole; this is the critical moment because the horse can see which way he has to turn after the pole and he will almost always strike off with the correct leg leading. If the horse still swings his shoulder in the air and lands incorrectly, on the wrong leg, a second pole may be placed on the outside of the pole (on the angle), leading the horse in the proper direction (*see* diagram 35). The rider must make sure that the most precise canter aids are

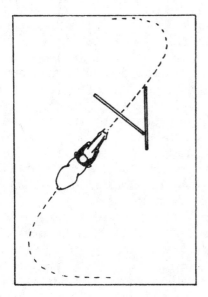

**35 To encourage a correct strike-off into canter** — *use the flowing movement of a change of rein in conjunction with a pole or poles to lead the horse to a position from which a correct strike-off is almost unavoidable: the poles should be placed off-centre, just past the E-B line.*

given, that the horse is driven forward into canter over the pole, and that the canter is established for a couple of circuits before another strike-off is attempted. Once the horse learns to associate the pole with the canter aid, the pole may be moved to other parts of the arena and used to make the strike-off anywhere. The rider must direct the horse with an open inside hand, preventing the shoulder from escaping with the outside hand; he must keep the quarters under control with a strong outside leg, but he gives the actual canter aid with the inside leg and with the weight on the inside seat-bone.

At all costs, the horse must be driven forward into his canter, and sometimes a really strong, almost fast trot will force the horse by balance alone to strike off correctly. The horse will want to lead on the correct leg for the sake of his balance . . . after all, how often do you see a racehorse go around a corner on the wrong leg? Watching the racing on the television teaches one an enormous amount about a horse's natural way of going; a racehorse will go around a corner with the 'wrong bend', but still be in perfect balance. This natural balance must always be remembered when riding on the flat or over fences.

### Tail-swishing
*Symptoms*: The horse whisks his tail either occasionally, at the moment he is given a specific aid, or almost continuously in a vigorous manner.
*Causes*: Resentment for one reason or another makes a horse react in this way. He may resent the rider's aid or even the rider's weight in the saddle; alternatively he may only show resentment when the rider asks him to work harder, or asks for a particular movement such as a strike-off into canter or a half-pass, both of which require not only a definite aid from the rider but also a specific effort from the horse. If the horse swishes his tail perpetually it may be an indication that he is in discomfort and not enjoying what he is being asked to do. This discomfort would normally be situated behind the shoulder. Indeed his behaviour may be associated with pain in the back – anything further forward than the shoulder would usually cause the horse to be unsettled in his head and neck.
*Treatment*: There is little that can be done to prevent a horse from swishing his tail and there should be no loss of marks in the dressage arena for the occasional flick. If the horse resents spurs, which are obligatory in advanced tests, the rider should use very small ones that will scarcely come into contact with the horse. The chronic tail-swisher, who is making it apparent that something is irritating him,

should be examined by a vet, who can ascertain if there is something amiss, be it a problem in the back region, or, in the case of a mare, an ovarian cyst. Some horses merely resent the rider's leg and the only action the rider can take in this instance is to be tactful, and to try to aggravate the horse as little as possible.

### Teeth-grinding

*Symptoms*: This is a resistance which results from the horse grinding his incisors together by moving his jaw slightly from side to side. He can also grind his molars together, but this is less common. Whilst grinding his teeth the horse drops the contact, and so falls behind the bit.

*Causes*: Resentment about or tension caused by either discomfort, excitement, temper or worry can lead the horse to develop this bad habit. The discomfort may stem from his mouth or from pain elsewhere, most commonly the muscles connected with suppleness along his back. A number of years ago, for instance, we were plagued in the yard by a skin infection, which occurred around the girth area in particular. One very thin-skinned horse started grinding his teeth, resisting the discomfort in the area of the girth and rider's leg but, once the 'spots' had cleared up, he then stopped grinding his teeth. This horse obviously had a natural tendency towards resentment, and throughout his career he has been a teeth-grinder when things have not quite gone his way; he also showed a certain amount of temper. Had he been aggravated in his training, he would no doubt have developed into a confirmed 'grinder', but because of sympathetic handling, it has not become a habit with him. A horse will usually start to grind his teeth when he becomes upset, and this is his way of telling the rider that he is unhappy about something. Often this resistance is triggered off by an attempt at a step forward in the horse's training which he finds difficult or uncomfortable; he is merely resisting in this way rather than in another. When a horse is slightly keyed-up and he knows that he might be going to do something exciting, he might grind his teeth, rather in the same way as a human might have a cigarette! (One top-class horse we have in the yard grinds his teeth when he is standing in the horsebox at an event: this is sheer frustration at being cooped up when he knows where he is. Once he has performed, he then relaxes and ceases to do it – thank goodness!) This is not so much a resistance, more a nervous habit, albeit annoying: it is infuriating to have to cope with a horse who grinds his teeth incessantly out hunting, for example, as the noise starts to grate quite heavily on one's nerves after a while!

*Treatment*: Teeth-grinding needs nipping in the bud because, if the horse becomes a confirmed 'grinder', there is little to be done to break him of the habit, even if the cause is removed. Number one step is to establish the cause. Few horses will grind their teeth in the stable, and it is only when the rider is aboard that the problem becomes apparent. This rather suggests that the horse is uncomfortable with the rider on his back: the first thing to ascertain, therefore, is whether the horse has any discomfort in his back, particularly in the saddle area. Check that the saddle fits correctly, that it is not pressing on the withers or spine, and that the pressure is well distributed. If the resistance *is* from the weight of the rider or from the saddle, one or even two thick numnahs may help. Thick foam under the saddle can help spread the pressure, and this should be placed between the saddle and a sheepskin numnah, which is warm and soft. The horse may also be uncomfortable in the girth region, either because the girth itself is made of rather harsh material for that particular horse, or even because inadequate grooming has led to a girth gall or sore particularly when the horse is changing his coat. Check the horse's teeth carefully, and look for any ulcers or sores in his mouth which could give him an excuse to resent the bit. If a horse, who is otherwise perfectly happy, grinds his teeth when he is asked to work harder, the rider must ask himself why the horse is becoming upset. Is the horse finding the work uncomfortable, or too difficult for his stage of training? Does he not understand what is being required of him, so that he becomes upset? Or is it merely his character, does he just resent being asked to work hard? Having answered these questions, the rider must act accordingly and, if need be, be more patient until the horse is more receptive to his increased workload. Teeth-grinding is undoubtedly a very unpleasant habit, and difficult to cure, but it must be the rider's aim – if he is to be successful in curing the habit – to make the horse feel happy and relaxed about his work, because, in this situation, he will not grind his teeth (*see also* Excitability, page 120, and Tenseness, below).

**Tenseness**

*Symptoms*: The horse appears unhappy in his work: he often has his ears back, a shortened, tight stride, a lack of forward movement and there is a general attitude of unease and lack of harmony between him and his rider. In extreme cases, the horse may refuse to perform certain movements of the dressage test; he will, for instance, fail to stand still in a halt, he will jog when he is supposed to walk, and he will canter instead of trotting. The horse may sweat profusely in his agitation and the whole picture will be one of tension and upset. Until a horse is relaxed both physically and mentally, he will be unable to work in a soft and supple way, and further steps in his training cannot be established until the horse is calm (*see* stage 1 of the Blueprint, page 18, and Typical schooling sessions, page 40).

*Causes*: If the horse is tense, it suggests that he is unhappy about something; that may be the rider, or what the rider is asking him to do. It may be outside influences, such as an exciting environment, or a frightening atmosphere. The horse may be fresh and unsettled, or he may not be confident about what he is being asked to do, and this worries him. He may be in discomfort – from the bit, or from the saddle, or from the weight of the rider, or from some other pain somewhere which is upsetting him. A tense rider can easily pass his nervousness on to his horse and even a normally phlegmatic animal may be affected in this way: if a horse is tense, he is not confident, and therefore he either is or will become worried.

*Treatment*: Since horses vary so much, it is difficult to state any definite method which works in combating tension; again, trial and error will establish the best method for each particular horse. The ways of settling a horse vary from working on a long rein, making the horse stretch down – so relaxing the muscles, which may then relax the horse's mind – to strong, determined riding. On the whole the problem is rider induced initially, and the greater his understanding of the cause, the more likely he is to be able to cure the problem. The less experienced the rider, the greater the problem will be, but even some very experienced riders become very nervous before a dressage test and, as a result, it suffers.

Try to ascertain the cause first of all. Ask the question 'what is he unhappy about?' – the rider must know the horse sufficiently well to be able to understand his behaviour and moods. If the horse is reacting to discomfort, then remove the source if at all possible – i.e. change to a milder bit, or use a better fitting saddle, or a softer girth. Ask the vet if he can find anything which could be causing him pain and upset. Only once all the concrete reasons have been thoroughly examined, can one set about trying to make the horse relaxed and settled in his work.

A rider must learn the appropriate warming-up period for his particular horse and must also discover the best way to make him relax before he is asked to work to his best ability. This may mean taking him for a walk on a long rein around the showground, or putting him on the lunge until he settles, or even just working him through the tense period, if there is one, until he is ready to concentrate fully on his work. Calmness is the first stage in any training programme, and it is vital that the horse is relaxed in every way before the work can progress. If the horse is not settled in his work at home, he certainly will not improve at an event, so the training at home must be established before the horse can be expected to produce good work away from home. One must remember that the horse never goes quite as well in an arena as he does elsewhere, as both outside influences and the rigid pattern of the test will usually contribute to a loss of form somewhere, so it is important that the horse's general work is as good as possible to allow for these lapses during the test itself. A horse will often work well outside the dressage arena at an event, but as soon as he enters the arena, the whole picture changes, so the more that can be done within the confines of white boards, the better. This way the horse becomes confident about performing his work in an arena. If a rider becomes tense as he begins his dressage test, the horse will immediately pick this up and so he will develop an association between dressage arenas and tension. All riders get nervous before tests but they must learn to control these nerves if they do not want to affect the horse. Experience is the greatest way of overcoming this problem, and mind over matter plays a strong part as well. I find that taking deep breaths every so often helps, and singing quietly too, as it is very difficult to sing and be tense at the same time – it takes one's mind off the job in hand a little! Smiling is very therapeutic too – providing the smile does not emerge as a grimace!

A horse must have confidence in the work he is being asked to do and if too much is demanded of him before he is physically and mentally able to cope, he will react by resisting or appearing tense. If the horse starts to get tense the rider should decide whether the horse is merely evading work by pretending to get upset, or whether he is genuinely not ready to perform the exercises at this stage in his training. If the latter is the case, the rider should return to simpler tasks and then reintroduce the more difficult movements gradually and carefully when he feels the horse is ready to try again. This may be during the same schooling session, or it may be a week later, depending on the horse. Calmness must be nurtured, as once the horse has become tense it is difficult to make him relax again. As soon as he becomes tense, the horse will tighten his muscles – especially those along his back – so any exercise to stretch and supple these muscles will help to relieve the tension. These exercises should comprise work on a long rein, with circles, transitions, shoulder-ins and shoulder-outs, and the rider should assume a soothing attitude, his aids should be tactful, he should use his voice and he should pat or stroke the horse's neck. Sometimes, however, it is necessary for the rider to exert some strong pressure on the horse to make him work hard in order for him to relax his muscles and the rider has to insist on obedience to obtain this relaxation.

If possible, the horse should learn that his training routine means concentration and a relaxed attitude towards his work. He should be rewarded for collaborating in this way by the rider, who should not be over-demanding or tense himself. Tenseness is a very common problem, and manifests itself more as the horse gets older and more experienced: most novice horses are quite happy to flop around the dressage arena, and it is only when they have learnt the precise routine of an event that they start to anticipate what will be coming.

### Tongue out

*Symptoms*: Either the horse pushes the tongue out of the side of mouth, twisting it at the same time, or it hangs out in a relaxed, floppy fashion. Sometimes the tongue may stick out forwards, with just the tip being visible. When the tongue is relaxed but hanging out, the horse can still remain on a contact, but if the tongue is moving, the horse will inevitably drop behind the bit (*see* page 101).

*Causes*: Discomfort, very much like the reasons for putting his tongue over the bit, is the cause here. Usually the horse will try to avoid pressure on his tongue which he finds uncomfortable by trying to move his tongue away from the contact. The over-relaxed tongue is often to be seen in a tired racehorse, for example, at the end of a long race, but in the dressage horse it normally arises from some previous discomfort in the mouth.

*Treatment*: First check that there are no sores or ulcers in the horse's mouth. Then see if a change of bit will help: try one which does not exert as much pressure on the tongue, such as the French-link snaffle, or Fillis. It is really a matter of trial and error, trying to find the right bit for a particular horse. When the rider is schooling, he must try to ensure that the contact is never so strong as to give the horse reason to resist, by trying to draw his tongue away from the bit. If the horse is carrying himself on a light contact, and provided that the right bit has been found, there should be no reason for him to feel uncomfortable in his mouth, and therefore he will have no reason for sticking his tongue out.

### Tongue over the bit

*Symptoms*: The horse does not accept the bit lying on his tongue, but instead draws his tongue back, and puts it over the top of the bit and the rider experiences a loss of control. The rider will be aware of a change of feeling in his hand; he may find that suddenly he either has no contact at all, or that the contact is completely dead and that he has no control, either to steady the horse or to turn him. Sometimes the horse may frighten himself by putting his tongue over the bit, and this might account for a horse suddenly rearing for no apparent reason: the discomfort involved in this action may be enough to cause the horse to 'flip' – i.e. rear straight over backwards with no warning. This is the worst kind of rearing as the rider is given no prior warning, and invariably he is caught under his horse as it goes over.

*Causes*: This habit is initially developed because the bit is too low in the horse's mouth, which encourages him to fiddle with it, at the same time making it easy for him to put his tongue over it. Alternatively, the horse is trying to find a way to ease some discomfort in his mouth arising either from a badly fitting bit, or pressure on his tongue, or general mouth discomfort which is then aggravated by the mere presence of the bit.

*Treatment*: If the bit *is* too low, raise it to the correct position, or even one hole higher, so that it is more difficult for the horse to get his tongue over it. Check that the bit is not too big, because, if this is the case, it will drop in the middle where the horse can pop his tongue over, even if the bit appears to be high enough at the corners. The horse does not necessarily have to open his mouth to draw his tongue back, so a tight noseband will not stop him, but it will make it more difficult. This may work both ways, however, because once he has put his tongue over, he will find it more difficult to bring it back again, and this is when he might rear. If the horse has a rather large tongue, which means that the bit acts rather strongly upon it, a change of bit may alleviate the pressure: a change from a plain jointed snaffle to a French-link snaffle which has less of a nut-cracker action often helps . . . or even to a Fillis snaffle, which has a double joint and an arch to give room for the tongue. Many horses do resent the nut-cracker action of the snaffle, and the milder action of the double-jointed snaffle (provided the central plate is flat and smooth) can be the answer. If the habit is established despite all causes having been dealt with, and all else fails, a removable rubber port will prevent the horse from being able to get his tongue over the bit. It will not stop him from being able to draw his tongue back, but it will stop him actually putting his tongue over and, in time, the horse may learn that in fact it is more comfortable to accept the bit in the correct place and it may then be possible to dispense with the port.

Sores or ulcers in the mouth give the horse ample excuse for evading the direct action of the bit and these must be treated before the horse can be expected to give up his bad habit. After all, the horse does not realise that he is being naughty by putting his tongue over the bit; all he knows is that he can evade its action, so it is up to us to make life comfortable for him so that he does not feel the need to resort to evasion.

### Tripping

*Symptoms*: The horse stumbles over something, but then can either pick himself up, or go right down onto his knees. The horse can also stumble behind by catching his toe when he brings his leg forward, and this means he puts his weight on the front wall of the hoof instead of on the sole.

*Causes*: Youth, weakness, or a lack of balance can cause a horse frequently to trip over his front feet. Foot trouble such as navicular disease is a possible, more sinister alternative. As far as tripping over the hind feet is concerned, weakness or sloppiness will be the reason.

*Treatment*: General schooling is necessary to correct the balance and make the horse come off his forehand and carry himself more on his hocks (*see* On forehand, page 152, and Leaning, page 142). There is a danger, if a horse trips, that he will either fall over altogether, or, more likely, fall onto his knees and this way he ends up with broken knees. A young horse tends to trip more because he has not yet learnt how to balance himself properly, and is very much on his forehand; and, for this reason, we always put kneecaps on our young horses for road work. The decision to dispense with the kneecaps is always a difficult one to make and one rides out in fear and trepidation on the day they are not worn, thinking that this will be the day that the horse falls onto his nose on the road. However, the horse cannot live in kneecaps; if they are worn for long periods every day, there is every chance that they will cause rubs and callouses, which may be a problem in themselves. Kneecaps have to be sufficiently tight that they cannot slip down but, at the same time, the pressure around the top of the knee may cause harm to that area.

In time, and with training, the horse will be well enough balanced that he will rarely trip, although the rider must always be aware that there is always the possibility he could trip, and, for that reason, a very loose rein is never advisable. A long rein is perfectly adequate, so that while the horse has as much freedom as he needs, it will still be possible to pick him up and remain in control if he should trip, or suddenly shoot off for any reason. A horse should know that he has done wrong if he does not pick his feet up, and a little kick – not enough to make him worried, but just to make him a little more alert and more careful about where he is putting his feet – does not go amiss. Do be careful, though, that the horse does not begin to associate tripping with something to fear – i.e. a smack or a big kick in the ribs; otherwise when he trips, he will shoot off, expecting a big reprimand . . . and the problem has been added to rather than solved.

## Unlevel

*Symptoms*: The horse does not take even strides. This is most noticeable in trot, but can also be felt in walk. The head will not necessarily nod as it would if the horse were actually lame, but still the horse does not bring one leg as far forward as the other.

*Causes*: This is a fashionable problem, and one that causes many heated discussions. Is a horse unlevel, or is he in fact lame? It is a very controversial question. Bridle-lameness comes under the 'unlevel' umbrella; some horses will 'back-off' a bit to such an extent that it will make them trot unlevel. A heavy-handed rider can also cause a horse to swing his head from side to side and so cause the stride pattern to become irregular.

*Treatment*: Finding the root of the unlevelness is the obvious starting point. I like to see a horse trotting loose, without any form of restriction, to study its action. If, by watching carefully, it is possible to detect any unlevelness, then it shows that there is some physical problem causing it, and, having ascertained whether it is behind or in front, right or left, it is best left to the vet to diagnose the exact cause.

If the horse only goes unlevel when the rider is on board, it must be discovered whether it is merely the weight of the rider which is triggering off the unlevelness or whether it is interference from a rider (who was too over-powering with the hand in the past) which has made the horse develop the habit of dropping short on one diagonal. Long rein work should establish the root of the problem in this case, but if the horse does not stretch on a long rein, he will probably still go unlevel. If he does stretch, however, and is still unlevel, then it is another matter for the vet. If the horse is perfectly level on a long–loose rein, then rider influence must be suspected, and working through the initial stages of training from stage 2 onwards again should solve the unlevelness. If this is the case, the unlevelness has been caused by the horse not driving through equally from behind; it may be that the horse has actually become less developed on one side, and finds it difficult to work evenly.

Training and time will help this enormously, but obviously, if a horse is one-sided to such a degree, one must also be suspicious of a weakness of some sort inherent in that horse.

There are vast numbers of horses, particularly in the field of eventing, who are slightly unlevel, although they may perform brilliantly cross-country and jump very well: they obviously compensate for the weakness (whatever it is) in other ways, and are quite happy to do so, for if they were in pain in any way, they would not perform so well. However, dressage work will highlight any unlevelness and more problems will probably emerge because unlevelness makes the half-pass and small circle work very difficult. There is no point in upsetting a horse by trying to force it to stay level in these movements if, in fact, he finds it virtually impossible. It is very much better to do the movement as best one can by trying as much as possible to maintain calmness and rhythm; making sure of the bend will help. Obviously any weakness can be helped by training, and the basic work is within the capabilities of any horse. He must be given the chance to learn and to develop sufficient muscle and strength to enable him to perform.

## Unsteady rhythm

*Symptoms*: Instead of maintaining the same rhythm throughout all the movements, the horse loses both rhythm and cadence: this normally happens during the more difficult movements – a 10-metre circle, for example, or medium trot, or half-pass.

*Causes*: Any loss of rhythm is due to a lack of drive from behind. If a movement calls for an increased hock engagement, particularly from the inside hind, and if the horse does not produce or use this extra power, a rhythm variation occurs. If the horse does not track up on the circle, this can exaggerate the above point, but also shows that the horse is stiff and unable to carry out that movement – either because he is not ready for it, or because the rider has not been sufficiently clear and firm with the aids to teach the horse to work correctly in rhythm. If the horse falls in on a corner he will lose the rhythm, and this basic fault will recur throughout his training until the horse learns to bend around the inside leg and consequently to track up, first on the bend and then on the circle.

A generally unsteady rhythm may be caused by tenseness or excitement, which may result again in a varied drive from behind.

*Treatment*: Back to the basics. Always in the rider's mind must be free forward movement, rhythm and suppleness. Balance will follow automatically from that, and then the more advanced stages will slot into place. Firmly establish the basics, though, even if it means going back to stage 1. Remember too, that the rider must think in rhythm for the horse to work in a rhythm.

## Yawing

*Symptoms*: The horse bears down onto the bit, with his mouth open, pulling the rider forward and/or even dragging the reins out of the rider's hand. Yawing is normally associated with little woolly ponies, who then either charge off, or grab a mouthful or two of grass, but alas it is all too common in horses too, and I am afraid these horses have to be labelled 'ignorant'.

*Causes*: This has to be lack of training and therefore ignorance on the horse's behalf. This does not come under the category of a resistance likely to be encountered during the five-stage training of a horse, but is a bad habit derived from poor discipline and moderate riding. Invariably it is a habit which forms its roots, not at a very early age, but when a horse begins to 'find his feet' and learns how he can get his own way. Unfortunately hunting can encourage this yawing and snatching at the bit, because the horse, in his eagerness to keep up with his companions at all times, will try anything to make sure that he is in control; when his rider goes to steady him, he pulls the reins with a quick jerk so that the rider momentarily loses control. Once the horse has learnt this unpleasant habit, he will continue to resort to it whenever he feels a contact with his mouth which he wants to break – a quick yaw downwards, and freedom is his. One very common cause of the problem is fatigue: the horse wants to stretch his neck when he is tired, but the rider restricts with his hand, and so the horse has to pull enough rein to allow himself to ease the cramped muscles in his neck. It is impractical to allow a horse a long rein when out hunting, as he can so easily trip, and normally he is not interested in staying on a long rein anyway, being far too excited about everything. The horse will find an occasional quick stretch of his neck sufficient to ease his aching muscles, and thus the bad habit is formed. This may then continue in the schooling programme when it becomes a problem to be corrected, but really it is a problem which should never have appeared in the first place.

*Treatment*: In a situation where the horse is displaying bad manners rather than a resistance related to stiffness or lack of engagement, he must learn that he is not allowed to behave in such a way, and that it is wrong. Initially, therefore, it is a matter of strength in not allowing the reins to be taken forward as the horse yaws, so that he learns that he achieves nothing by his action. This sounds easier than it really is, as a horse is very strong, particularly in a snatching motion; but the rider must ensure that he does not let the horse feel that he has gained anything, but instead has met with a solid block. The horse should encounter the same feel that he would if he had side-reins attached, as the side-rein will not give but, at the same time, it will never pull back: pulling back at a horse is a sure way to make him pull and yaw at the reins. If the rider is not strong enough to *create* this hold, then holding on to the saddle flap, grabbing hold of a piece of his breeches (if not too tight!) over the thighs, or holding a bridge (*see* diagram 36), when cantering in forward position, will give him added strength, and the horse will soon realise that he gains nothing by yawing and will cease to do it. If the problem is a serious one, then some work on the lunge with side-reins – working through the transitions – will teach the horse some respect for the bit, and will help to teach the horse to work in a good shape, and maintain that shape throughout the upward and downward changes of pace which is when yawing is most common. In his flat work, the rider must make sure that he drives the horse forward very strongly every time he tries to bear down on the rein; he must not allow the horse to increase in speed, by which he will have run through the rider's hand (*see* page 159). The rider's legs and seat must be sufficiently strong to keep the horse in a stable rhythm, even when not allowing him to take the contact in a snatch; this all teaches him the basic discipline without which training cannot proceed. If the horse yaws at the bit, a good rhythm cannot be established, and stage 3 will not be achieved.

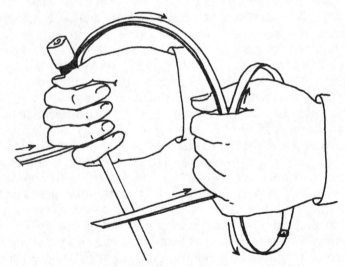

**36 The correct way to hold the reins in a bridge** — *which allows the whip to be carried easily.*

# FOUR

# Show-Jumping

Before I discuss the specific problems which occur in the show-jumping phase, I must emphasise again that with jumping, whatever the fence may be, or from whatever pace the horse is asked to jump, the principles are exactly the same as those worked on in dressage. Provided that the horse is able to maintain forward movement, balance and rhythm at all times, whatever the speed or terrain, the training has been correct and, as a result, the jumping should follow naturally. Experience is everything in jumping and that only comes with time, correct training and confidence. The well-trained horse should be a pleasure to ride not only on the flat but also over a variety of fences.

I always find it difficult at an event to associate a very good dressage mark on the result board with a rather mediocre exhibition cross-country or in the show-jumping phase from the same horse. To my mind, the whole reason for working a horse on the flat is to make him supple and obedient for another end, whether that be more advanced dressage, jumping, or hunting, to name but three examples. The rider should be seeking obedience but, by saying that, I am not suggesting that the horse should be a robot and unable to think for himself; far from it, in fact, because an obedient horse is a balanced horse with forward movement, rhythm and suppleness. As such he is in harmony with the rider and therefore physically able to help the rider on many occasions. Note that I say physically able to help the rider, for here lies the difference between the good horse and the brilliant horse. Virtually all horses can be trained to be good horses, but the brilliant horse is trained to a high level, and then really wants to do the job; he is very alert and determined to please; he will strive at all costs to comply with the rider's demands, however difficult. The good horse may be trained to the same level, but in moments of stress does not have the same mental attitude and perhaps gives up, instead of 'having a go'.

The horse must be trained to be athletic and so able to undertake all the requirements of the rider not only on the flat but over fences as well, and if this groundwork has not been correct, then the faults will be emphasised during the jumping work. When I discuss individual problems in this chapter, the reader is often referred to sections in the dressage chapter (where relevant), or to the Blueprint earlier in the book.

Because there is no judge marking the show-jumping round for style and correctness as there is in the dressage phase, and provided that most of the time there is a nought on the scoreboard, there are many people who do not work hard enough on the actual jump of the horse. Unless the jumping runs hand in hand with the progressive work on the flat, however, the horse will eventually be caught out as he moves up the grades, or rather IF he moves up the grades. Even Intermediate cross-country courses are becoming more technical and therefore more difficult, and they require more precision by both rider and horse. I feel very strongly that unless a horse can jump a close-to-classical round over fences about a metre (3 feet 6 inches) high, he should not be hurtling round a cross-country course at speed, but it seems, when I watch the show-jumping phase at the average one-day horse trial, that I am, alas, in a minority. Whereas a show-jump does fall down if 'taken on', a cross-country fence does not and this is where accidents happen; the more controlled the show-jumping round, the more controlled the cross-country round will be. It seems sensible to me to perfect the horse's jump at a slower pace before expecting him to jump at speed; unless the horse is disciplined in jumping fences from trot and canter, he will certainly be a danger both to himself and to his rider if he is asked to jump from the gallop.

It is worth bearing in mind too that penalties for a fence down, a refusal or a fall in the show-jumping phase are almost always the result of incorrect training, although there are occasional hard luck stories.

## Problems encountered

### Always landing on the same leg

*Symptoms*: The horse lands on the same lead irrespective of the direction to be taken after the fence.

*Causes*: Which leg the horse lands on is all to do with balance, and if the horse can see that he is to turn right after a fence, he will normally land on the right lead, and vice versa for the left. If he persists, however, on always landing on the same lead, one of several things may be at fault. One is that he twists in the air, so that he is forced, by balance alone, to land on a particular lead; if he twists his quarters to the right in the air, for example, he will land on his left front leg to compensate, and this will mean that he will continue on the right lead, although sometimes, if the horse jumps a little faster, the twist may be less obvious and he will be able to land on either leg. When he jumps slowly, the horse does not carry his jumping through and consequently he lands not going forward and will then favour a particular lead. If the jump is ridden through by the rider – i.e. the rider drives the horse forward on the landing side – the horse will be balanced automatically in the direction he is going.

The rider's balance in the air can have a bearing on that of the horse, so that if the rider perpetually swings more one way than the other, the horse will have to compensate by shifting his weight to the opposite side. If the horse arrives at a fence not quite straight, with his outside shoulder falling out, the horse will already be veering slightly that way and, as he jumps, will continue on that line – landing on the inside fore with the outside leg leading. The final reason may be that the horse is in some discomfort as he lands and avoids landing on a particular leg to lessen the concussion or jarring.

*Treatment*: I have found that one can become rather paranoid about horses always landing on the same lead. One always notices this far more at home than at a competition when, because of the fluency connected with riding a course, the horse seems to 'screw' less in the air, and lands on the correct lead each time. It is at home where this fault seems most in evidence, when the horse is not being asked specifically to land either way and so is not driven forward on the landing side of the fence. The jump must be a continuous movement, with a flowing feeling not only on the approach to the fence but also as the horse goes over it and away the other side; it is a common fault to see a horse 'die' as he lands and have no impulsion at all in the first few strides after that. The rider must insist right from the early stages that the horse lands and 'goes' in his jumping – in other words, that he lands and immediately picks up the rhythm, balance and forward movement in preparation for the next fence. It is important that the horse is driven forward at this stage, and on no account should the rider try to snatch up the horse with his hand, because this will create a hollow horse on landing, and might even affect the jump itself – the horse may prepare himself for the action of the rider but, in so doing, he will have no chance to find his own balance on the landing side. This balance is important when it comes to cross-country jumping, and the horse meets all sorts of unusual terrain on the landing side. If he has never been given a chance to learn how to balance himself as he lands, he will be more likely to encounter problems (with drop fences and the like), as he will not know how to bring his hocks underneath him as he lands. Landing on the wrong lead is a symptom of the horse's lack of balance on landing, and the rider must be aware of what consequences this might have when he thinks about sorting the problem out.

There is an excellent exercise (shown to me by Pat Burgess) which helps enormously in perfecting not only the horse's correct strike-off on landing but also the whole aspect of his jump. The exercise is simplicity itself, consisting of a small grid on a turn (*see* diagram 37), but requires perfect riding and perfect performance from both parties to be executed as it should be. It consists of a cross-pole, with a placing pole 2.5–2.75 metres (8–9 feet) away and a pole on the landing side 2.75–3.00 metres (9–10 feet) away, with poles either side to keep the horse on the true circle as he lands. This is to be ridden in trot coming off whatever size of circle or turn the rider wishes; a 20-metre circle is probably about right although the circle may be made bigger – all that matters is that the rider meets the placing pole straight, so the angle of the placing pole will determine the size of the circle. The horse must be brought in to the exercise in perfect balance and rhythm; he must be allowed to stretch his head and neck over the pole; he must be given total freedom in the air, and then driven forward on landing to bring the hocks under the horse and re-establish the rhythm and balance. The rider should open the inside rein fractionally in the air, in order to lead the horse onto the required line as he lands, but he must be careful not to restrict him as he does so. The legs of the rider should remain in the correct position for the turn, which will ensure that the horse stays on the circle shape and has to land on the correct lead. This exercise shows up many imperfections in both horse and

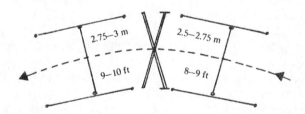

**37 Pat Burgess's grid on a turn** — *to be approached from a circle in trot: poles are placed on the landing side of the fences to keep the horse on the correct line, encouraging him to land on the correct lead in canter.*

rider, and as such is invaluable. For the horse who twists in the air and lands unbalanced, there is no better exercise, and once he has perfected his technique over this jump, he can then be asked to work with less of an angle and fewer poles, until he is able to reproduce the same jump over a single, straight fence. Without the poles to guide him he may, of course, revert to jumping crooked or twisted again, but if the exercise is used now and again as a tool to insist that he jumps correctly, his natural jump will improve quite considerably.

The rider should have the same attitude when he jumps a horse over a fence as when he asks the horse to make an upward transition, from trot to canter, for example. He must drive through and forwards into the next pace, and not draw back; he keeps the horse working from behind. Jumping works on exactly the same principle: the horse is driven up, over and away from the fence with the same degree of continuity as would be required in a transition. The horse is, after all, being asked to react similarly – he is being asked to release potential energy from a round, rhythmical and balanced position at a given moment, with no loss of impulsion on completion of either transition or jump. With the flowing action encouraged by this exercise the horse must remain in balance, and the problem of incorrect leads on landing should be eradicated.

### Ballooning the fences

*Symptoms*: The horse jumps high over the fence, wasting effort and time in the process; often he will leave his legs dangling when he jumps in this way instead of folding them up neatly.

*Causes*: Youth and inexperience will make a horse jump big; because he is unsure of what he is jumping he will give everything extra clearance. The horse who lacks bravery may jump every fence very high too, because he does not want to hit anything: this might mean that the horse is just particularly careful (which is the requirement for a show-jumper), but he may not be brave enough when he is asked to jump larger fences – knowing that he cannot give big fences the same clearance he gives smaller ones.

A horse with poor front leg technique will have to jump higher to clear a fence than the horse who is neat and tidy in front and folds his knees correctly. As the fences get bigger the horse may learn that he has to fold his legs in order to clear the fence, and his jump may become less extravagant as his training is furthered.

*Treatment*: I would far rather have a horse jumping too high than one who does not jump high enough! A young horse *should* balloon his early fences although his technique should still be neat and tidy

– with bent knees and legs staying together rather than with one knee up and the other down – as he will soon learn to jump more economically as he gets older. Obviously he is far less likely to hit fences if he likes to make sure of them by jumping high. Ballooning also shows that the horse has a spring, is athletic and powerful, and is prepared to have a go and not chicken out. If, however, he jumps extra big in a dubious, hesitant way he may need a tap from the whip, a reminder that he must commit himself in his jump and not be half-hearted. He will prove whether he is really bold enough in time, but this cannot be discovered initially as any impatience may wreck his confidence. Even when he is mature and experienced the horse may suffer a fright and suddenly start to doubt what he is being asked to jump, so the rider must be very careful about facing a horse with too big a problem too soon, and he must make sure that the horse is both physically and mentally prepared for any question. A horse might jump round Badminton, the Grand National, or a Nations Cup course on his first attempt, for instance, but is never the same again: this suggests that the horse's adrenalin carried him round at the time, but that when he had a chance to think about what he had done, his nerve and confidence disappeared. If the horse's confidence is severely shaken, he will probably never fully recover his faith and trust in his rider but, in order to restore as much confidence as possible, the horse should be restricted to small, undemanding courses which will build up his enjoyment again.

Provided that the horse is ballooning his fences from over-jumping and not from over-caution, I actually do not consider it a problem, because he will flatten out in time. Never complain if the horse gives his fences too much daylight because it is far more difficult to make a horse who jumps flat become round!

### Cat-jumping

*Symptoms*: The horse's forward motion stops just before he takes off, so instead of moving fluidly into the normal parabola over the fence, he jumps up in the air with little or no forward movement. He may seem almost to land back feet first, and certainly he will land too close to the point from which he took off, perhaps on or even in the jump itself. At best a cat-jump is very uncomfortable.

*Causes*: A horse cat-jumps mainly because he is badly presented at a fence which means he arrives there on a bad stride; even if a horse is meeting a fence wrong, provided that he is balanced and rhythmical, he will be able to adjust his stride to enable him to clear the fence in good style. The outside influences which can affect the horse's approach include the rider, who perhaps asks the horse to stand off too far away from the fence; slippery conditions which make it difficult for the horse to balance himself whilst attempting to adjust his stride; and a lack of basic training which means the horse cannot actually adjust his stride before he reaches the fence. Not only does he not understand how to adjust his stride but he is also not capable, therefore, of doing so. All these things invariably lead the horse to lose confidence in his jumping, and a cat-jump is certainly an illustration of a lack of commitment on the part of the horse and possibly on the rider's part too. Poor general riding may also be to blame for this problem: if the horse receives a jab in the mouth over the top of the fence, for instance, he is likely to start cat-jumping.

*Treatment*: The answer here is to go back to the basics. The horse's confidence must be restored, which means that he must be asked to jump only small fences until he is perfectly happy and jumps enthusiastically. His flat work must be worked upon so that he is able to balance and adjust himself, lengthening and shortening his stride with ease. To retain this confidence even in slippery conditions, and remembering that firm ground may be just as slippery as soft ground, the rider should use studs whenever appropriate so that the horse does not feel his feet sliding as he takes off. The rider must make sure that the horse has maximum freedom with his head and neck over the top of a fence at all costs, and particularly when he meets the fence wrong, and has to make a huge effort to clear it. If he receives a jab in the mouth at this point, because the rider loses his balance, he will be unwilling to jump correctly in the same situation next time.

## Crooked

*Symptoms*: The horse deviates from the straight line dissecting the fence at ninety degrees by veering either to the right or left as he takes off. This, of course, affects his line to the next fence and may even cause a run-out in a combination of fences.

*Causes*: The most usual reason is that the horse is not using his back in a sufficiently supple way to enable him to trace the correct parabola over the fence. By drifting to one side or the other the stiff-backed horse is able to give himself more distance, which means that his shape can remain somewhat flat over the fence. At times jumping crooked can be helpful as it gives the horse more room to manoeuvre off a bad stride – because the horse's arc over the fence is shallower, he finds the jump easier.

The distribution of the rider's weight over the fence can play a large part in making the horse keep on a true line and, by leaning one way or another, he can influence the direction the horse takes both over the fence and away the other side.

A rather spooky horse may jump to one side when jumping a fence he is not sure of; he will try to jump away from a frightening object such as a ditch beneath a fence, or a brightly coloured filler.

The horse may jump crooked because he is in pain, so that he jumps away from the site of discomfort: if the horse has a pulled muscle in his back, for instance, he may try to get away from the pain of the injury. The horse who rushes his fences behaves in a similar way but here the horse avoids the pain by moving sideways rather than jumping faster.

*Treatment*: The cause of the problem must, of course, be ascertained, but even so, the horse must be taught that he should jump every fence straight, rather than drifting to one side. By jumping crooked, the horse will eventually run himself into trouble. From the earliest days of introducing poles and small fences, it is the rider's task to make quite certain that the horse learns he must not deviate from the straight line over a fence, and, to achieve this, the rider must keep his own eyes straight ahead both over the fence and going away from it, so that he can drive the horse forward onto the straight line. Always bear in mind that the landing of one fence is the approach to the next one, so this straight, forward riding is important; it encourages the horse to use himself correctly over the fence and to supple his back in order to help him do so. He should be worked regularly over grids – the cross-pole to parallel being one of the most beneficial in this instance because the parallel helps to stretch the horse's shape and this, in turn, loosens his whole body. If the horse persists in jumping crooked, some 'V's, either placed on the ground in front of the fence, or leaning on the front (or back) pole, will make him stay on the straight line (*see* diag. 38, p. 190). When these 'Vs' are first introduced to a fence, the arms of the 'V' must not be too close together as the horse may not understand that he must jump between the two poles. However, once he has realised, the angle of the 'V' may be closed up gradually until the horse jumps through the fence on a precise line. Because the horse is not allowed to jump to one side or the other, he is forced to use himself more fully over the fences, and, once he has learnt how to jump with a correct parabola, he will be both more able and more willing to repeat in this way over different fences. If a horse is not naturally athletic and supple, the rider must help him by working him through the appropriate exercises, whilst at the same time being patient and not asking the horse any difficult questions until he is ready. Difficult

**38 To encourage the horse to jump straight — the 'V' on the fence**

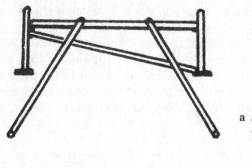

a *initially the arms should be wide apart*

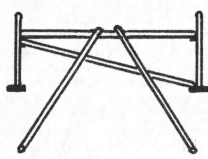

b *the arms of the 'V' close as the horse becomes used to the idea of jumping straight*

questions are big fences or demanding exercises which require a great deal of suppleness and athleticism and which the stiff horse will find beyond his capabilities, giving him ample cause to start jumping to one side. Whatever is causing a horse to jump crooked the above treatment should be considered and, in every case, time and training should bring about considerable improvement. If the horse is very stiff in his back (*see* Stiff in the back, page 239), it is unlikely that (even with training) he will be as supple as the naturally elastic horse. He should be able to cope with the rider's wishes in time, however, provided that his flat work is well established and he learns to use himself to the best of his ability.

There are times when the horse gives himself more room to take off by drifting slightly one way. This can be a great bonus when jumping at speed and may be the difference between hitting the fence hard and jumping it clear. However, this is only recommended in moments of emergency, as an athletic horse should be able to back off and jump any fence correctly at whatever speed the rider proposes. All the hours spent training over grids and small fences should have taught the horse how to use himself in such a way that any increase in speed or size of fence should provide him with no difficulties as his career advances.

**Difficulty in turning before or after a fence**
*Symptoms*: The horse is disobedient to the rider's aids to turn. This may well mean that he misses the true line into a fence and this will inevitably lead to problems in jumping the fence itself. The horse will either resist the aids by putting his head in the air, or by bearing down on the rider's hand, or, alternatively, by swinging his shoulder or quarters outwards, which will prevent him from turning when asked.
*Causes*: The horse's flat work is not sufficiently established. If a horse is unable to carry himself correctly on the flat, he will find the adjustment of balance necessary for jumping too difficult to manage; he should be balancing himself by bringing his hocks even further underneath him but, if he is unable to do this, he will lack agility in his jump.
*Treatment*: Back to the basics! The rider must concentrate upon the turns and circles, and he must be particuarly insistent that the horse learns to turn onto a straight line. This is invariably where the problem originates, as the horse drifts in the turn and overshoots the line into the fence. I always imagine that I am executing a turn onto the centre line when turning into a fence, because that way I am very aware not only of the straightness required, but also of the control necessary to obtain it. It is the outside hand and leg which are important in this precise exercise, but, at the same time, the rider must be careful that he is not unconsciously restricting the forward movement with the inside hand – this would cause other problems because the horse would not be going forward to his fence (*see* Rushing, page 232, Refusing, page 220, Knock-downs, page 201).

Some horses are reluctant to turn into or away from a fence because they are naughty, not wanting to leave either other horses or home. Sometimes this disobedience requires a slap down the shoulder with the whip, but, in the end, the situation will only be cured if the horse is willing to obey the rider's demands. This, of course, will only be achieved through correct basic flat work, as this will enable the horse to comply with his rider's wishes.

**Falling**
*Symptoms*: Falls over non-fixed obstacles usually occur when the horse catches a pole between his forelegs, which gives him no chance to recover his balance. It is rare for a pole caught between

the hindlegs to cause a fall.

*Causes*: It is when a horse fails to clear the fence for one reason or another that he will fall. He may fall at an upright if, at the point of take-off, he is totally indecisive, and consequently paddles through the fence, barely rising at all. The same situation may arise with a parallel, but more usually the horse falls when he fails to make the spread, and either comes down on the back rail with his forelegs, or puts one foreleg over the back pole but fails to bring the other one forward with it. This means that the horse has the pole between his legs and this will trip him up as he lands.

The actual take-off point and the requisite impulsion to jump a fence are crucial factors in jumping but the scope and ability of the horse has a large bearing on whether a horse will fall if all goes wrong in the approach and take-off. A horse with a vast amount of scope will still somehow be able to jump the fence from the sheer power of his spring. If a horse has limited ability, on the other hand, and arrives at the bottom of a spread fence with no impulsion to take off, he will either stop, or try his best to jump the fence with the inevitable result of crashing over the fence. The horse who does not really want to jump the fence, but is respectful of his rider's wishes to a certain extent, may also find himself with no impulsion at the take-off point; by backing off the fence, and not committing himself to the jump, his half-hearted attempt may well mean that he does not make the necessary spread and falls. Of course, this will make the horse even more reluctant to 'have a go' next time, and so the situation is aggravated.

*Treatment*: Fortunately falls are rare, particularly over small unfixed fences, but they do still happen. The main thing is to prevent them occurring again and even to prevent them happening in the first place! The horse does not want to fall any more than the rider does, and so, provided that he is given every chance to jump the fence safely, he will try his utmost to do so. Rhythm, balance and forward movement must be established because a horse will not fall if these three things are working correctly; as soon as one of these aspects is lost, the horse is in danger of being unable to clear the fence. Of course the horse will only be able to maintain the three 'necessaries' if his flat work is correct and consolidated at the standard at which he is working. There is obviously more chance of a horse falling over a fence measuring 1.5 metres (5 feet) than one measuring 91 centimetres (3 feet), but it is the rider's job to ensure that the horse is ready to undertake the immediate demands. The horse's general standard of training should be on a par with the level of competition, and the rider should not make the mistake of asking him to run before he can walk. Correct training will mean that accidents will happen only rarely, but the rider must be patient and diligent in order to achieve the necessary standard and quality of ground work.

It is up to the rider to assess any situation which may lead a horse to fall. He has to decide what evasive action to take when the horse is on the wrong stride for a wide fence, for instance – the most common cause of a fall. The pace and impulsion needed to cope with the varying distances involved are things which a rider will only learn from experience, but forward riding and a good rhythm will ensure that the horse has every chance to jump with as much scope as he possesses. On no account should the rider panic and over-ride, thereby affecting the horse's balance and rhythm and making everything far more difficult for the horse. It must always be remembered that speed is not impulsion, although, when faced with a big, wide fence, a slight increase in pace will assist the horse to make the spread, provided that the horse is not pushed out of his rhythm.

Again, with a long combination, a slight increase of pace will help carry the horse through the distance, and similarly, with a tight distance, the horse should be brought into the first element in a slightly shortened form, to discourage him from making up too much distance in the jump. He will land short over the first element, which will then make the distance ride correctly, lessening any risk of the horse trying to take one less stride between elements, which may well result in a fall. It is a moment of indecision (from the horse) which will lead to problems, and so the rider's job is to try to reduce the chances of this happening as much as possible, by positive, confident riding.

**Fighting the hand**
*Symptoms*: On the approach to a fence the horse, attempting to increase his pace, raises his head and fights the rider's hand. As a result, the rhythm is lost, the horse becomes unbalanced and the jump itself suffers; the horse will refuse or, if he does manage to negotiate the fence, it will probably be an unhappy experience and the chances are that he will hit it.
*Causes*: Lack of training and restriction from the rider will instigate the problem. If the horse feels the need to fight for freedom with his head and neck, the rider is probably restricting him on the approach to the fence. The horse feels that he has insufficient impulsion to jump the fence from this energyless state, and so he struggles for freedom in order to increase his pace, which will at least give him the confidence that his impetus will carry him over the fence despite

his lack of impulsion. One can say that the beginnings of this problem are rider orientated because, if the horse arrives at a fence in a balanced, forward-going rhythm with plenty of impulsion, he will not need to increase his pace to be able to jump the fence. Even if a change of rider should occur, however, the horse is unlikely to stop fighting the rider on the approach right away, as it is probable that the habit will take time to be corrected.

*Treatment*: If the horse has nothing to fight, he cannot fight, in the same way that it takes two to pull when a horse is pulling. The rider must be aware of this on the approach, and, if the horse tries to resist remaining in a rhythm by trying to raise his head and fight the hand, the rider should increase the leg, give fractionally with the hand, and then hold again – giving and taking with a half-halt – so that the horse has nothing to resist and brings his hocks underneath him. The basic flat work must be correct before the horse can be expected to approach a fence without resistance of any sort, and, once he is able to increase and decrease his pace in canter without resisting the hand, he will find his jumping much easier. The rider should prepare the horse for jumping a fence by cantering over a single pole on the ground, making sure that he strides over it in balance and rhythm. The pole can then be raised gradually until the horse can perform the exercise over an actual fence. Asking the horse to canter over several poles scattered around the school without losing his rhythm or without fighting for his head provides an excellent schooling exercise: he should remain balanced and rhythmical and be able to change direction with ease, landing naturally on the correct lead. This simple exercise is remarkably difficult to perform perfectly, but if the horse is unable to execute it without fighting, he cannot be expected to negotiate a course of fences without problems.

If a horse can canter round an arena without resisting and fighting the hand, then there is no reason why he should start to fight just because a fence is put in his path. Jumping is only a continuation of dressage, and if riders keep that in mind as they train their horses (through grid work and cantering over fences), this sort of problem should not occur.

## Flat

*Symptoms*: The horse, instead of basculing over his fence and making the correct parabola (*see* diagram 39a), makes a shallow arc, invariably with a hollow back and high head-carriage (*see* diagram 39b). If the horse jumps flat the likelihood of hitting the fence is increased because, the parabola being shallow, the horse will either

**39 The difference between the correct parabola of the bascule and
the shallow arc of a flat jump**

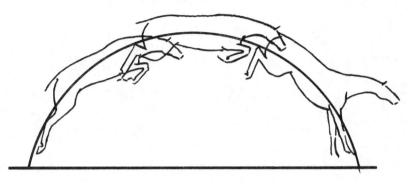

a *correct arc — the bascule*

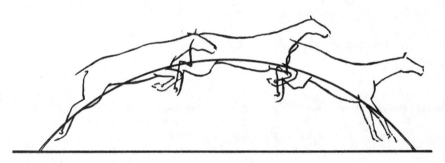

b *incorrect arc — the horse makes a shallow jump, with a hollow back
and high head-carriage*

hit the fence on the way up (because he needs to take off further
away in order to reach the top of his parabola), or – even if he is
meeting it right for his parabola – he will roll the pole with his toes,
unaware that he is doing so. The horse who jumps flat will also roll
poles off behind, because the shape of his arc means that his
hindlegs will trail. A horse must use potential energy to spring over
his fences (*see* diag. 40, p. 196), rather than merely to lift his legs –
while seeming scarcely to lift his body at all (*see* diag. 41, p. 196).
*Causes*: On the whole there are three reasons why a horse jumps
flat. First, it is to do with the way he has been ridden and trained. A
horse who is always made to stand off his fences will not learn how
to round over a fence and use himself athletically, because the arc is

**40 The correct take-off — the gathering and release of potential energy in a spring** — *when the horse's hind feet are together, he is able to spring upwards, lifting his shoulders, rounding his back and lowering his head and neck . . . because the energy is available*

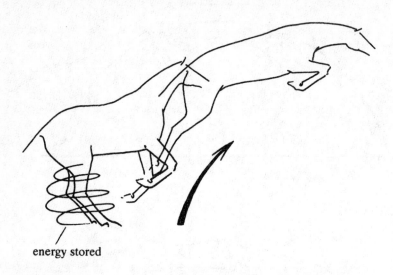

energy stored

**41 The incorrect take-off** — *when the hind feet are spread, the horse loses some of his energy potential, he lacks spring, and consequently he jumps flat, with his head high and his shoulders low*

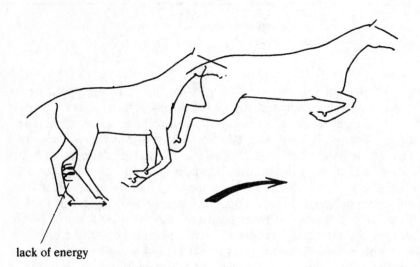

lack of energy

so shallow that little movement in the neck or back is required. He has no need to lower his head and neck to follow the arc over the fence, but if he always jumps like this he will begin not to be able to use himself in a supple way. Many people feel that it is safer not to get too close to a fence for take-off, and, with a horse who cannot use himself over a fence, that may well be true for the immediate future; but eventually the unathletic horse will be caught out. Some fences will require him to take off at a deeper point, and, unless he can round over the fence, he is likely to fall. The further away the take-off point, the less quick the horse needs to be with his front legs. The danger is, however, that the rider then consciously asks the horse to take off further and further away, until there comes a point when the horse tries to put in another stride, and this may result in a knock-down, stop or fall. It is, of course, a great advantage if the rider can help the horse with his stride (remembering to remain within the rhythm and balance of the horse), but if a round, active stride is maintained on the approach to a fence, a round – and not a flat – jump should follow naturally.

The horse with back trouble who physically cannot round himself over a fence will also jump flat. This type of horse will tend generally to be rather hollow in his shape and will lack muscle along his top line. He will be unable to round himself on the flat and his jump will be an extension of that problem.

The third category comprises the rather faint-hearted horses who do not enjoy jumping and who try to slither to the other side of a fence rather than springing over. A horse who is frightened of jumping would rather not jump any higher over a fence than he has to and, as a result, he prefers to sneak over as quickly as possible (*see* Rushing, page 232).

*Treatment*: The first category of horse, whose training is at fault, has to be returned to the basics and taught how to jump again from scratch. The general flat work must also be corrected and the horse worked in a round shape (*see* Hollow, page 132, and Above the bit, page 83, in Chapter Three). The horse should be worked over a grid comprising a cross-pole to a parallel, and he should be given maximum freedom with his head and neck, allowing him to use himself to the full. The placing poles in the exercise will make the limits of the take-off point much tighter than those to which the horse is accustomed, and he will need to learn how to jump athletically to clear the fences. This will take time and patience and the horse cannot be expected to change his style of jumping overnight. By using longer grids which incorporate uprights and parallels, still at a distance of 5.5 metres (6 yards) (with poles in between so that the horse is not tempted to try to bounce through), the horse will gradually learn that he can use himself and that jumping will be far more comfortable for him as a result.

The horse with back trouble can be helped by suppling exercises. These can take the form of grids, which will gently work the muscles in the correct way, but they should be used in moderation, and the horse must not be expected to be as athletic and supple as his sound counterpart. He must be allowed to adapt his style according to his ability and must merely be given the opportunity to round if he can. This horse should not be expected to perform at high levels because his lack of suppleness and agility will lead to problems over the big, demanding courses. There is no reason, however, why he should not cope up to a certain standard, if he is happy to do so. Signs which show that the horse is not happy will vary depending on his character, but may range from stopping and napping, to rushing at his fences, or even a general tenseness: the rider must understand his horse to interpret the signs.

Similarly, the 'chicken' horse will perform up to a certain level and then decide that he has had enough. Working this type of horse over grids may help to give him confidence in himself and his jumping, and he may eventually grow to enjoy it. Jumping must be fun for both horse and rider: a horse should want to spring over his fences, not sneak over in a pathetic fashion. The horse who really enjoys his jumping will jump with agility, enthusiasm and exuberance, often giving the fence far more room than he needs to. This is not because he is frightened of the fence, but because he loves jumping and, as soon as he shows signs of losing this love, he should be returned to smaller fences until he recovers his enthusiasm. Alternatively, this could be the moment to perk him up with some hunting in good jumping country, so that he associates jumping with enjoyment, but he must know the basics of jumping to reap the full benefit of this.

**Frightened**
*Symptoms*: The horse either refuses to jump, backs off or whips round on the approach, runs out, or, if he jumps the fence, he either jumps very big or he hesitates and then climbs over it, or he rushes at it, or dashes over in a sneaky fashion.
*Causes*: The horse may have had a fright from either falling at a fence, or landing in the middle of one. Alternatively, the horse may be particularly careful by nature and the rider may not be accurate enough to ride a horse who prefers to take off at a specific place. The horse may not actually be brave enough to be taken jumping,

and genuinely has a fear of leaving the ground. There are not many horses of this type whose temperament is limiting; if they are produced correctly, they can usually achieve a certain level, although a horse who is made bold enough – through schooling – to jump round Badminton, for example, is not a common animal.

*Treatment*: To introduce a horse to jumping, the rider should familiarise himself not only with the Blueprint on Jumping but also with the separate sections relating to the symptoms, in order to see how best to overcome these interrelated problems.

A 'chicken' horse cannot be made brave, any more than a nervous rider can be made bold, but confidence has a large part to play in both cases. For instance, one would not ask a young horse to jump huge fences; he would be unlikely to be sufficiently well prepared for the task, and so, he would soon lose his enjoyment of jumping and start to refuse or crash through them. He would then start to view jumping with fear and trepidation, instead of as part of life which is fun and to be enjoyed. The training stages of jumping must be gradual so that at no moment is there a chance of the horse being frightened. Of course, he is bound to view a new fence with suspicion, but the rider must make him realise that it is not going to hurt, and he should make sure the new spooky fence is of such a size that the horse could step over it if necessary. It is 'overfacing' the young horse which does all the damage, and also asking him to jump from a faster pace than he is confident in or ready for. Hunting can help enormously in giving a horse a little more heart, although (*see* Introduction) it does not make a horse brave, it merely stimulates his adrenalin which makes him enjoy his jumping at the time. A horse must, really, be happy to jump in cold blood, otherwise he will never make a truly successful horse. Although one does not school over big fences, I always feel that one should be prepared to jump almost any fence on a cross-country course whether one is in competition or not, and I think that a horse's mentality should be the same.

A change of rider may help improve the confidence of a horse who has been frightened by the mistakes of a less experienced and less accurate rider, but this horse is unlikely to be an absolutely top-class event horse, because his courage will probably fail him when he really needs it. A half-hearted horse will almost invariably give the rider a fall, by only semi-committing himself at a big fence, or trying to bank it. An accurate rider can make all the difference between a successful show-jumper and a horse which is labelled a confirmed stopper.

**Hocks trailing**

*Symptoms*: If the horse does not engage his hocks on the approach to a fence, he will not have any impulsion or energy to jump it. Various problems will occur simultaneously because of this fundamental fault: the horse will not be propelling himself from behind – because he is not carrying his weight on his hocks – he will not be going forward, a rhythm will be difficult to establish, and he is likely either to resist in his mouth or to be on his forehand. The rider will find that he is unable to meet the fence well, which means, inevitably, a knock-down, stop or an uncomfortable jump. The horse's springboard is in his hocks (*see* diag. 40, p. 196) and to enable him to spring from here, they must be well under his body and working correctly.

*Causes*: A horse trails his hocks because he lacks training or because he is young and weak. However, there are some horses who, through the physical abnormalities of their conformation, are unable to bring their hocks underneath them.

*Treatment*: Study the Blueprint on dressage, and the discussion on the horse's refusal to engage his hocks in the chapter on dressage problems. In many instances, a horse is actually easier to ride once he starts jumping than he is on the flat. The enthusiasm he has for jumping will give him more reason to work from behind, and he will automatically start to carry some weight on his hocks, because he knows that he has to use his hocks in order to jump. On the flat, this horse is probably rather idle and unmotivated, but, when he sees a fence, he perks up and becomes much easier to ride, because he actually takes a hold of the bit and goes forward far more willingly. This is where jumping can help the flat work so much, as the horse, by learning to use his hocks when he jumps, will then start to engage them more in his flat work. The two disciplines can complement each other. I certainly find with the 'babies' that when they start to jump from canter, and perhaps jump a small course of fences, their flat work suddenly improves. This helpful situation will only occur if the flat work and jumping are treated in the same way – i.e. jumping being flat work with a fence in the way.

In order for a horse to bring his hocks underneath him, he must be supple in his back, and grid work will help supple and loosen a horse over his back. By stretching the horse and making him use himself in a grid, one is teaching him how he can use his muscles to the most advantage, and all these muscles are the same whether the horse be working on the flat or over fences. As a result, the horse will be more athletic in his flat work as well as in his jump, and so again each discipline will help the other's progress. Patient schooling, giving the horse time to adjust his balance and to learn to bring his hocks underneath him, will stop the horse trailing his back end, and a horse who was hitherto labelled 'careless' will suddenly start to jump clear rounds.

## Knock-downs

*Symptoms*: The horse hits the fence, either in front with his toe, hoof, shin, knee or forearm, or with the toe, hoof or shin of his hindleg . . . or else he completely crashes through the fence. Depending on the cause the actual knock on the fence may vary – from a slight rub to a complete demolition job. Sometimes the horse can hit a fence hard without a pole falling, and other times he will barely touch the pole, but will roll it off by dint of the way he hits it.

*Causes*: Horses will hit fences for a myriad of reasons but, on the whole, they do not like to hit them as one can see by watching horses jumping loose. Of course they may hit fences occasionally, but we have discovered over the years that the horse who hits most fences is the horse who is reluctant to jump in the first place. If the horse does not actually want to jump the fence, he will have his mind on anything but jumping; his ears will not be pricked and his mind will not be concentrated on the fence because he is looking for an escape route. For this reason he will not be going forward to the fence and will find that he invariably arrives there on a bad stride, which will give him even less encouragement to make a good, confident jump. Jumping, for both horse and rider, is very much a matter of confidence and this must be kept boosted and be protected at all costs. Once confidence is lost, it is virtually impossible to build up the same amount again, although in most cases it can be rebuilt to enable the horse to perform satisfactorily. As an honest horse does not want to knock fences, the rider must decide why he is unable to clear them; or he must decide whether he is one of the unfortunate few who rides one of the small number of totally insensitive horses who really do not care whether or not they hit fences. I would like to stress that this type of horse *is* in the minority, however much people like to claim that the reason for their horses hitting fences is that they are careless or lazy. Nine times out of ten a horse will hit a fence because he is physically unable to clear it – be it because of rider error, horse error, the horse's weakness or lack of training – and not because the horse is clumsy.

Problems associated with the approach to a fence invariably lead to a knock-down. If, for example, the horse is not going forward, rushing at the fence, backing off the fence, fighting the bit, is stiff in his back, is spooking, trailing his hocks, or crooked in his approach – all of which are discussed in separate sections – the chances of his clearing the fence are greatly diminished. If the approach to the fence is correct, which means that the horse is going forward in a balanced manner, in a rhythm, and with hocks engaged, then he is being given every opportunity to jump the fence cleanly, and he will do so, provided that he is athletic and his technique is good.

When deciding whether a horse is athletic or not, watch him on the approach to a fence, as well as in the air and away the other side, having landed. This is best done when the horse is loose, without the hindrance, or help, of the rider. The horse must be quick on his feet and must be able either to put in a short, snappy stride if necessary, or to stand off without losing any power at the take-off point (and so jumping flat). He must be quick-witted and able to decide where and when he wants to take off, although this will improve, as will every aspect of his jumping, as he gets older and more experienced. The spark will be visible, though, however green he may be. A young horse who shows signs of being slow-witted and indecisive will take longer than the sharper horse, and may or may not be as good in the end. This is something which no one can foretell but which will become apparent in time.

As for technique, the most important aspect is that the horse lifts his knees high and bends them well as he jumps the fence. The hindleg technique is not so important for the eventer as for the show-jumper. For the event horse, the wide fences will be cross-country fences, and the most important fact is that he clears them with his front legs; his increased speed will enable him to clear them with his hindlegs. The show-jumper has to be able to jump big, wide, square parallels, which means that he must be quick and neat in front and able to throw his back end into the air to clear not only the front pole, but the back pole as well. A show-jumper's technique should be excellent, although there are a few who are very good despite their slightly unorthodox method of jumping. The event horse must have a big, scopey jump, together with a quick brain and a bold attitude. This boldness comes from confidence and from correct and patient training throughout the horse's competitive career, so that he is not asked for too much too soon.

Unfortunately, it can be said that ninety per cent of knock-downs stem from rider error. Faulty schooling may mean that the rider's errors are of long standing; this will cause such problems as rushing, trailing hocks and resisting . . . but the errors can be more immediate – when he interferes, for instance, on the approach to the fence. This attempted assistance can be helpful, but it is rather dependent on the rider's ability to see a stride. The accurate, non-fussy rider is far less likely to miss the point of take-off (thus helping the horse without dominating him), therefore, than the rider who does not know whether he is right or wrong or can only see long strides. If he pushes the horse to the wrong take-off point the horse has little option but to hit the fence. If the horse takes off too close to the fence, he will hit it in front, and if he stands off too far, he is likely to trail his hindlegs, as his parabola over the fence will be shallow and flat (*see* diagram 42).

The approach to any fence is important and the rider must ensure that the horse is straight when he is presented at the fence. A crooked approach, whether it be the horse itself or the line he is taking to the fence, will almost certainly lead to trouble of some sort at the fence. A horse cannot be expected to jump a fence unless he is straight, because only that way can he push equally with both hocks. It is only when a horse has reached a high standard of training that he can be expected to jump off a tight turn.

Outside influences such as the going or a distraction may have a bearing on whether a horse hits a fence, particularly with the young, inexperienced horse who has to cope with so much at his first few

**42 How different take-off points affect whether the horse hits a fence**

a *correct take-off points for an upright and a parallel*

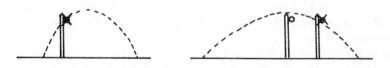

b *incorrect take-off points — taking off too close to an upright will mean it is only too easy to hit it on the way up while standing too far off a spread fence will increase the chances of hitting it on the way down* shows. Loose, deep or slippery going will be very difficult for the young horse and he will have to learn how to adjust in these conditions. He will also have to learn to concentrate at his first few shows, as he will probably be quite bemused by all the different sights and activities going on around him. A course of new fences, particularly in an indoor school, come upon him very quickly, and he will take time to grow accustomed to thinking fast enough to be able to jump clear rounds.

A physical disability will affect a horse's jumping performance, and any source of pain which is evident on the flat will become all the more apparent when the horse jumps. There may be a problem in the back or sacroilliac region, or discomfort in the mouth, shoulders, legs or feet. If it hurts the horse to push to take-off and also to land, he will not throw a big jump over a fence: sometimes this pain will be greater than that of hitting a pole and he will put in an even smaller jump, not really worried about jumping the fence clear at all but more concerned about the pain.

Fear of jumping will make a horse reluctant to go any higher off the ground than he needs to, but, if he knows that he will be punished if he refuses, his fear of reprimand from the rider will be greater than his fear of jumping the fence for a time at least. His attitude will be to get to the other side as quickly as possible, and this may mean that he takes the poles with him. This is the type of horse who will eventually fall on the cross-country; when he meets a fence he really does not want to jump, he may half-heartedly attempt to jump it – being wary of the rider – with the inevitable result. In the same way a horse who is thwarted by the quick action of the rider when he tries to stop or run out at a fence will be unable to throw a good jump, and faults may well be incurred.

*Treatment*: A knock-down being the end result of so many problems, the rider should study the discussions of these in their own right, as they each have a section to themselves. Look at Crooked, Frightened, Losing rhythm, On forehand, Not backing off, Not going forward, Over-backing off, Resisting, Rushing, Spooking, Stiff in the back. This section will discuss the treatment of the more direct reasons, and will provide possible remedial exercises for lack of athleticism and poor technique.

The horse will, with time and experience, learn to cope with the outside distractions he will encounter at a show, and the rider must be patient and give the horse time to accustom himself to the surroundings (*see* Blueprint – Jumping, page 54). The horse must also be given the chance to adapt to difficult conditions underfoot. The rider must help the horse with stronger riding which will drive the horse together more than usual, in order to gain the increased impulsion necessary for the horse to be able to spring over his fences even if the going is heavy. If the ground is slippery, studs should always be employed to give the horse extra purchase, particularly as he takes off. If the horse slips when he is jumping, he will not only be likely to knock down a fence but also to lose confidence. Under these circumstances the horse may be labelled 'clumsy' or 'careless', but this would be an incorrect judgement.

A young horse must always be given time to develop all aspects of his strength, and his weakness and inexperience will become most apparent in jumping. The rider must ensure that he does not work the horse for too long over fences, or expect him to jump well if he is tired. Training and patience will eventually be rewarded – the horse will jump regular clear rounds.

To improve a horse's athletic ability and technique over a fence, he should be worked over grids (which are covered at length in Chapter Two in the Blueprint on jumping). These grids will prove invaluable for correcting numerous different problems, but the rider must maintain the balance and rhythm achieved by them when he jumps single fences. He must keep the horse's concentration focused on the fence by riding him forward and saying mentally, 'Come on horse, look at the fence', and he must never be tempted to use more hand than leg to attract his attention.

An interfering rider will cause a horse to have fences down, particularly if he interferes by putting the horse wrong at a fence – i.e. missing his stride – when, had the horse been left alone, he would have been able to alter his stride himself. The situation when the rider insists that the horse lengthens his stride into a fence, thinking 'one, two, three . . .', but the horse suddenly puts in a short fourth stride into the fence, is the perfect example of negative interference because, had the rider sat still, the horse would have been able to pop over the fence. The rider, trying to commit the horse to three strides, when in fact he should have taken four to the take-off point, gives the horse no option but to hit the fence, because he has then gone in too deep. When the horse does need to lengthen his stride a little to meet the take-off point, provided that he is up to the rider's hand, he will *automatically* draw to the fence (stretch his stride a little), but he must be going forward to be able to do this . . . and forward does not mean fast.

Two other points to discuss when talking about knocking fences down are the use of the whip and rapping. I am firmly against both of these. Question number one to ask is why the horse knocked down the fence, and the answer rarely suggests that he requires punishment. If the horse hits the fence as a result of an idle jump, then the preparation was inadequate, and, in this case, the horse needs to be woken up before the approach – but not *over* the fence. If the rider hits the horse for knocking a fence, the horse will merely learn to associate the whole concept of jumping, rather than hitting the fence, with punishment. The horse will try to jump the fence faster next time to avoid the punishment which he is expecting: a faster jump will be a flatter jump, and this will lead to a knock-down . . . so a vicious circle has been created. The only time to hit a horse is if he is thinking about refusing, or jumps the fence in a very sticky fashion, which portends a stop next time. A smart reminder will let him know that he must never consider stopping.

Rapping, to my mind, has no part in a schooling programme, although I am sure that there are many people who would disagree; perhaps it has sometimes proved successful for them. I still maintain that if the horse is produced on the correct lines and presented at his fences with every chance of jumping them, he will try far harder than if he has reason to mistrust the fences (proven perhaps by the horse who refuses to go anywhere near a fence where anyone is standing). One appears, by reverting to rapping, to be tackling the problem from the wrong end, so that if one studies horses who hit fences, it is easy to see why they hit them and surely correcting the cause is better than forcing the horse to jump higher by frightening him.

If a horse is casual about his jumping and is not trying very hard because he is bored of working at home, then a change of pole or the addition of a filler will invariably help to add interest.

Some horses find specific fences more difficult than others; planks, for instance, are a common problem because of their upright appearance (as was mentioned in the Blueprint). If a horse has hit planks more than once or twice, a rider may then develop a mental block in his approach to them, and he may become rigid and tense in his effort to make the horse jump them clear. The rider must prepare the horse as best he can – according to the horse's stage of training – by driving the horse's hocks underneath him as much as possible, in order to enable him to make the maximum effort. Planks will catch out the young horse until he learns to carry himself on his hocks, and he realises that there is no ground-line for him to adjust himself. A ground-line may be introduced at home because it will help keep the horse away from the fence, and this will assist his judgement about take-off, preventing him from running in too deep. A course which is slightly twisty will, in fact, be far easier to ride than a course built in straight lines, because the rider will be able to drive the inside hindleg up underneath him on each corner (which may be more effective than a half-halt on the straight). The long straight courses will allow the horse to drop further and further onto his forehand, and the rider will have great difficulty trying to fit in enough half-halts between the fences. Indoor jumping is really good for both horse and rider as far as preparing for fences is concerned, because their reactions have to be quick, whereas out in the open there is room to manoeuvre. Some horses are much easier to ride indoors, the enclosed space making them back off the ends of the school and gather themselves together; the hocks are brought underneath almost inadvertently, whereas in the open space, the horse runs onto his forehand, and there is nothing to set him up.

If there is any suspicion that the horse is knocking down fences because he is in discomfort or pain, I would suggest that he is examined by a vet to ascertain the problem. The event rider must be particularly aware of this possibility; he must remember on the third day that the rigours of the preceding day's cross-country round are quite likely to affect the horse's natural show-jumping ability. The show-jumping phase often being the key phase in a three-day event (as regards the result), the rider should always ride the cross-country with this last discipline in mind; he must reserve an extra stock of energy, so that he can compensate for the inevitable stiffness and fatigue which will become apparent on the third day – even in a very fit horse, and even after a 'sound' judgement at the vet's inspection. In general, however, if the vet is unable to find any specific source of pain, it can be assumed that, with training, the horse will learn to adapt to jumping with the problem – by suppling and strengthening up and gaining confidence in his ability.

Every horse is entitled to hit a fence every so often, for horses are not machines, but it is up to the rider to present the horse at a fence in a way so that he is able to clear it. The higher the fences to be jumped the more technical one can become regarding pace and strides, but in order to jump a course of up to 1.2 metres (4 feet) high, nothing more than rhythm, balance and forward movement are required provided that the horse works obediently and correctly on the flat.

### Making up too much distance
*Symptoms*: When a horse jumps in with too big a parabola over the first of some fences set at related distances, he lands a long way out from it, and the intervening distance before the subsequent fences is apparently shortened. If it is shortened dramatically, and the horse is not sufficiently quick or athletic to react by shortening his stride,

a stop, knock-down or fall may well result. This could occur in any related distance, from a bounce to a three- or four-stride distance, although obviously the further apart the fences, the more chance the horse has to shorten his stride between them to arrive at a take-off point which enables him to clear the second fence.

*Causes*: The size of the parabola over the first fence in a related distance is invariably the root of the problem, although some horses may make up too much distance in the actual canter strides between the elements. The size of parabola over the first fence is dependent upon the pace of the approach, the take-off point, and the horse's general scope of jump: a fast approach will mean that the horse will jump well in, as will an early take-off point, which gives a shallow, flat jump. A horse with a big, scopey, bold jump and a long stride, therefore, is far more likely to encounter problems with his combinations than the cautious, economical jumper, or the horse with a naturally short stride length (*see* diagram 43). The horse must learn to back off in his combinations when required, and the horse which has not learnt to do so will find that he runs himself into trouble. This is where the use of grids in the horse's early jumping education is so vitally important, because the short distances used in correct grid work will prepare the horse for the sort of combination fences he will meet later.

Some horses will try to rush through their combinations which will cause them, in effect, to make up too much distance: the horse may find combinations difficult and, as a result, will want to get through them as quickly as possible. Unfortunately in so doing, he makes the combination all the more tricky for himself, and a vicious circle ensues.

As the horse's schooling progresses, he will learn to be able to shorten his stride whenever necessary, and the long-striding horse must learn this lesson particularly well when he starts to jump, in preparation for short related distances, in the cross-country especially (which will seem very short after a fast, long-striding approach). However, in the early stages, when his stride is probably long and sloppy, the size of fence he will be jumping will make the distances in doubles, and general related distances, seem about right. The smaller the fence, the smaller the parabola, and therefore the smaller the chance that the horse will jump in too far in a combination. As the fences get bigger, so the distance in the middle becomes proportionately shorter, and the horse needs to be all the more athletic.

*Treatment*: The horse must be taught how to cope with these combination fences by using grids and poles, which will encourage

**43 How the shape of the horse's parabola over the first element affects the way he jumps the second element of a double**

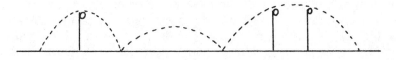

a  *correct arcs*

b  *coming in on a long stride, the horse stands off the first part; his parabola is long and flat, and he lands too close to the second part, which means he knocks off the front rail of the second element on the way up*

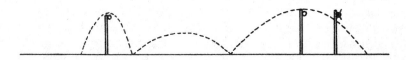

c  *making a very up-and-down jump over the first element, the horse drops in very short after it, making it virtually impossible for himself to reach the second element off one stride, and he therefore hits the back pole on the way down*

him to throw the necessary jump into the related distance, and also to keep his stride short and round throughout, so that he is then able to back off the succeeding elements as necessary. The rider must work out at what pace he must approach these fences to give his horse maximum assistance. This depends upon the horse, his scope and range of jump, and his ability to be quick on his feet between elements: practice, and trial and error are required. The slower the pace and the more bouncy the stride into a combination, the less chance the horse has of jumping too far in. The rider must be very careful not to stop riding forward in the approach, however, no matter how worried he is about the horse jumping in too boldly; this will make the horse try to rush through even more, because he will feel that he has insufficient impulsion to cope with the multiplicity of fences.

The basic grid of trot-pole to cross-pole, pole on the ground followed by either one (or more) upright(s) or parallel(s) – all with placing poles on the ground equidistant from each element – will be enormously helpful in teaching the horse to be athletic and cope with his combination fences. He will not be able to jump so far out with the poles on the ground, or he will tread on the pole, which most horses will avoid doing at all costs. By making his jump shorter, it should also be made rounder with more bascule, which, in turn, will help to maintain the correct shape throughout the line of fences. If the first jump is flat, then subsequent jumps will be the same, so it is important that the horse jumps the first element (or any fence for that matter) in a round shape. Once the horse is working through a grid correctly, the same principles may be applied to a line of fences at related distances. A pole on the landing side of the first element will ensure that the horse jumps within the correct parabola, and a pole on the take-off side 2.75 metres (3 yards) away for cantering, or 2.3 metres (2½ yards) for trotting, will help the horse to keep his rhythm down the line of fences. The distance between the fences can be varied until the horse learns how to adjust himself as necessary. The rider is, of course, vitally important in these cases; the temptation is to pull the horse back and away from the second and subsequent elements, and to try to lift him over them, making him jump less extravagantly. By this action, the horse will be made to form a hollow shape from which it will be impossible for him to make a round jump. Correct flat work is the only way to make the horse remain round between fences; the correctly executed half-halt must be employed. Unless the horse knows how to bring his hocks underneath him, which he should have learnt through the half-halt in his general flat work, he will be unable to adjust his stride between fences on related distances. The rider must apply the half-halt after the first stride of landing, repeating the aids until the horse has re-established a balanced and rhythmical canter. If the horse is snatched up too soon on the landing side, he will have had no chance to balance himself, and will be forced to adopt a hollow shape for the first stride, which will mean that the rider will be unlikely to correct this in time for the next fence. It is easier to correct a horse who is slightly on his forehand on the landing side of a fence than one who jumps hollow. The horse on his forehand can still maintain a round shape, and just needs to bring his hocks underneath him, whereas the hollow horse has not only to bring his hocks underneath, but has also to alter his tight and stiff outline.

I find that the voice is of great assistance in these cases: saying 'steady', or even 'whoa', in the middle of a combination can make a great difference to the horse's attitude, and will probably help with the horse who tries to rush through his combinations in particular. The horse should understand the voice commands, and issuing the steadying ones whilst the horse is actually jumping will have the effect of slowing the whole procedure down, giving the horse the chance to back off and jump more slowly. Any soothing influence with the nervous or excitable horse can only do good, and the voice has one of the most beneficial effects.

The fact that the horse has a big, scopey jump is a comforting thought, despite the fact that he must be trained to restrain his jump so that he does not jump himself into difficulties. It is the horse who cannot make up distance who gets himself into more troubles in the end rather than the horse with vast scope. This scopey horse's range of jump has to be channelled in the right direction, stored until it is eventually required; once the horse is asked to compete at high levels, this ability will be gratefully accepted by the rider.

### Not backing off
*Symptoms*: On the final few strides before a fence, the horse may have to shorten his stride without losing his rhythm or forward movement in order to reach the necessary point of take-off. If the horse is unable to adjust his stride, he will arrive at a point too close to the fence, and this will result at best, in an awkward jump, and otherwise a knock-down, refusal or fall. However accurate the rider may be in seeing a stride into a fence, the horse must still be able to assist the rider by being able to back off, and he must have the ability to shorten his stride just before take-off when he comes to jump very big fences. This quick shortening of the stride allows the horse to bring his hocks underneath him, gathering the spring for take-off (*see* diags 40 and 41, p. 196).

If a horse has not learnt the art of shortening his stride when necessary, the rider will find that the horse stands off his fences when jumping . . . which may be fine for a while. The moment will come however, when the horse arrives at a point too far away from the fence for take-off, but, because he has never learnt to shorten his stride, he feels there is no room for another stride: there will, practically without exception, be a crash of either poles or horse and rider.

*Causes*: In order to back off, the horse must bring his hocks underneath him, in the same way that he does in any downward transition or shortening of stride. If the horse is unable to engage his hocks any more on the approach to the fence than within his normal canter, he will be unable to back off correctly. He will be able to prop into the fence, but because he is merely slowing down and not bringing his hocks underneath him and creating the necessary impulsion, he will not be able to jump a fence of reasonably large proportions. It is perfectly possible to negotiate small fences when the horse is not working correctly, but the faults will soon become apparent once the fences become more difficult, so it is preferable to train the horse to approach and jump his fences (right from the very beginning) in such a way that he will find no problems as he progresses. For many reasons the horse may fail to engage his hocks as he tries to back off, and the reader should consult the Hocks trailing sections (*see* pages 131 and 200), and work from there. He may not back off because he is over-keen to jump the fence, perhaps he is just displaying excitement and freshness or anxiety and nerves. In his haste to get to the other side of the fence as quickly as possible, the horse tends to forget about the take-off and may well end up right at the bottom of the fence, which will give him little or no chance of jumping the fence well. The nervous horse will succeed only in aggravating the worry in his mind about jumping by tackling a fence in this way, and it will probably make him rush all the more the next time (*see* Rushing, page 232).

The final reason is that the horse is unable to judge the take-off point of the fence, and therefore does not realise that he must shorten his stride in order to arrive at a suitable take-off position. This inability to assess the situation may be due to inexperience and greenness in the young horse, or a certain lack of thought in the older animal, although, like riders, horses will naturally differ in their ability to judge distances into fences. In the same way that some horses are quicker to learn in every way, it must also follow that some horses are brighter than others at sorting out where to take off; but, at the same time, I still maintain that physical ability is closely linked with quickness of thought, and the agile, athletic horse tends to be that way both mentally and physically. The less quick-thinking the horse, the more training and help he will require, and the longer he will take to learn how to cope with all the situations he meets in his educational life. The horse with good judgement and agility will prove to be the easiest ride. It must be stressed that this good judgement from both horse and rider does improve with practice and experience, although the natural talent, if lacking, can never be implanted.

*Treatment*: In order to teach a horse that he must back off at times before a fence, he must learn how to shorten his stride while maintaining his rhythm and without losing any forward movement. Apart from working on the basic flat work, and teaching the horse how to use his hocks to slow down (and change pace) by making plenty of transitions both up and down, and changing the stride-length within the paces themselves (trot and canter), the horse should also be worked through many grids, which will teach him to keep his stride short and active throughout the jumping exercise. Using poles on the ground which ensure that the horse does not lengthen his stride between elements, and which place the horse in a position for take-off which is relatively close to the fence, the horse learns the correct foundations of jumping – i.e. rhythm, balance, forward movement, ideal take-off point, and how to use himself to the maximum. Grid work coupled with loose jumping will give the horse a tremendous foundation for his jumping.

When he is jumping loose, the horse does not have the distraction of the rider on his back, nor the problem of balancing himself with the rider's weight. The handler's task is to encourage the horse to maintain a good rhythm on the approach and on no account to chase the horse, which would give the horse no chance to back off if need be. The horse must be left alone as much as possible, being given the opportunity to think for himself and judge the fence; the only help he needs is the necessary encouragement to keep him going forward with impulsion. This encouragement may only need to be a click, or the handler may need to crack a lunge whip: on no account should the horse be hit with the whip nor should the handler ever make any action which will make the horse frightened of him. A healthy respect is the desired response, certainly not fear.

A useful way of preventing a horse from running himself too deep into a fence is to place a pole on the ground at the base of a fence, some 60–90 centimetres (2–3 feet) away (*see* diag. 44, p. 214). The horse will not want to tread on this pole and will back off this rather than the fence. The rider will be confident about relaxing his hand, knowing that the horse is unlikely to run into the fence, and this, coupled with the fact that the ground-line will make the horse look down on the approach, will help keep him round in his outline. By backing off the pole on the ground, the horse is kept slightly off the fence itself, which gives him more time to fold his front legs and throw a good jump if he has been running himself in deep. This comfortable jump will give the horse confidence and give him less cause to rush at his fence. The rider can ride the horse forward to the ground-line, which makes the horse shorten his stride, as he tries to avoid standing on it at take-off, and this gathers the horse and teaches him how to use his hocks and spring to take off.

A change of poles or fence will give the horse something else to look at and help him to back off, and the use of 'V's on a fence will

**44  To encourage the horse to back off his fences**

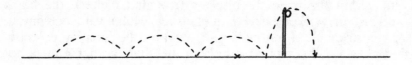

a  *the horse fails to back off and runs himself too deep into the fence*

b  *a pole placed on the ground 60—90 centimetres (2—3 feet) in front of the fence makes the horse back off, shortening his stride and gathering impulsion, and he springs over the fence with a better arc*

possibly have the same effect (*see* Crooked jumping, page 188).

One of the most common traps to fall into on the approach to a fence is to stop riding and almost freeze in the situation when the horse is meeting the fence all wrong. This is the moment for the rider to work much harder to help the horse bring his hocks under him, in order that he might make a supreme effort to jump the fence. Whatever the horse has to do at this moment, whether it be stand off a little, or back off with a short stride, he needs a vast amount of impulsion to jump and if, at this point, the rider has given up with the attitude of 'oh dear, we're wrong', the horse is literally left entirely on his own with no assistance at all from on top. The rider should be working hard on the approach by driving the horse strongly up to the hand: if he then sees that the horse is not meeting the fence well, he should increase the leg without 'dropping' the horse. This way he creates a sudden increase in activity from behind, and therefore gives the horse a choice about what he wants to do, whether it be to back off or stand off. If the rider throws the horse at the fence and the horse chooses not to pick up, disaster will strike and, similarly, if the rider approaches the fence pulling, the horse may well grind to a halt. Provided that the horse approaches the fence in a rhythm, balanced and full of impulsion, and his flat work has been well established, he will be able to adjust his stride with no trouble at all. If his flat work is poor, then his jumping will be too, and it will probably get worse unless the flat work is improved. As is true of so many of the problems discussed, once the one root trouble is sorted out (flat work), the secondary problems will no longer exist.

**Not going forward**

*Symptoms*: When a horse is not going forward into a fence a number of interrelated problems appear and, once the horse goes forward, they will cease to exist. For instance, if the horse is not up to the rider's hand on the approach to a fence, the rider will have difficulty finding a stride to the fence, and the horse will either creep into the bottom of the fence and then cat-leap over, or find himself too far off the fence to take off at all. The rider must always feel as if he is being drawn towards the fence in a forward-going, balanced, rhythmical stride, out of which it is easy for the horse to jump. If the horse is not going forward on the approach, he may also start to back off his fences some distance away (*see* Over-backing off, page 218) – with a shortening stride and further loss of forward movement and rhythm.

*Causes*: This is invariably rider error, whether the horse be green or well-trained. The rider must always be driving the horse up to a non-restrictive hand, allowing the energy to flow forward, without letting the horse increase speed. Speed is not impulsion, which is potential energy: indeed, if the horse is allowed to go faster, all the energy created will immediately be used up, rather than being stored in the hocks as impulsion. Often, the rider falls into the trap of hanging onto the inside rein which causes the horse to lose his forward motion; by protecting the bend with the inside hand the rider is unwittingly blocking the horse's forward momentum, which immediately stops him going forward. The horse will either rush at his fences (*see* Rushing, page 232) as a result of this, or he will drop behind the bit on the approach to the fence. Either way the horse has no impulsion to jump the fence. An untidy jump here – for the horse is bound to land unbalanced – will affect the next fence and since the landing of one fence is always the beginning of the approach to another, the rest of the course of fences will probably be adversely affected.

*Treatment*: The rider must establish a good, swinging canter before he attempts to jump. In this pace, the horse must be in a state of self-carriage; he must be well balanced and propelling himself from behind, so that the rider has a good contact in his hand. He should always have the feeling that if he gives a little with his hand, the horse will be able to take bigger steps without losing his rhythm or dropping onto his forehand. One can draw a parallel here with driving a car, the driver needing to be in a low gear and have high revs, in order to be ready to overtake or accelerate (which would not be possible quickly with low revs). From a canter full of impulsion and forward movement, the horse can be made to maintain his rhythm all the way to the fence, and, if he should try to back off too much, the rider can then ride him through that stage; he cannot, on the other hand, spring over a fence with no impulsion coming from his hocks.

In order to obtain this forward-going canter, the rider should make some increases and decreases of pace in canter, to check that the horse is totally responsive to the leg aids and is ready to move forward and come back immediately. If the horse does not respond quickly to these aids on the flat, then it is most unlikely that he will be ready to cope with adjusting his balance as he would have to in order to jump and land over a fence, and to be ready to jump another fence shortly afterwards. It is important to establish the forward movement early on during the approach to a fence, and the horse must be driven up to the rider's hand at least ten or twelve strides before it. In some instances the horse may need a little kick to wake him up and engage his hocks, and it is too late to wait until a stride before the fence to do this. Apart from the fact that the horse cannot suddenly engage his hocks at the last minute, it will encourage the rider to get in front of his horse on take-off. The old saying of 'throw your heart over and the horse will follow' is all very well to teach the small child on the virtually infallible first pony, but, to be safe, the rider should always stay in behind his horse until the horse has actually taken off . . . and this is particularly important when it comes to cross-country riding. If the rider has the horse strongly up to his hand on the approach, there will be no need for him to feel that he has to 'give him a kick' to take off; instead he can just keep an even contact on the reins with the leg squeezed on, and the horse will then be able to take off out of his rhythm.

The rider must aim to have the horse 'on his toes' and ready to obey the rider's commands to change either pace or direction. With this in mind, the rider must maintain the driving force on the approach to every fence (with the words 'balance' and 'rhythm' firmly imprinted in his mind), and the actual jumping of the fence should follow automatically.

## Not making up enough distance

*Symptoms*: As with making up too much distance (*see* page 207) this occurs with related-distance fences, when a horse struggles to make the correct distance between elements. If the horse does not arrive at a take-off point within his capabilities at the second or third of the related elements, he will either stop, or try to put in an extra stride, which will result in an awkward jump or a knock-down. If this take-off point is too far away, it may well result in a fall because the horse may try to 'paddle' his way over the fence.

*Causes*: The jump over the first part of the element, the pace of the approach, and the scope of stride and jump of the horse will have a direct bearing on the ability to make the correct distances (as was true of the opposite problem). If the horse throws a rather 'up-and-down' jump or cat-leap at the first element, the lack of forward movement will mean that he will be struggling to make up the necessary ground between the elements. A horse with a big scopey stride will not find this any problem, but the rather short-striding horse will be unable suddenly to make up the distance. In the case of a combination fence (i.e. three elements) he may well have lost further ground by the third part, because he will have landed 'flat-footed' after his effort at the second part, and will have lost all impulsion by the third (*see* diagram 45 below).

In order to make the requisite distance, the horse must be going forward, so a spooky horse, because he will be lacking forward movement, will have trouble in making the required ground in combination fences. Rider error may well cause the horse to struggle in his combinations too – from general lack of forward riding, to deciding on an incorrect pace, or misjudging the take-off point. If the rider 'misses' the take-off point whilst riding a horse with a lot of scope, it will be immaterial, because the horse will be able to make up the lost ground with his length of stride; but the less talented

correct arcs                                    incorrect arcs

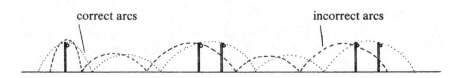

**45 The treble combination**— *if the horse gets too close to the first element, he will have to stand off the second element and he will have lost even more ground and all his remaining impulsion by the final element: at best both second and third parts will be knocked down.*

horse will not be able to help the rider out, and difficulties will follow.

*Treatment*: First, the rider must make sure that the horse is going very strongly forward on the approach to any related-distance fences. If the horse lacks natural scope both in his length of stride and his actual jump, then he *must* be going forward with a little bit of pace. This does not mean that he should be asked to approach his combinations at a flat-out gallop – or even fast – but that he must have an abundance of potential energy (in the form of impulsion), which will carry him through. Once the horse has been ridden strongly through his combinations a few times, he should have more confidence in his ability to make the distance. Often a horse will back off excessively in his related distances, knowing from experience that he is going to have to put in a short stride in order to make the true distance. Sometimes, the horse may have to be given a quick reminder, either from a pair of spurs or from a whip, that he must keep going forward to his fences, and that he must not start backing off as soon as he is presented with a line of fences, so that he loses impulsion rather than storing it.

It is beneficial to work this type of horse through slightly longer grids to encourage him to jump out a little further, and to make up distance. The grid must not be so long, however, that the whole purpose of it is wasted: the main reason for grid work is to make the horse as athletic and supple as possible, and an overlong grid will not do this – quite the reverse! The elements of the grid only need to be pulled out 30 centimetres (1 foot) or so, to make the horse work harder and to make him jump in a more scopey fashion. Unless this fault is corrected in the early stages, the horse will never be able to cope with bigger courses; as the fences get bigger, the horse must be going forward more, with more impulsion, in order not only to jump the fence, but also to make the requisite distances after it. The horse may get away with putting in a little stride over small fences, but he will not do so over wider, larger ones.

### Over-backing off

*Symptoms*: The horse shortens his stride before the take-off point to such an extent that he slows down and manages to put in several extra strides. The result of all this is rather a laboured jump, or perhaps even a stop or a knock-down. In this case, the horse shortens his stride by propping with his front legs, rather than by using his hocks as he would if he were backing off correctly in order to arrive at a suitable take-off point. There are many situations where a horse must back off a little in order not to arrive too close to a fence, and if he does not back off by bringing his hocks underneath him, he will undoubtedly either hit the fence or fall. However, if the horse is backing off automatically on the approach, by losing his forward movement and rhythm before he can see whether he needs to or not, he will have little or no impulsion to jump the fence when he does eventually arrive there. With a small fence, this may not be too disastrous, but impulsion is vital with a big, wide fence. A horse who backs off a big fence too much will generally stop; if he does attempt to jump it, he will probably land on the back pole and this will give him cause to be even more suspicious of a similar fence next time.

*Causes*: These are various. The young horse is probably backing off because he is spooking at the fence (*see* Spooking, page 237) and is highly suspicious of what he is being asked to jump: it is quite acceptable at this stage, because the young horse is asked to jump all sorts of strange things which he has never seen before. It is natural that he should want to look carefully at what he is about to jump but, having seen it, he should be quite happy to jump it the second time. The older horse maybe backs off either because he is not quite brave enough (which comes across as being permanently spooky), or otherwise because he has not been ridden forward to his fences for most of his jumping career: as a result the stride will have got shorter and shorter on the approach to the fence, with a consequent loss of power (*see* Not going forward, page 215). The wise old horse or pony who has had to look after himself over the years when jumping will have discovered that he will be able to adjust his stride for take-off more easily by backing off than by standing off and flying the fence, which probably is not in his nature anyway if he is a cautious horse.

*Treatment*: In the case of the young horse, the rider must quietly insist that the rhythm is maintained on the approach; should the horse try to back off and spook at the fence, the rider must ride very strongly to give the horse confidence that all is well, and that nothing will hurt him. Once the horse has seen a variety of fences, he will realise that he must jump whatever is put in front of him at the first time of asking, and to prevent a refusal the rider must always be quick enough in his reactions, to keep behind the horse, and drive firmly. The horse should be allowed to back off a little, as this is something he must *be able* to do: the rider should concentrate on getting the horse going forward in a rhythm on a medium-length stride, from which the horse can back off a little if he needs to – but correctly, from his hocks. The horse must learn how to shorten his stride before a fence, and be quick on his feet, but he must not be allowed to slow down to do it for that way he loses rhythm or forward movement.

The same principle must apply to the older horse, who must be driven strongly up to the rider's hand all the way to the fence, particularly when he tries to prop; this does not mean, however, that the rider must chase the horse, as this may only worry the horse and make him jump flat. Similarly, if a horse is being really naughty, a smart reminder with the whip may be necessary, but the rider must be careful that the jump is not spoilt as a result. It is firm but quiet riding which will give the horse confidence (although some horses may benefit from a pair of spurs just to keep them up to their work). This cautious type of horse is obviously reluctant to stand off his fences, and the rider should appreciate that when jumping him, especially as standing off fences is not the ideal way to jump. He must be taught to jump out of a rhythm, and the rider must keep the horse going forward – balanced between hand and leg – on the approach to any fence, whether it be a show-jump or cross-country fence. . . . The only difference is the pace.

### Refusing

*Symptoms*: The horse stops either some way away from the fence by gradually slowing down to a halt, or otherwise stops at the last minute, when he is likely to demolish the fence as a result. If he stops suddenly in this way, he may find that his back legs slip underneath him, and he may fall, either into the fence, or, losing his balance altogether, toppling over completely.

*Causes*: The reasons why a horse refuses are as various as the reasons for his knocking fences down, and they can range from disobedience to genuine fear. Many of the reasons are inseparable from other, more basic faults, and once these faults are ironed out – most of them being flat work problems – the refusals will cease.

If we start from the beginning, the very young horse may stop at a fence through suspicion and fear. The first time he is asked to jump a colourful filler, for example, he may spook and shy at it with an attitude of surprise that he is actually expected to jump over something so strange. However, once he has been persuaded to pop over, he will accept many different types of filler with little fuss or bother. Some horses, however, remain spooky all their lives and are very untrusting of any new fence, and this is particularly evident when they have not been jumped for a while. This spookiness goes hand in hand with the horse being naughty, and the rider must be sufficiently strong in his riding to counteract it.

If the rider is only half-hearted in his approach to a fence, the horse will soon grasp the idea that he is lacking determination, and will take advantage of this weak, non-purposeful riding. The rider must ride *over* the fence, and not just *to* it, and he should be mentally throwing his heart over, although he should physically stay in behind the horse until he actually takes off. If a rider just rides to a fence, he invariably drops the contact just before take-off, and consequently the horse is no longer between hand and leg – 'Dropping the horse' is one of the most common causes of stops.

There are further rider errors which cause refusals such as poor approaches, where the horse is either brought in on an angle, or he is unprepared to the extent that the horse is taken so much by surprise that he stops, or, finally, he is presented at a fence at a take-off point from which he is unable to jump. The rider may have asked him to take off too far away, or otherwise he has 'hooked' him into the bottom of the fence, and either way, the horse has every right to refuse. This is why in show-jumping a refusal is only three penalties, as opposed to the four of a knock-down. The horse is showing discretion by stopping, as, if he tries to jump from an impossible take-off point, he may cause injury to himself or his rider – either by crashing through the fence, or by falling.

In the same way if a horse loses ground in the middle of a combination fence, (*see* Not making up enough distance, page 217) he will find himself too far away to take off, and he will have to stop. Alternatively, if he jumps too far in (*see* Making up too much distance, page 207), he may find that he is on top of the next element, and will still be unable to take off.

Slippery conditions underfoot are common causes of refusals. The horse may slip as he goes to back off the fence a little, which then makes him lose all rhythm and balance, and puts him in an impossible position for take-off. Alternatively he may mistrust the ground to such an extent that he is nervous about jumping out of it. A horse does like to feel secure about where his feet are, and any surface which moves (or on which his feet cannot get a good purchase) is bound to make him slightly diffident. The most hazardous going is hard ground with newly-fallen rain on it, because this makes it extremely slippery. This, coupled with worn shoes, can be disastrous. At least in deep going, which is when most people think to use studs, the foot goes into the ground some way and this gives a certain amount of grip, but on hard, slippery ground there is no chance of making an imprint at all. On the contrary, if the horse knows that he is able to back off, pat the ground and spring over a fence with no danger of his feet slipping on the ground, he has no cause to doubt the terrain, and will jump boldly and confidently. It is surprising the number of people who do not use studs, except perhaps in the jump-off, when they feel the horse needs grip on tight turns . . . quite apart from the corners, the horse needs to have a firm hold on the ground for the last few strides in front of any fence, when he is gathering himself to jump.

For all show-jumping competitions, we would advocate studs both in front and behind, screwed in on the outside of the shoes. Experience will tell you which studs are best for which going, though of course one must avoid large studs on firm ground – especially in front, as these can cause jarring and bruising.

Some all-weather surfaces are quite unsuitable for jumping because the surface is loose and will not pack down firmly enough, so that every time the horse goes to take off by patting the ground with his front feet, the surface moves underneath him, and gives him the feeling that someone is pulling the ground away from underneath his feet as he tries to jump. To comprehend fully the effect a slippery surface has on a horse's jump, one should try running and jumping over an object in icy conditions. . . . It is perfectly clear then why the horse is not confident about his job!

A rather ungenerous-natured horse which has grown rather 'doggy' (ungenuine) over the years may refuse too. The horse is behaving in a disobedient manner, and must be treated accordingly; disobedience shows a basic lack of discipline and so flat work is the problem. If this same horse can just be encouraged to enjoy his jumping, however, any punishment will be unnecessary, and this would obviously be by far the best answer.

*Treatment*: The number one issue to establish is why the horse stopped in the first place. Until this is ascertained, the treatment cannot be carried out and the fault corrected. Giving the horse 'two round the tail' is not the answer, although in some cases it may be necessary to let the horse know that he has done wrong. Refusals should not be part of the horse's vocabulary – particularly in the case of the event horse – but it is up to the rider to ensure that he never presents the horse at a fence in such a way that he *cannot* jump it. It is true that horses soon learn that stopping is the easy way out, but the stop itself is ninety per cent caused by rider error in the early stages when, presenting him badly at fences the rider gave the horse ample reason to stop. If the horse persists in refusing, despite the fact that he is always presented at a fence in such a way that he can jump it (even if it takes some effort to do so), he may be given a quick reminder with the whip or spurs, to tell him that he must not give up unless the position is totally hopeless. He must be obedient and do as he is asked, whether it be movements on the flat, or jumping over fences.

From the early stages, the horse must not be asked to jump something with which he is not ready to cope; that way he is never overfaced. Every young horse is entitled to spook at his first filler; the rider must be quick enough, however, to drive him forward with plenty of determination, so that even if he manages to stop, or whip round the first time, the second time he knows that he must jump over it. Once this initial small battle has been won, the horse soon accepts all the little fences to be put in front of him, and happily takes them in his stride. The horse's flat work must be fairly well established – so that he is responsive and obedient to the steering and leg aids – because otherwise the rider has no chance of making the horse go where he wants him to go, and the horse will realise that there is a distinct lack of control and will capitalise upon it.

The spooky horse who shies at something which he has jumped regularly is probably the sort of animal who needs jumping almost every day ('a jump a day keeps refusals away', don't forget!). It need not be anything huge, but just something small to remind him. The more little shows this sort of horse can be taken to, the better, so that he becomes more confident about the whole aspect of jumping different fences. It is obviously easier to give a horse with these characteristics a fright than it is to intimidate the naturally bold horse.

Bad presentation at a fence is fundamentally rider error, although, if a horse has not been trained to a standard consistent with the rider's demands, then the approach to any fence cannot be controlled, and will probably lead to poor presentation. The line into any fence, at the early stages at least, must cut the fence in half at right-angles, so that the horse is given every available opportunity to judge the fence correctly. In order for the rider to make a proper turn into a fence, he must make sure that he looks at the fence before he makes the turn, otherwise he will be unable to hit the true line to the fence. Also, for maximum judgement on the approach to a fence, the rider must look straight at the fence, and not look at it out of the corner of his eye; it is impossible to judge distances correctly in this way.

Many riders seem to be reluctant to turn their heads to look for their direction, but it is absolutely necessary to do just that in order to make a precise turn into any fence . . . and the tighter the turn, the more the rider must turn his head. Your eyes will always take you to the correct point: when riding a bicycle, for instance, one does not look at the road immediately in front of the handlebars, but one looks well ahead and pedals in the direction in which one is looking. Riding horses is exactly the same, and the rider should ride his mount in the direction his eyes are looking. In the more advanced stages of jumping, fences may be jumped on the angle, but far more precision is required, and this is only achieved when the horse is more able to adjust his stride for take-off. If a fence is approached at right-angles, the horse is able to drift slightly either way in emergencies to give himself more take-off space (*see* Crooked jumping, page 188), whereas if the fence is already being approached on an angle, there is only one way that the horse can drift safely, while there is a great danger that the horse will run along the fence, and so run out (*see* diagram 46).

Not only is a straight approach very important, but also the manner in which a horse is brought to a fence is crucial to the production of a good jump. Here the basic correct schooling of the horse must be in evidence, the horse must be able to maintain a balanced, rhythmical, forward-going canter with plenty of impulsion. He must be between the rider's hand and leg all the way to the fence, the rider lightening the contact slightly as the take-off point is neared. On no account should the contact be dropped, because the horse will immediately lose his feeling of security; because the impulsion is no longer contained, the horse is free to stop if he wishes. He must be carrying himself on his hocks with energy stored ready for use in order to be able to alter his stride as necessary, and spring up and over the fence, but the rider must always have the feeling – at the same time – that the horse is drawing him into the fence. The rider is responsible for this, and should be riding strongly forward, in particular on the turn prior to the fence: it is on this turn where a good jump is either made or lost. If the rider restricts in any way with the inside hand, the forward movement will be immediately curtailed and the jump will automatically suffer. I cannot stress enough the importance of riding *through* this corner, so that it is used to advantage in the preparation of the horse for the jump ahead. If the rider tries to protect the bend with the inside hand or, with his hand, tries to keep the horse in too round a shape, then he will have fallen into the trap of stopping the forward movement. Having a horse who is not moving into a fence is similar to trying to overtake quickly in a car without changing down a gear – the car has no acceleration; in the same way, if the horse is not going forward, he has no impulsion. The rider should always be confident that he has impulsion at his fingertips in the same way that the driver has acceleration, because this stored impulsion might be needed to adjust stride patterns, and it certainly forms the spring of the jump itself. It is up to the rider to make sure that the pace too, whatever it might be, is correctly established well before the horse is presented at any fence. It may take a couple of circles to find and

**46 How different angled approaches to fences can increase the risk of a run-out**

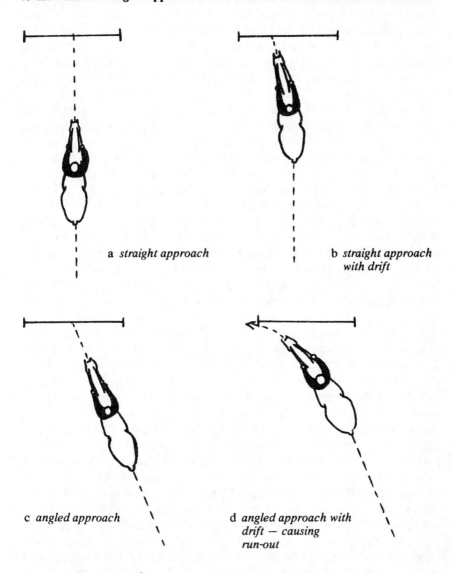

a *straight approach*

b *straight approach with drift*

c *angled approach*

d *angled approach with drift — causing run-out*

maintain the correct canter, but the rider should aim to be able to obtain this canter immediately, and not have to spend ages cultivating it. The horse is then in a position – from this good pace – to be able to jump the fence from a rhythm, and, provided that the rider keeps riding forward, the horse can then decide whether he will stand off a little, or shorten his stride to arrive at a suitable take-off point. The horse should always be in a position to jump a small fence, at whatever pace, and often, when working on the flat, it is a good idea to turn and pop over a little fence to keep the horse alert and to perfect jumping from a rhythm. If the rider interferes by altering the horse's rhythm, he will also affect his balance, and should the rider make a misjudgement, the horse might be unable to help him out.

It is difficult to be dogmatic about 'seeing strides' because the rider who has a naturally good eye will, of course, be able to help his horse quite considerably in reaching an ideal take-off point. However, the *very* good rider will be the one whose horse seems to meet the fence perfectly every time, but with seemingly no help from his rider. Do not be fooled into thinking that it is the horse who is making all the adjustments, for the rider is making considerable adjustments too; because they are being made subtly, within the horse's rhythm, it is barely noticeable to the average onlooker. By helping the horse to lengthen or shorten his stride within a rhythm the rider is not dominating the horse at all, and the horse is therefore trained to help the rider as well as vice versa. Many times, no adjustments are necessary in any case, and the horse meets the fence perfectly, simply by keeping on an even stride. It is disappointingly common, however, to see riders 'hooking' before a fence whilst looking for a stride. The horse loses all forward movement and all rhythm, and so lacks impulsion. If the rider should then 'miss his jerk' – i.e. either asking the horse to stand off too far or hooking him into the bottom – the horse has no chance of helping the rider out, because he has been committed to jump the fence on an impossible stride. The golden words in the approach to any fence must be *rhythm* and *balance* and *keep coming* . . . coupled with 'keep them on the ground for as long as possible' for those who always go for long ones. These should help enormously all riders who panic about finding strides. One so often hears a rider say, 'I know when I'm wrong, but I don't know what to do about it.' One will not meet a fence wrong if the horse is strongly up to the hand with his hocks well engaged, as there will always be a stride; but the rider only obtains this perfect state with correct flat work and forward riding, concentrating, I repeat, on the corner preceding any fence, which is the crucial factor. Ride the corner *correctly* and the fence will be negotiated without problems. Ride the corner badly, and the fence will be met all wrong. Bad riding is at the root of all manner of faults from lack of forward movement, by restriction from the inside hand, to missing the line and consequently approaching on an angle which is caused by not looking towards the fence, and to losing the rhythm, by not working hard enough with the leg. If the rider concentrates on the approach, rather than worrying about whether he will meet the fence right, he will find it all happens much more easily, and with gained confidence the whole situation will improve by degrees still more.

The less experienced rider must make sure that he is very positive in his approach to jumping, however diffident he may actually be feeling. The only way to make a horse jump a fence is to let him know in no uncertain terms that you are both going to get to the other side in one piece. It is hopeless to ride half-heartedly at a fence, as the horse is strong enough to be able to take immediate advantage and stop if he feels so inclined. Once a horse realises that the rider means business, he will cooperate quite willingly, but the initial determination has to come from the rider.

The immediate cause for a refusal based on fear is obvious: the horse is being asked to jump a fence which he deems to be too big or frightening for him. He may also be equally frightened of jumping because he carries with him memories of bad experiences when jumping. Either way, the horse's confidence must be restored before he can be asked to progress with his jumping training. This probably means that the horse must be returned to smaller, easier fences, these being built up as the horse regains faith in himself and his rider. Jumping is very much a case of confidence, and if this vital aspect is absent, the combination of horse and rider will not proceed very far at all. I do stress, however, that if the training has been undertaken seriously with every forward step taken at the right moment, there should be no cause for the horse to lose his confidence. Fear of jumping stems from overfacing of some sort. The horse does not have to stick to jumping fences of 91 centimetres (3 feet) for years, but he must have the foundations of correct flat work which will enable him to cope with bigger, wider fences with ease. It is his manoeuvrability on the flat which will affect his jump more than anything else, and his capacity to alter his stride in front of the fence in a balanced, rhythmical way, in the same way that he alters his stride pattern within the confines if the dressage arena. . . . Flat work is so important!

Normally, if a horse is refusing to jump because he is in pain or discomfort, there will be other signs to indicate that there is a problem. The horse is unlikely to work well on the flat if there is something amiss, and jumping will merely exaggerate this problem. An experienced horseman will be able to identify any significant problem, but otherwise, if nothing specific is apparent, the veterinary surgeon should be consulted. If nothing of any great importance can be found, and all other reasons have been ruled out, the horse has no excuse for stopping and perhaps a small reminder is all that is required.

Stops caused by losing or gaining too much ground in related-distance fences are dealt with under those separate headings; other headings to study in connection with refusals are Not going forward, Over-backing off, Rushing, Stiff in the back, Frightened, Hocks trailing, Fighting the hand, and Spooking. As can be seen from these headings, refusals are closely interlinked with many basic faults, and if these faults were not allowed to develop in the first place, refusals would be less common. A correctly produced horse will have little reason to refuse, and the horse must be educated to realise that he must jump whatever is asked of him, that refusals are not to be tolerated. It is very important to stress what a responsibility the rider has in the training of the horse: he must try not to let his own inadequate riding cause any of the problems under discussion. A horse cannot be expected to jump every fence at which he is presented if he is not given a chance to do so: it is our duty to train the horse slowly and properly so that he can help us as much as we try to help him; if we have not done our ground work with him, we cannot expect him to do more.

### Running out

*Symptoms*: The horse runs past the fence instead of jumping it, and this may be a last-minute action or a deviation which manifests itself quite some distance from the fence. The horse drifts off the straight line into the fence by cocking his jaw and leading away from the fence with his shoulder. The rider suffers a complete loss of control as the horse decides to run out, although prior warning may or may not be given, depending upon the reason for the horse's disobedience. Whereas a refusal indicates a definite NO, by running out, the horse is almost saying, 'Well, if you'd presented me properly, I would have jumped it.'

*Causes*: Running out is a disobedience, and the obvious reason for it is that the horse does not want to jump the fence. Although running out and refusing are penalised in the same way both in the cross-country and the show-jumping, the reasons why a horse will opt to run out rather than refuse need consideration. To my mind, a run-out can be more a case of rider error than a stop, although a horse refuses or runs out for similar reasons (*see* Refusing, page 220). When a horse runs out, he is not refusing point-blank to go forward, but for various reasons feels that he is unable to jump the obstacle put in front of him. He does not lose courage sufficiently, however, to stop at the fence; by skirting round the fence, his attitude is less of a firm resistance, but more of a half-hearted commitment. Running out does not bear the same stigma as refusing, and, whereas a horse may be known as a confirmed stopper, who should be avoided, if he is known to 'nip out the side' it is normally accepted that training and more definite riding will result in a cure. This does rather suggest, therefore, that the horse's presentation at the fence by the rider has a large bearing on his evasion, and that his courage is not necessarily the root cause. To approach a fence on a line which invites a horse to run out is asking for trouble; the rider should always jump the centre of a fence and meet it on a line which is at a right-angle to the fence itself (*see* diags 17 and 46, pp. 57 and 225). To approach a fence on an angle, or jump it anywhere but at the centre, requires a well-trained and obedient horse, and even then the horse's honesty is put to the test. There is always a slight risk involved in angling any fence, especially a difficult one, and it is these risks which have to be considered when the rider is walking a course. He should seriously question whether the risk involved is really worth the time and effort saved.

Running out can often be attributed to the horse just being rather cheeky, when he does not have any other concrete reason for doing so. Of course, had the rider been alert, the horse would not have had the chance, and this merely emphasises the importance of presenting the horse correctly at every fence every time, never relying upon the horse merely to carry the rider over. A complacent rider will always invite naughtiness from the horse, and the danger of a lapse from the rider on one occasion is that it will lead the horse to believe that he can get away with running out on subsequent occasions. As with refusing, running out should never enter a horse's repertoire, and it is up to the rider to train the horse correctly and ride him in such a way that he is never given the opportunity to learn these disobediences.

*Treatment*: The most important thought for the rider to keep in his mind is that prevention is better than cure, and so, starting from the beginning, the young horse who is introduced to jumping must never be allowed to think that he can do anything but jump straight over whatever is put in front of him. It is quite natural for a youngster to try to nip round the edge of a new, rather spooky-looking fence, or to run out at the second part of a double, so the rider must be absolutely ready to drive the horse forward between hand and leg, staying in behind the horse rather than getting in front of the movement (where it will be impossible for him to have maximum control). If the rider anticipates having problems, he should always aim to be one step ahead of the horse in his mind, while remaining fractionally behind him in action. However, if the horse is introduced to new fences gradually, so that he gains confidence about tackling anything big, there should be no specific problems incurred. Bear in mind that any potentially frightening new object should be tiny, so that – even if the horse shies and backs off violently – the rider can make the horse jump it even from a standstill without frightening him in any way. If the horse should try to run past the fence, he must always be turned away from the way he has tried to go – so if he runs out to the right, he must be turned left – and re-presented at the fence as quickly as possible, so that he does not think that he has won a moral victory. It is important that the horse is responsive on the flat before he is asked to jump fences from canter, because if it is difficult to steer the horse on the flat once he gets into canter, then it will be impossible to control him over fences, and this is when bad habits may well ensue.

A young horse will often try to run out at his first show: it is a strange place with strange fences and there are so many things going on to distract him. It is this loss of concentration which may cause him to try to run past his fences. Strong, determined riding is the only answer, with perhaps a tap down the shoulder with the whip on the side to which he is hanging. The nature of this tap with the whip is vitally important because it must not be used in such a way that the horse will then jump flat, or run away from the stick, so that he deviates from the straight line of approach. The whip must only be used at the precise moment when the horse *thinks* of running out – if the rider applies the whip *as* the horse runs out it will be too late, and if he uses it too early, the horse will only run away from it. Only if that split-second timing is caught will the whip be of benefit. With forward riding – while the horse is being kept between hand and leg, but allowed the maximum freedom of his head and neck over the fences – the young horse will soon learn to jump whatever he is asked, thoroughly enjoying himself at the same time.

If the older horse runs out the disobedience has probably become somewhat confirmed; he has learnt from being ridden in a rather ineffective way that he can run out at will. If a horse does cock his jaw and really decide to go, there is little that a rider can do about it at the time. The answer is that the horse must be disciplined more thoroughly on the flat before being asked to jump fences where he is likely to duck out. When a horse runs out, either he will normally not take a contact on the approach to a fence but then suddenly snatch one and go, or otherwise he will come in to the fence pulling or fighting and then run out, with the rider completely out of control. The rider must therefore concentrate on taking the horse back through the dressage Blueprint (*see* Chapter Two) and ironing out any problems which occur (discussed under individual headings) as he encounters them. The types of exercises needed to check that the horse is in control and ready for jumping are: circles in canter and transitions – from canter to trot, and working canter to medium canter and back again – making sure that the horse remains light and non-resistant throughout. It is particularly important with this type of horse, who will take advantage of any flaws in his training, that this flat work is consolidated, otherwise the rider will not be able to maintain control in the jumping phases.

The question of martingales arises here, for, as the horse cocks his jaw to run out, he invariably raises his head beyond the point of control. A correctly fitted running martingale will come into action when the horse raises his head, helping to keep him between the rider's hand and leg. If the martingale is too tight, it interferes with the direct contact the rider has between himself and the horse, which can be damaging, so the correct fitting is essential. The rider must also check before he mounts that the martingale will only come into action when the horse raises his head to an uncontrollable position, bearing in mind as he does so the position of the rider's hand and the consequent line of the reins.

If a horse is too strong for the rider and this leads to running out, a stronger bit is worth considering: there is a bewildering number of combinations of bit and noseband from which to choose. As has been mentioned in other sections, the bit is the key to the comfort of the horse's mouth and it is a matter of finding the right combination of bit and noseband for every individual horse. The snaffle family does offer a wide variation for most problems, and the strong horse may be tried in a Dr Bristol, a twisted snaffle, or a roller snaffle – what I would call 'sharp bits', because they have rather narrow surfaces and may cause discomfort in a tender-mouthed horse. A vulcanite pelham gives more control through chin-groove and poll-pressure action, and this may suit other horses. One can then move back to the snaffle family, a gag perhaps, with the gag rein used like a curb rein – although two reins may be too much of a handful. Of course, the natural successor to the snaffle bridle is the double bridle, but the horse must be going correctly in the snaffle first of all, and the rider must be able to ride confidently and correctly with the double bridle himself, managing the two reins not only on the flat, but also over fences. It is quite impossible to advise anyone on paper on the subject of bits; it is only by seeing the individual horses that one can make a reasonable suggestion as to what type of bit might be best employed.

Some horses perfect the art of running out to such a point that it is very difficult to stop it happening, and the rider has to learn to anticipate the horse, taking preventative action. The rider must be even more insistent that the horse stays strictly between the hand and leg, and he can, on no account, relax this feeling for one instant. The moment the horse feels any release he will be able to react at will and, by the time he has decided to run out, it will be too late for the rider to stop him.

Most horses are genuine enough to jump any fence provided that the rider has prepared satisfactorily for the type of fence. A bigger, more difficult fence, for instance, requires a more exact presentation than a small, straightforward obstacle, and so it is up to the rider to give his horse every chance of jumping his fences with ease, and not to make his task impossible. Not only must he ride carefully and confidently at a fence but he must also improve the horse's basic flat work, in order to eliminate the lack of discipline which underlies running out.

### Rushing

*Symptoms*: Instead of maintaining an even rhythm on the approach to a fence the horse increases his speed. Depending on the severity of the problem, a horse may accelerate over the last few strides or he may make an uncontrollable dash into the fence from a long way out. Apart from the fact that the rider lacks control on the approach, the effect on the jump itself may be quite dramatic too. By rushing in, the horse gives himself little opportunity to alter his stride and will be in trouble should he need to shorten in order to arrive at the correct take-off point. The result will be an untidy, unbalanced jump; the horse may hit the fence, and this may also cause a fall if the fence is solid. Alternatively, the horse may refuse at the last minute when he suddenly realises that he has no place to take-off, and this quick refusal is a type which is unseating. It is the effects caused by a horse rushing in jumping which are dangerous, rather than the rushing itself.

*Causes*: Although it is commonly believed to be the only reason, it is only in a few cases that the horse rushes at his fences because he is eager to jump. I strongly believe that, apart from a few, very rare exceptions, the horse who charges at his fences only does so because he cannot wait to get to the other side – not necessarily because he loves his jumping, but more because he associates jumping with something rather uncomfortable, and is therefore desperate to finish the job. This unpleasantness may be caused by fear or pain – stem-ming from a problem in himself – or may be rider induced. He might have pain in his back, for example, or the rider may cause him pain by yanking him in the mouth over the fence. A horse will always run away from pain, and jumping will inevitably exacerbate any discomfort, because the sheer effort of taking off intensifies the action of the muscles necessary for jumping. If, every time a horse jumps a fence, he receives a resounding yank from the bit, this will incite him to jump the fence as quickly as he can, as he is trying to avoid the pain by running away from it.

A horse who is over-fresh and exuberant may try to 'get at' his fence and then jump it in an exaggerated way, possibly giving a buck afterwards, but, once he settles down to his jumping, he will no longer rush. The horse who finds jumping easy will have no reason to try to increase his pace as he knows that he can jump the fence out of his stride. A horse might feel, however, that he has to increase his speed to give himself the impetus to jump. Restricted by the rider on the approach, this horse is not going forward on the flat. He tries to give himself the necessary impulsion and freedom by raising his head and rushing at the fence, thereby taking control of the situation.

It is always fascinating to watch a horse jump loose if he tends to rush at his fences when he is ridden. Invariably, as soon as they feel that they no longer have the rider preventing them from going forward to the fence, these horses will give up rushing. The horse who is in pain will probably still try to jump his fences rather fast, although back pain is often aggravated by the rider's weight, and if this is the site of the discomfort the horse may be more settled when jumping loose.

The final category of horses who rush their fences are those who are basically frightened of jumping. A 'chicken' horse will often want to get over the fence as quickly as possible, and charges at it in the hope that the frightening experience will be short-lived. This type of horse has probably been reprimanded at some stage for stopping and, for the time being at least, is more worried about being punished by the rider than frightened of the fence; he dare not stop but wants to get over the fence as quickly as he can. There comes a point when the fence seems as frightening to these horses as the possible chastisement and this is when they stop, or, in their half-hearted attempts to take off, fall. We can all picture the horse (strapped down with metal pelhams and martingales) who charges at his fences at an alarming rate, only to stop dead at the last minute. This horse is frightened not only of the pain in his mouth but also of the fence and the act of jumping, and, whereas the initial reaction is to charge at the fence to get over it quickly, his courage fails at the last moment, even though he can expect a punishment for stopping.

*Treatment*: A young horse will not rush his fences provided that he has been trained correctly, the jumping phases running hand in hand with his flat work. He will have no reason to rush as long as he is not asked too much too soon which would cause him to lose confidence in his jumping. All progress must be gradual, remaining within both the mental and physical capabilities of the horse. For this reason, some horses may progress quicker than others because of their temperament, and the rider must understand his individual horses in order to know how much he can ask of each horse. On the whole, therefore, one tends to be dealing with an older horse rushing at its fences, rather than a youngster. If a young horse does start to try to increase his pace approaching a fence, the habit can be quickly nipped in the bud by going back a stage, re-introducing the trot-pole before a fence, and dropping it in size to restore any loss of confidence. Quietly schooling young horses over fences makes them learn that jumping is not something to get excited about, but part of their everyday work, and it produces obedient, confident horses who enjoy their jumping . . . and this is the ultimate aim. Generally a horse will happily accept jumping from a rhythm as a continuation of his basic flat training, but he must be disciplined, and if, at any time, he tries to alter the rhythm, the rider should take a half-halt, just as he would on the flat (in order to maintain his canter or trot rhythm).

With the older horse who has become accustomed to rushing at his fences, the rider must return almost to stage one of his Blueprint: the horse has to re-learn the basics of his flat work so that these can be put into practice over fences. A horse who is going correctly on the flat is unlikely suddenly to start rushing at his fences, so the rider must consolidate the work on the flat before he can start to correct any problems arising in the horse's jumping. The horse must respond to the half-halt; he must be able to increase and decrease his pace within a rhythm without resisting; and he must be supple and responsive. All this should be fixed in the horse's mind before jumping training is attempted, because if the horse is disobedient on the flat, he will get his own way jumping too.

When the rider feels that the horse's flat work has improved sufficiently to start jumping, trotting poles should be incorporated into the basic flat work. Until the horse trots quietly over poles, there will be little chance of his cantering quietly over a fence. The rider must bear in mind that if the habit of rushing is firmly ingrained, the horse will have a mental block about jumping. The rider has a mental problem to iron out as well as a training fault, whatever the reason might be. Even the horse who finds jumping difficult may learn to cope with his disability if, with patient schooling, he is given the opportunity.

Once the horse is trotting in a happy and relaxed way over poles on the ground, a small cross-pole with a placing pole taken in trot should be introduced. This should be a separate exercise, rather than at the end of the line of poles (*see* Blueprint – Jumping, page 54). The horse must be kept in a forward-going rhythm to the fence, and the rider must be very careful not to restrict the movement with the inside hand. The inside hand being too strong is one of the most common faults of riders on the approach to a fence, and it has the effect of totally blocking any forward movement (*see* John's Tunnel, diag. 9, p. 31). Whether it is in an effort to keep the horse 'on the bit', or to protect the bend, the rider restricts with the inside hand, and this stops the forward movement and makes the horse feel that he has to grab his impulsion and freedom by rushing at the fence. The horse has to be at a very high level of training to be able to jump a fence from the shape described in dressage as 'on the bit', and the most natural way for a horse to jump a fence is from a round shape, when the horse's nose is not perpendicular to the ground, but when the horse is up to the rider's hand with plenty of impulsion and drive from behind. The horse then has some freedom to use his head and neck on take-off, which he cannot do if he is forced into a tight shape. The horse's nose needs to be in front of the vertical on the approach, so that he can lower his head and neck a little and feel confident that he can use himself to the maximum in his jump. Study the top riders in action to see this point, whether they be event riders or show-jumpers.

The trot-pole to cross-pole should be used to exercise the horse over a fence while putting into practice the work done on the flat – teaching the horse obedience. Should he try to increase his speed on the approach, the rider should half-halt repeatedly, until the horse learns that he is expected to jump the fence out of a rhythm, and that he *can* do so because he is arriving at the fence with no restriction. From this basic exercise, the rider can canter to a small fence, again insisting – by the use of the half-halt and forward riding – that the horse jumps the fence out of a rhythm. This exercise should be repeated as necessary. The horse will, by now, begin to understand that the leg aid not only means forward but steady as well; without this basic training it will be impossible to maintain control on the approach as hands alone will have no effect and may well aggravate the situation.

It is common practice to circle in front of a fence until the horse has settled before jumping it. Indeed, this may work in certain cases; the horse, who has a mental block about rushing at his fences, may learn that, in fact, he can jump a fence slowly and calmly, and this then gives him confidence and so helps the problem. In other cases this method may surprise the horse, not giving him enough time to gather his wits and rush, but the horse's training is not progressing as such in this case, because he is not being truly obedient. It is better, surely, to persevere – by working over small fences until progress is consolidated there – with trying to make the horse understand exactly what is required of him.

When bigger fences are introduced, the horse may start to rush again because he needs more potential energy (impulsion) to jump a bigger fence, so the rider has to be sure that his approach is correct for the size of fence. The bigger the fence the more impulsion the horse must have, and it is the rider who must make sure that his horse is going forward, particularly on the corner preceding the fence.

Many horses try to rush through grids as they get older and this is because they find them difficult: at this stage, the grids the horse is asked to jump are probably quite big and demanding, and they will expose his stiffness and lack of athleticism. He cannot avoid using himself to the full in a grid, whereas over a single fence he can adapt his jump to suit himself; if he finds difficulty in this, he may become worried and try to rush down the grid. A small amount of grid work will not harm any horse but it is best to avoid long sessions which may only aggravate him. Any athletic exercise can only be of benefit but one must use judgement to decide how much and how often. Indeed, the rider must decide whether the grid is being beneficial or merely upsetting the horse, possibly spoiling his jump for the future. A grid used correctly is a wonderful training aid, and it also presents an ideal opportunity to watch other horses and riders in action. It is better to have several people working over a grid as this allows the horses a short break in between work. On no account, however, should horses follow each other down the grid, as this will merely provide a further incentive for the horse to rush.

There are two exercises which may be used to help prevent the horse from rushing at his fences. The first one is intended to make the horse relax and it involves a 20-metre (or slightly bigger) circle with either one or two (equidistant) fences on the circumference. The horse is asked to canter round over the fence or fences (which should be uprights 91 centimetres (3 feet) high with a good ground-line), and the horse should be encouraged to find his own balance and rhythm with as little help from the rider as possible. Obviously, the rider must half-halt to establish the required pace if the horse tries to go faster, but he should help the horse to realise that there is no need for him to rush his fences, and eventually the horse should settle into a sensible rhythm. This exercise must be repeated until the horse is relaxed, and able to canter round quietly over the small fences. The rider may have to show a fair amount of patience in order to achieve this, but, until the horse accepts this little exercise with a relaxed attitude, he cannot be expected to progress over different fences without reverting to rushing.

Another exercise, which must be used with caution, involves asking the horse to halt approximately half a dozen strides in front of the fence every time he tries to increase his speed. The horse should then be moved forward either to the right or left, driven forward into canter again and re-presented at the fence. The rider must sit quietly, making sure that the horse is going forward on the corner preceding the fence, and this time allowing the horse to pop over. The rider must keep the horse going forward to the fence and not start to draw back on the approach, because this may aggravate the problem as the horse loses his forward movement. The purpose of the halt is to make the horse engage his hocks on the approach, and make him obedient to the aids (to reduce his pace). These same aids can then be used, but to a lesser extent, if the horse tries to increase his speed. On no account should the rider halt in front of a fence and then proceed immediately to jump it, as this will almost force a horse to rush at his fence; he will, in effect, be jumping virtually from a standstill with no impulsion.

If one is in any doubt about the reasons why horses rush at their fences, I feel one should study the best horses in action. Do we see the winners of Badminton or the King George V Gold Cup rushing over their fences? The answer is, of course, no. However much a horse enjoys his jumping, he should not rush at his fences if he is correctly trained. If the rider tells himself that his horse is rushing because he loves his jumping, he is only kidding himself. . . . He is not looking deeply enough into the reasons.

## Spooking

*Symptoms*: The horse wants to have a good look at the fence before he jumps it, normally shortening his stride and wavering on the approach. Consequently he lacks forward movement and rhythm, and often jumps crooked as he shies (mid-air) at the fence.

The rider will have great difficulty creating a fluent stride as he approaches the fence because the horse will drop the bridle, the hocks will no longer be engaged and the horse will lose all his impulsion which he needs to jump the fence. Some horses who spook on the approach will then dash over their fences as quickly as possible, causing the whole jump to lack fluency and balance and making it most uncomfortable for the rider, who will also have difficulty maintaining his balance.

*Causes*: Horses spook at their fences initially because they are inexperienced; often when a brightly coloured filler is introduced for the first time, the horse will try to run out or refuse, possibly even declining to go anywhere near it. There are some horses who will continue to spook at new fences all their life and these are difficult horses to ride, because the rider is unable to keep any rhythm, balance and free forward movement on the approach. These spooky horses, apart from being rather irritating, are often not brave enough when it comes to more demanding questions.

There are, however, many very bold horses who will spook at fences before they are presented at them, but when they are asked to jump them, they attack without any hesitation at all. This is the ideal sort of horse, because he is aware of everything around him, and yet quite fearless of whatever he is asked to jump. This is the type of horse who pretends to be terrified of plastic bags by the side of the road, and then, asked to jump a row of them with a pole on top, sails over without a second thought!

*Treatment*: In order to overcome the loss of impulsion caused by the horse spooking and propping at the fence (*see* Over-backing off, page 218) the horse must be made to learn to be completely obedient to the rider's aid. Only then can the rider insist that the horse stays in a rhythm, and keeps going forward to the fence. The rider must approach the fence well; he must be straight and must give the horse sufficient distance to assess the fence before he is asked to jump it. The horse must learn that he can still look carefully at the fence if he wants to, but that he must maintain his forward movement and rhythm at the same time – he must always remain responsive to the rider's leg. (*See* Crooked jumping, page 188, for those horses who try to jump across their fence.)

Spooky horses will normally make a fuss at small fences as well as bigger ones, so it is best to practise over small fences, making the horse maintain his rhythm in a straight approach with very strong riding. If the horse is kept strictly between hand and leg he cannot deviate from his straight line. Remember that it is always preferable to prevent something happening in the first place, than to allow it to happen and then have to correct it: the rider must be forceful, therefore, about not allowing the horse to shorten his stride, or lose his rhythm on the approach, making him remain obedient and responsive to the aids instead. The rider must be sure that the horse is really going forward on the flat (*see* Not going forward in Chapter Three, page 149), otherwise the horse will certainly not go forward to his fence, particularly if he is by nature spooky.

The more outings to shows the spooky horse has, the more confident he will become. Chasing the horse over fences will serve no purpose as it will only make him worry about the rider as well as the fence, and the resulting tenseness will add to the problems. A horse's character cannot be forcefully changed; but he can, with the right training, be taught to overcome his natural reactions.

### Stiff in the back

*Symptoms*: The horse does not bascule correctly over a fence; instead he jumps in a flat – although not necessarily hollow – shape. The result of this is that the horse loses some of his athleticism; he will probably find combination fences rather difficult, and will often jump crooked to avoid using himself and also to give himself more room to take off. The horse must be able to curve his body over a fence when he encounters more demanding questions as his training progresses. A horse with a stiff back may well cope reasonably up to a certain level, but his lack of athleticism may well find him out when a higher level is attempted.

*Causes*: A stiff back may be caused by rider error. If the rider has not allowed the horse sufficient freedom in the air, the horse will have got into the habit of jumping with a restricted head and neck, and this will, in turn, affect the suppleness of the back. Alternatively, the horse may be naturally stiff in his back and, despite training on the flat, he will be lacking in flexibility over fences: the horse with a rather short back will be less flexible in the spine than a correctly made horse, and as many suppling exercises as possible should be done to help him. A young horse may be stiff in his back when he is first introduced to jumping because he is slightly nervous of the rider's movement.

*Treatment*: Working the horse through grids will obviously help to supple his back and make the horse work through from behind, but there is no magical cure to make a horse use himself more in the air, and some horses, despite flat work and grid work, are still rather stiff in their backs over a fence. This may stem from nervousness as a youngster, or just general lack of movement in the back (*see* Stiffness in Chapter Three, page 165, Crooked jumping, page 188, and also read stage 4 of the Blueprint – Straightness, page 26). As the horse's flat work improves, so should his bascule, and the rider should carry on giving the horse every opportunity to round over a fence by giving him maximum freedom with his hand. Some horses actually need a loose rein over a fence before they will stretch to the full, so the rider must experiment to find out what works best for his horse. The horse who is quick with his legs, compensating in that way for his lack of suppleness, may still be a very successful horse; but the rider should still try to encourage him to be more supple, as he will find jumping far easier if he is more flexible and athletic.

**Strong/Pulling**

*Symptoms*: The rider has difficulty holding the horse both on the approach and between fences, and this may lead the horse to go too fast and to jump flat. The horse will be trailing his hocks as the speed is not controlled by the rider and therefore no energy is being contained.

A horse who is heavily on his forehand will also demonstrate the symptoms of being strong when, in fact, he is merely relying on the rider's hand for balance and support. The rider will have problems adjusting the balance throughout a course: this heaviness on the forehand will become worse during a round of fences because each time the horse jumps a fence, he will drop further onto his forehand and if the rider cannot hold his horse, he will also waste time on the turns and because he has lost control on the approach, he will be fighting just to keep the horse in rhythm and balance.

*Causes*: Lack of training and discipline is probably the most common reason for lack of control. However, some horses do naturally produce excess impulsion when they start to jump – through keenness and enjoyment – and if the rider is not sufficiently strong to contain the energy, he will soon be struggling to maintain control. Many riders think that because their horses are strong, they must be keen; in fact, the horses are trying to run through the rider's hand because of nerves. As the horse lands over one fence (which of course is the approach to the next fence) and rather rushes away from an experience which he has not enjoyed – almost like a dog running away with its tail between its legs – it is obvious that the horse is not pulling with enthusiasm but because there is a problem.

*Treatment*: The rider must be able to define the difference between a strong horse and an evading one – be he leaning, on the forehand, running through the rider's hand, or rushing and yawing (which are dealt with elsewhere). The rider must be in control at all times but it is especially important when jumping that the horse is strongly contained between the rider's hand and leg, indicating plenty of impulsion or 'petrol in the tank': the horse has to learn not only to remain obedient, however much impulsion is being created but also to wait for the rider's commands and not to take matters into his own hands.

Basic flat work must be correct if the jumping work is to be executed with control: the horse must be responsive to both the leg and the hand (*see* Dressage section: Leaning, On forehand, Pulling, Running through rider's hand, and Yawing). Faults in the flat work will become exaggerated once the horse starts to jump, and in order to retain control over fences, the horse's work must be established on the flat. To my mind, flat work is not an end in itself but should be used to produce an obedient and athletic horse over fences.

One of the most vital training aids to which the horse must respond is the half-halt, because whilst jumping a course of fences the half-halt will be required many times; it sets the horse up and brings his hocks underneath him in readiness for the approach to the next fence. The half-halt will adjust the horse's balance and help him to maintain his rhythm whilst jumping a series of fences; if the horse does not understand the half-halt, however, the rider will struggle either to get the horse's hocks under him or to lighten the forehand.

If, despite trying to establish correct, basic flat work, the horse still runs through the rider's hand as soon as he starts jumping, a stronger bit may have to be employed. This increased control (in the form of a bit) must be carefully used, though, so that the horse does not start off being too strong and end up being behind the bit and therefore not going forward. The main aspect to consider when changing bit is whether the horse has any reason to be frightened of it; for that reason it is best to steer clear of any sharp mouthpiece.

The circling exercise which is advocated for the horse who rushes at its fences will also benefit the strong horse who needs settling over a fence, and who has problems in interrelating flat work and jumping (*see* Rushing, page 232). He must realise that, as with his flat work, the exercise will be repeated until he does what he is asked, arriving at his fences in a balanced rhythm on a firm but steady contact. Whereas it is easier to ride a horse who is taking the rider into the fence – as opposed to one who will not take up a contact – the rider must still be able to adjust the horse's stride or direction at any given moment. I am not advocating interference on the approach to a fence, but it is comforting . . . and essential to know that one is in control before one is able to ride confidently over fences.

**Water Jump problems**

*Symptoms*: The horse must make a wide shallow arc in order to clear the necessary width of the water (normally 3.65 metres (12 feet) at the lower levels of competition). The horse may either refuse to jump it or fail to clear it, incurring penalties for landing either in the water or on the landing tape.

*Causes*: Fear of the water will cause a horse either to stop or to spook and over-back off, which will lead to a jump lacking in impulsion, and therefore having insufficient power to make the width. The young horse may be frightened because he has little experience of jumping water, but the older horse who has had a fright in his early training and has not yet recovered his confidence will react in the same way. A rider who panics during his approach to a water jump – making his horse gallop at it – is more than likely to miss seeing his stride. This will cause the horse to take off too far away and this means the horse has a far greater distance to jump (*see* diagram 47).

*Treatment*: The greatest problem with jumping water is lack of practice. If a horse is used to jumping coloured poles and is suddenly subjected to an entirely new hazard, he is entitled to express surprise and caution, so it is important that he is slowly introduced to a water jump and gradually taught how to cope with it. Few people have water jumps, but a stretch of blue polythene and a brush filler can be used as a substitute. This is not ideal, but it will teach the horse to jump out over something which will give him some idea of how to jump water confidently. The young horse will be suspicious initially and must be given time to accept what he is being asked to jump before any great degree of width is introduced; but once the horse has learnt how to jump a low, wide fence it may be necessary to place a fence midway over the water jump to encourage the horse to increase his parabola, to jump a little higher over the water, and lessen the risk of his landing on the tape. These fences are often used in Foxhunter classes to help the young horse to jump over the water which is good practice for the inexperienced horse and much recommended. The rider should approach a water jump in the same way he approaches any other fence, increasing the pace without altering the rhythm or balance. All too often, one sees riders galloping in to a water jump and hoping for the best, which gives the horse little chance of adjusting his stride. The rider should avoid asking the horse to stand off, as this gives the horse a far more difficult task, and he has to put in an enormous effort to clear the water.

When walking distances in doubles or combinations one allows

**47 The water jump — the importance of the approach**

a *correct approach to a water jump — medium canter with pace and spring*

b *incorrect approach — galloping in on a long stride, committing the horse to a take-off point, standing off too far and landing in the water*

Note: *The three approach strides in the correct approach cover the same distance as two in the incorrect approach.*

3.65 metres (4 yards) for a horse's stride (which is 12 feet) – the width of a novice water jump. The horse has only to make an extension of his stride to clear this distance, and if he arrives at a take-off point with plenty of impulsion going slightly faster than he would approaching a normal coloured fence, he should be able to clear the water with ease. The most common reason for any problem is that the horse lacks this all-important confidence, so this must be built up and nurtured from the beginning.

This procedure should be followed when the horse is being introduced to water ditches, banks or any other natural features that might be encountered in the ring. If the horse meets any such obstacle for the first time during a round in the ring, the rider is inviting problems and is placing unreasonable demands on the horse by asking him to jump such strange fences without prior intro-duction. The fright the horse might possibly receive could be enough to put him off jumping water or ditches for a very long time and he could never fully recover his confidence.

FIVE

# Cross-Country

There are a number of books available which explain the art of cross-country riding and I do not intend to add to them by trying to give exact procedures on how to ride the different types of fences likely to be encountered on a cross-country course. What this chapter will show is how dependent the cross-country phase is on successful dressage and show-jumping training, and that when problems apparently specific to these two phases are solved, the cross-country will improve in parallel.

A car is more difficult to control at high speeds than low and a horse is the same. Any defects in training become intensified at faster paces, and the speed of cross-country is such that these defects will be exposed. The rider must have increased control the faster the speed he demands from his horse, although it sometimes appears at events that some riders are unaware of this, and watching their cross-country performances can be a frightening experience.

The majority of horses do have a strong sense of self-preservation and do not want to fall any more than do their riders, but there are times when poor presentation at a fence, inexperience of the horse or the influence of poor conditions may prove too much unless the rider is able to be of assistance. He should ride at a correct speed having taken into account the extent of his own and his horse's experience, the state of the ground and the severity of the fences, and should keep the horse balanced and in rhythm throughout.

Most event riders find the cross-country phase easier to ride than the show-jumping because the extra speed gives the impetus which allows for a greater range of take-off points than in show-jumping, where impulsion and greater accuracy are required to jump fences from a slower pace. Most horses enjoy their cross-country work and take a good hold, which means that they are at least going forward, and a rider feels more confident to drive strongly into the fences in the knowledge that even if the horse jumps a little flat, a fault cannot be incurred by the fence being knocked down.

However, the principles for jumping any fence are identical from whatever pace the fence is approached – free forward movement, rhythm and balance.

## Problems encountered

Before any other causes of cross-country problems are considered, the rider should ensure that the horse does not have any pain in his back, since this could well be the cause of many of the following problems, especially if the difficulty manifests itself after a fall.

### Ditch/water aversions

*Symptoms*: The horse refuses or is reluctant to jump either hazard, or another fence in conjunction with them. He may well display nappy signs.

*Causes*: The reaction of a horse presented with either water or ditches for the first time does depend upon the individual. Some horses hardly look twice and pop straight over a ditch or water while others point blank refuse to even look at them, let alone jump them. This inherent fear differs from horse to horse and some horses get over it while others never do. I firmly believe that horses who have been a real problem initially at either water or ditches will always let one down eventually. It seems that they never forget their early fears and when asked to jump a fence which requires a very bold jump, they say 'no'.

*Treatment*: The initial introduction to these hazards is of vital importance if the horse is not to be given a fright at the very beginning. He must be started over ditches so small that he can walk over them, and gradually, but only when he is confident, be asked actually to jump them. Puddles make a good start for water education and the horse should be splashed through as many as possible at every opportunity. He should be taught that splashing through water is fun and gradually he will accept that the water will not harm him. Firm riding is essential to tell the horse that he must go wherever he is asked, yet he should not be hassled and upset, as this will hinder progress. Giving young horses a lead with a more experienced one is a good idea, but the young horse must go on his own by the end of the session. Hunting will help the horse to cope with mud and puddles, although it will not necessarily cure ditch aversions, for he may jump enormous ditches in the company of other horses but will not attempt little ones on his own. In this case one must persevere with time and patience and realise that with experience the horse will manage, at least up to novice level, even if he lacks the courage to go beyond.

**Exaggerated backing off**
*Symptoms*: The horse shortens his stride into fences, losing the forward impulsion and creeping into the bottom of the fence for take-off. He may succeed over small fences by jumping this way but will be unable to cope with the bigger courses.
*Causes*: The frightened or spooky horse may behave in this way (*see* pages 198 and 237), or the horse which has been ridden by someone who lacks attack in his cross-country riding.
*Treatment*: The lack of forward movement in the approach will allow the horse to creep into his fences instead of jumping them freely. The rider must insist that the horse maintains his rhythm all the way to the fence and picks it up again immediately on landing. Many riders ride *to* a fence, instead of riding *over* it, and the horse who backs off particularly requires strong, attacking riding to keep him attacking the fences too. The rider must be careful not to get in front of his horse at any time, as his driving effectiveness will be less and, if the horse should refuse, there is the danger that the rider might jump the fence on his own! Always stay in behind the horse until he actually takes off and in this way the balance will always be preserved.

If the horse persists in backing off, a sharp reminder with the whip might be required. The effect of a whip, however, depends entirely on timing and this timing in these situations comes with experience and 'feel'. Perhaps the best way to describe it would be to say that the horse should have a smack as he thinks about doing something, rather than once he has already done it. My motto is 'prevention is better than cure', and a quick whack does far more good in nipping an evasion in the bud than a couple of whacks once it has happened.


**Excitability at the start**
*Symptoms*: The horse becomes very unsettled as his turn to start draws near and he leaps around, jogs, naps or sweats profusely in his anxiety.
*Causes*: The horse may be either genuinely keen to get on his way or very worried about what is to follow. Alternatively he might just be affected by his rider's nerves.
*Treatment*: It is natural that every rider has nerves at the start of a competition but it is important that these nerves are not transmitted to the horse since they will add to his own excitement. Before the start the rider should allow the horse to walk quietly round on a long rein, giving him a reassuring pat and talking to him if he shows signs of tension. There is no need to take up a firm contact until the

starter says 'Go', at which point the rider should adopt the forward position and take up the rein as he does so. If the rider shortens the reins too obviously before that moment, the horse will become even more wound up and is in danger of jumping the first couple of fences in a tense manner. This quiet attitude is all the more important before the start of a three-day event cross-country. The ten-minute halt is to allow the horse's pulse and respiration rates to recover, so by exciting him before he sets off cross-country, these rates will increase, which will hardly help the horse to cope with the ordeal to come.

### Falling

*Symptoms*: Since cross-country fences are solid, if the horse meets one in such a way that he hits it hard in front, he may either turn a complete somersault or lose his balance on landing. The horse is less likely to fall if he hits the fence with his hindlegs, as his front legs will be free for landing and his balance will not be so adversely affected. Drop fences and changes of terrain call for even more demands on the horse's ability to balance himself on landing, and whereas a horse may get away with hitting a fence on the level, he will not do so when the fence has a drop or is sited on a downhill slope.

*Causes*: The same as for show-jumping apart from the fact that, since the fences are solid, a horse will not be tripped up by catching a pole between his legs. The horse will fall because he has not jumped high enough and has hit the fence with either his knees, forearms or shins, or he may have left one foreleg dangling which unbalances him sufficiently so that he falls on landing. The increased speed at which cross-country fences are ridden means that the horse must be even quicker on his feet even though the impetus from the speed gives him more chance to stand off if he needs to. The horse must be agile enough to put in a short stride and still clear the fence, although he will probably survive hitting the fence with his shins or toes provided that the rider maintains balance on the landing side. The rider's position can play a large part in the horse regaining his balance after jumping a fence and this correct position is of vital importance if the horse is jumping a downhill fence, a drop fence, or if he hits one. If the rider's weight is too far forward it may well cause the horse to over-balance on landing and therefore fall; alternatively, if the horse pecks, the rider will probably fall off. The lurch caused by jumping at speed coupled with a sudden halt in momentum if the horse hits the fence is enough to shoot the rider forward, particularly if his weight is not situated correctly. Correctly

**48 The rider's position seen from behind**

a  *correct, straight, in balance*

b  *incorrect — crooked and with insecure lower legs, the rider is prone to lose balance, which will cause the horse to lose his balance too.*

is *slightly* behind the movement with the heels down and the lower leg at the same angle as the horse's shoulder; this is the practical cross-country seat which should be adopted for safety (*see* diagrams 48 and 49). The horse may still be allowed maximum freedom in the air and sometimes the rider may have to slip his reins to give the horse enough length without being pulled forward himself. The horse must be allowed to use his head and neck as much as he wants in order to preserve his balance at difficult moments, although the rider must maintain contact throughout.

The conditions underfoot and the constantly changing terrain which is invariably to be found on a cross-country course are instrumental in contributing towards a fall. Courses do vary considerably in their severity and the type of terrain and the ground, if affected by adverse weather conditions, add to the difficulty. Any situation which prevents the horse from using his agility to jump a fence may cause him to fall. Hilly terrain will affect his balance and put more demands on his ability to alter his centre of balance quickly, and deep, holding going, or water, will affect his movement and agility. We know how difficult it is for us to walk through deep mud, or wade through water and, although a horse is infinitely more powerful than we are, he is still affected by testing ground conditions. All his movements will require greater effort and more emphasis will therefore be placed on his ability and training. Deep going and difficult terrain will also place extra demands on his fitness and stamina by increasing the effort involved, and a tired horse is much more likely to fall than a fresh one, which underlines the need for having a very fit horse.

**49 The rider's position seen from the side** — *if the lower leg is on the girth and the heel is down, the rider is secure in his seat, no matter how the horse jumps the fence. The knee and ankle joints must be able to absorb stress from above and below.*

a *correct position with centre of gravity over the heel and the lower leg on the girth and the back flat*

b *correct — with shorter stirrups: the rider's seat moves back to maintain balance and the flexion in the knee is increased so that the lower leg can remain on the girth*

c *incorrect — behind the movement: centre of gravity now behind the heel, the lower leg shoots forward — toe down and the angle at the knee too open — and he falls back, his back slightly rounded, landing heavily on the horse's back*

d *incorrect — in front of the movement: centre of gravity is in front of the rider's foot; he collapses forward onto the horse's neck as his lower leg swings back, the angle at the knee too open and the toe down once more*

It is sometimes assumed that the over-bold horse will be more likely to fall than the cautious one but I have come to the conclusion that the horse lacking in boldness is the more likely candidate for ending up on the floor. With a lack of commitment at the crucial moment of take-off, the chicken horse loses power and impulsion and fails to make the necessary size of jump. Alternatively, he will paddle the fence in his efforts to regain the ground as quickly as possible, or simply fail to jump high enough because he dare not launch himself into the air. The bold horse, however, may encounter difficulties in combination fences cross-country by jumping too big over the first element and giving himself little or no chance to jump the subsequent elements (*see* diags 43 and 45, pp. 209 and 217, and section on Making up too much distance, page 256). The distances in cross-country combinations are comparatively short compared to the show-jumping ones, especially when one takes into consideration the difference between the length of stride necessary to jump a short combination and the length of stride the horse has been taking in his gallop. Course builders test the horse and rider by alternating straightforward or wide fences with combination fences, which places maximum demands on obedience, agility and athleticism from the horse and thoughtful riding from the rider.

*Treatment*: A cross-country fence is unyielding and must therefore be respected. The rider should present the horse at the fences so that he has every chance of jumping them clear however much of a hurry he may be in. A few time faults are preferable to a fall, which not only will give sixty penalties, but may damage horse or rider both physically and mentally. Reducing the speed does not necessarily mean that the horse will not fall, but arriving at the more difficult fences at a sensible pace gives a better chance of clearing them successfully.

A well-balanced, well-trained horse is far less likely to fall than the undisciplined horse which will lack agility and knowledge of how to extricate himself from trouble if he is meeting a fence wrong (*see* Making up too much/not enough distance, page 256). Grid work and flat work are the foundations for safe cross-country riding and the more jumping the horse does correctly, the better he will become. This will help him to adapt himself to the changes of terrain and footing which will affect his balance and his jump cross-country. Hunting will teach him to cope with all sorts of different goings and will speed up his reactions, but it is the basic flat work coupled with experience which will stand him in greatest stead in adjusting his balance and learning to jump cleanly whatever the conditions. All jumping executed correctly will benefit the horse in athleticism and experience, and the bonus of extra show-jumping is that it is less strenuous for the horse than the faster paced cross-country. Jumping against the clock requires speed and agility, and turning short into fences speeds up the reactions of both horse and rider. It is his speed of reaction that prevents a horse from falling and allows him to assess situations to avoid hitting the fences.

The rider has to think carefully whilst walking the course to decide which fences are potentially hazardous (they all are!) and which are most likely to cause problems. Bear in mind that the horse has no chance for a preview and your first impressions of a fence will be what he sees as he approaches it, except that he will be going much faster with less time to discover what he is being asked to jump. As a rider, one tells the horse by the pace at which one approaches the fence what he is likely to expect. A big, straight-forward fence needs bold, attacking riding, whereas a tricky fence requires the horse to be bouncing on his hocks and full of impulsion, ready to pop and be nimble. The wrong approach will be asking for trouble and it is unfair to the horse to present him poorly when he has no idea what is ahead.

It is probably safe to say that the majority of falls are caused by the horse taking off at a point which is unsuitable for the particular fence. The rider who is able to help his horse is obviously at an advantage here by altering the horse's stride yet maintaining rhythm and balance and free forward movement on the approach. The horse will be able to help the average rider provided he is given the chance to do so and is presented at his fences on a medium-length stride which gives him the choice of either putting in a short one or standing off a little if he is meeting the fence wrong. If the rider interferes on the approach and asks the horse to stand off too far, or otherwise over-rides to the point that the horse is pushed to the bottom of the fence, the horse is committed to a certain stride pattern and, if that leads him to an impossible take-off position, he may well fall. A horse will rarely fall if he is allowed to back off and jump his fences, but if the rider perpetually asks him to stand off further and further until the day comes when the horse tries to put in a short stride and fails to pick up in time, a bad fall will inevitably occur. It must be repeated that forward movement, rhythm and balance are the key words to correct, safe jumping.

The horse who falls through lack of courage is best forgotten as an event horse. A bold horse will always 'have a go' and jump higher over a fence if need be, but the horse with no courage will fall if he will not commit himself to a large leap, and the more worried he is, the lower he jumps. Lack of courage can make a horse almost 'freeze' in take-off and if he sneaks over the fence he may well land in a ditch on the other side. Any horse who has second thoughts about jumping will rarely, if ever, make a top event horse and although he may get away with this attitude at Novice level, he is unlikely to progress further with any degree of safety. Although a strong, experienced rider will obviously have more chance with this type of animal than will a novice rider, to be really successful in jumping, the horse and rider must have confidence in both themselves and each other, and if there is any doubt in either mind, problems will undoubtedly ensue.

### Flat

*Symptoms*: The horse jumps his fences with a hollow back which may present problems in combination fences (*see* Standing off too far, page 265).

*Causes*: A rider may instigate a flat jump by asking the horse to stand too far off his fences. A horse will tend to jump flatter cross-country due to the speed and parabola he makes over his fences, but he must have the facility to round himself when necessary, either when meeting a fence on a deeper take-off point or when jumping combination fences.

The speed may encourage a rider to ask the horse to stand off his fences so that the horse is unable to make a round arc over them, and this is not improved by the rider frequently not giving enough freedom with his hands to allow the horse to stretch his head and neck. Provided that a horse jumps correctly over a fence in canter there is no reason why he should start to jump flat just because the pace is increased, as long as the rider does not change his way of riding. Dressage, show-jumping and cross-country must all go hand in hand.

*Treatment*: This is the same as for show-jumping. The rider has to remember to keep rhythm and balance in his mind when he rides cross-country and wait for the fences to come to him rather than 'fire' the horse into them on long strides. Provided that the horse has impulsion, rhythm and balance on the approach, he will be able to jump the fences correctly. The rider's job is to control the pace and ride a good approach to the various fences (*see* diagram 50), avoiding arriving in a position for take-off which invites a flat, shallow parabola.

### Frightened

*Symptoms*: The horse is worried about jumping the variety of fences he meets cross-country and either over-backs off, spooks,

**50 How the rider can adversely affect the horse's jump in
his attempts to help on the approach**

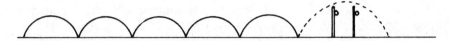

a *correct rhythmical approach leading to a well-formed parabola*

hooking back      firing      short one

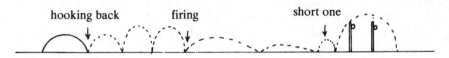

b *rider 'firing' horse and missing stride leads to a 'short one' when the horse gets
under the fence*

c *rider sees a 'long one' and pushes the horse on to that stride, making him stand
off and jump flat*

2.8m (3 yards)

d *correct approach for a bounce: the canter stride should be short, bouncy and
rhythmical*

refuses, or falls in his reluctance to tackle them (*see* Chapter Four).
A nappy horse may also suffer from nerves and be frightened of
jumping the different types of obstacles at speed.

*Causes*: There are three reasons for a horse to be frightened of
cross-country: he is simply not brave enough to jump fences with
ditches in front or underneath, as this does require a bold nature; he
has had a fright and lost his confidence, perhaps by being hurried in
his training or by having had a fall; he lacks experience and is bound
to show signs of apprehension when presented at strange, new

obstacles. If the horse is badly presented at these initially, instead of becoming confident to jump them happily, he will learn fear and mistrust which may or may not eventually be overcome.

*Treatment*: There is little to be done to change a horse's character provided that he has been given every chance to overcome his fear by thorough and patient training. If, despite every effort to produce him correctly, he is still lacking bravery, he should pursue a different career from eventing.

To regain confidence after a fall, the horse must be jumped regularly over small fences until his courage is restored. It depends on the individual horse how much a fall will affect him but if he is a confident horse and fell from over-boldness or slowness of reaction, it might give him a fright but should not alter his attitude; if, however, a horse falls because he was in two minds whether to jump the fence or not, his confidence will be further shaken or even wrecked, which indicates a long, slow road to recovery. A horse's boldness must never be abused and the rider must safeguard this precious attribute as much as he can and not be persuaded to hurry the horse's career or progress in his quest for success.

### Hanging

*Symptoms*: The horse is reluctant to go in a particular direction, normally away from home or other horses, and tries to edge back that way. He will be difficult to steer and will be strong and heavy in the hand, giving the rider the impression that if he relaxed his hand for an instant, the horse would veer off one way; this may present steering problems in the approach to a fence (*see* Running out, page 260).

*Causes*: The horse is either napping slightly or he has a problem in balancing himself in the gallop by carrying himself evenly on his hocks. This will cause him to rely on the rider's hand to support his weight and, depending on which side is affected, he will be heavier in one hand than the other. If the right side of the horse is the problem, the horse will be unable to bring that hind-leg underneath enough to take the weight for the one beat of canter which will make the horse veer off to his left.

*Treatment*: In either case the rider must insist with strong aids that the horse remains on a straight line. The rider must make use of both hands and both legs to help the horse carry himself more on his hocks. If the horse is veering off to the left, he is leading with his left shoulder, so the rider must use as much left hand as right to control the shoulder and try to stop it from swinging further out. He may even exaggerate this by turning the horse's head slightly to the left to move the shoulder to the right and then give and take strongly, even to the extent of giving a little tug, with the right rein to straighten the horse and dissuade him from hanging on that rein to such an extent.

If the rider suspects that there is something amiss, he should consult his vet to confirm his suspicions or allay his worries. If there proves to be nothing wrong with the horse physically, it suggests that more work must be undertaken on the flat to discipline the horse, and learning how to gallop in a balanced manner is part of an event horse's education.

### Hitting fences

*Symptoms*: The horse raps the fence either in front or behind. Although cross-country fences are solid and no fault can be incurred for a knock-down, the horse may fall as a result (*see* Falling, page 247) or lose balance to such an extent that he would be unable to jump a fence closely following.

If a horse regularly hits solid fences, his legs will suffer damage which may be immediate or apparent in the long-term.

*Causes*: A horse hits a fence because he does not jump high enough, so one has to decide why the horse is unable to make sufficient effort to jump cleanly. This may result from a poor approach and bad presentation to the fence, the approach lacking either balance or rhythm, being crooked, being too fast or with insufficient impulsion; other considerations may be deep going, the drag of water, difficult distances, false ground-lines, inexperience or lack of concentration by the horse.

*Treatment*: In all cases, the answer to jumping any fence without problems is correct presentation and an obedient, supple horse who is trained correctly for whatever he is being asked to perform. All the basic training dealt with in this book leads to this end and there are no short-cuts. It is impossible to train every horse never to touch a fence and some horses are naturally more careful and/or talented than others, but a rider has to give his horse every chance in his preparation for jumping to learn to be athletic and to cope with the situations he will meet cross-country.

If there is a fence on a course which tempts the horse to hit it, such as an upright fence with no ground-line or out of deep going, the rider must be even more meticulous in the way he rides the approach. He must ensure that the horse has his hocks well engaged, that he is balanced and in a forward going rhythm with impulsion and that he is concentrating on the centre of the fence. The rider himself must sit up and keep his balance and position throughout the jump and landing, and must on no account get in front of the movement at any time, so that he is prepared to pick up the speed and rhythm straight away on landing. Good cross-country riding involves careful thought and preparation and the more difficult the course, the more demand is placed on this. A horse's attitude towards cross-country can be severely affected by the way he has been ridden in the past and whereas schooling and re-training can reform a horse on the flat and for show-jumping to a large extent, once a horse has been badly ridden cross-country it will be more difficult to re-school him to top-class level. Confidence plays such an enormous part in an event·horse's success and if the horse has ever had reason to doubt his rider, he may let the rider down by losing faith in him at a critical moment.

**Making up too much/not enough distance**
*Symptoms*: The problem of not making up enough distance arises less often cross-country than when show-jumping, as the rider can use speed and impetus and allow the horse's jump to be rather flatter in its parabola, without the risk of incurring penalties for knocking down the fence. The horse who makes up too much ground will find this exacerbated cross-country as he will naturally be jumping his fences with shallower arcs and will have to be made to reduce his parabola. The reason why this second problem is encountered less in the show-jumping is because the horse keeps the same length of stride throughout his round, whereas on the cross-country he has to alter the length of his stride considerably depending on the type of fence, which will obviously prove more difficult for a horse with an expansive stride. By jumping into a combination too deep and not giving himself enough room for take-off over the subsequent elements, the horse is in danger of hitting them with his front legs – particularly if he is the type who is not quick at folding his front legs – which is just the sort of situation that causes a fall. If a combination fence takes a horse by surprise, he may 'leave a leg' on the second and third elements, which again may result in a fall.
*Causes*: These problems in cross-country differ from the show-jumping ones due to changes of terrain and the variety of combination fences likely to be encountered, which often include ditches and banks. It is these types of fences which may catch out the cautious, undisciplined or inexperienced horse by causing him to lose forward movement and impulsion on the last few strides preceding take-off, thereby having the effect of making him lose ground in between the elements (*see* Exaggerated backing off, page

246). A horse who jumps with a lack of fluency and lands not going forward will have problems making up distances in combinations. It is of vital importance that the rider is able to stride out the correct distances between elements when he walks the course because these distances affect the pace of approach and, if the pace is incorrect for the relative distance, the horse will not be given the best chance to cope with the combination.

A horse with a big, scopey jump and naturally long stride will find short distances a problem unless the rider is meticulous in his preparation of the horse for the fences. This type of scope can be used to great advantage over big courses but must be controlled unless needed.

*Treatment*: The horse who is rather restricted in his jump and stride may be presented at combination fences with more pace in order to carry him through. The rider should aim for the horse to land further out, which then shortens the distance before the next element. If the horse should land short over the first element, the rider must vigorously attack the next element in order to keep the horse going forward on landing and make him engage his hocks immediately. The rider must not be tempted to sit there with a negative or defeatist attitude, for if he shows no determination in extricating himself from trouble, the horse is unlikely to take the initiative and a stop or a fall may occur. If the horse has tendencies to spook or over-back off, the rider has to make sure that the approach is full of impulsion and the horse going as strongly forward as possible so that even if he should lose some impulsion at the last minute there is still sufficient energy to carry him through the combination.

The opposite type of horse must be brought into combinations on as bouncy and short a stride as is necessary for the distances between the elements. The shorter the distance, the shorter the horse's stride and the slower the pace, but the rider must be careful not to shorten from the hand alone but to use his legs to engage the horse's hocks and so lighten the forehand. If the horse lands unbalanced, he will have no chance of adjusting his balance before the next element and with the weight on his forehand will be unable to be quick and agile. The rider's aim should be to pop the first element from this short, bouncy approach, giving the horse the chance to assess the rest of the elements of the fence (*see* diagrams 43 and 45, pp. 209 and 217).

The whole purpose of walking a cross-country course is to decide how best to approach and ride each fence. All combination fences need particularly careful walking for the rider to assess all the possible pitfalls and decide how to avoid them on the horse he is riding. Advice from fellow competitors will only be helpful if adjusted to take account of one's own horse, since the method of riding a particular fence may be perfect for one horse but totally incorrect for another, so always take this into consideration before making any decisions.

**Refusing**
*Symptoms*: The only difference between the two jumping phases is that the horse will meet many different types of fence on a variety of terrains across country which he will not encounter in the show-jumping arena. This calls for a bold attitude, quickness and mental and physical agility and adaptability in altering pace and balance to cope with the ups and downs of the terrain.
*Causes*: These are the same as for show-jumping, but poor presentation by the rider (not taking account of the type of fence to be jumped), and lack of experience or courage in the horse can also be held responsible. A big, bold cross-country fence requires riding with attack and gusto and a faint-hearted approach will lead to a stop. A tricky fence such as a coffin or a bounce requires a different approach whereby the horse is gathered together with impulsion on a shorter, bouncier stride so that he can pop over without fear of landing either in the ditch of a coffin or too close to the next element of a combination fence (*see* diagram 51).
    The problem of balancing the horse for different types of terrain does not occur in show-jumping where the fences are normally built on relatively flat land with perhaps the odd undulation. The horse will be a difficult ride until he learns to carry his weight on his hocks and adjust his balance quickly. If he approaches fences on his forehand which call for agility and speed of reaction, he may be unable to cope and will therefore refuse. Due to the unlevelness of the ground and the placement of some of the fences, the rider must be exceptionally careful in the line of his approach if he wishes to avoid a refusal. The horse must be given sufficient time to evaluate the situation and the experience of the horse must always be taken into account when walking the course and deciding on which lines to take.
*Treatment*: For the general causes of refusals the reader should continue to study the show-jumping section for methods of correction. In the case of the horse which lacks courage, the rider must decide whether the horse refuses because he is inexperienced and does not fully understand how to cope with jumping the fence

**51 The coffin — the importance of the short bouncy stride on the approach**

a *correct approach — short, rhythmical, energetic canter results in an arched jump over the first element which allows enough room for a stride before the ditch, but which also sets him up for a correct jump over the third element*

b *incorrect approach — the stride may be too long or the pace too fast; the horse jumps with a very flat parabola which lands him close to the ditch; and thinking that he will land in the ditch, the horse then stops*

or fences before him, or whether he is a coward (*see* Frightened, page 252).

Since the horse is penalised only for refusing or falling and not for knocking fences down, it is imperative that he is taught from an early stage that it is not permissible for him to stop and have a look first, but that he must jump everything at the first time of asking. It is the rider's duty never to present the horse at an obstacle which is beyond his present capabilities, thereby giving him just reason to refuse. Provided that the horse is trained and ridden correctly, he should never be given the chance to stop and it should almost never enter his head that he could. (*See also* Ditch/water aversions, page 245.)

The attitude when riding a young horse over cross-country fences is to prevent a refusal by firm, understanding riding, but in the case of an older horse which has learnt to give up in difficult moments rather than make an effort, the rider is entitled to adopt a more aggressive attitude. Firstly, the rider must make sure that he approaches every fence at the correct pace with the requisite amount of impulsion. If the horse then stops, he should be given a sharp reminder with the whip to make him realise that he has to jump when asked and has to learn to think more quickly to assess the obstacle. This type of horse does not necessarily lack bravery but is slow in his reactions and must generally be sharpened up.

Grid work and practice over small versions of different types of fences will teach the horse how to cope with coffins, bounces, in-and-outs, and similar tricky fences which demand agility and athleticism. With practice and training, the horse will learn how to balance himself on undulating ground, although some horses, being naturally better balanced than others, will find it easier. The more work done on the flat to teach the horse to balance himself on his hocks, the more he will be able to reproduce this when ridden up and down hills and on the approach to fences sited in awkward situations.

When riding a cross-country course the rider must remember that he has had the advantage of previously walking the course and knows what each hazard entails. The horse is presented at strange fences involving different problems that he must assess on the spur of the moment. The rider's job is to present the horse at the obstacle with the maximum chance of jumping it and he must have clear in his mind what pace he must be in and what line he must take to arrive at the necessary take-off point. If the horse arrives too fast at a fence or lacks impulsion, he will have no chance to assess the fence, to gather himself and jump, and may have no alternative but to refuse.

## Running out

*Symptoms*: The increase in speed from show-jumping to cross-country demands more precision in the approach, and the angle at which some fences are built is designed to test the obedience of the horse in jumping on the oblique. Any lack of control will be exposed and once the horse learns that he can run out, the danger is that it may become a habit whenever he is presented with a difficult problem.

*Causes*: Lack of control in meeting fences sited on an angle, made worse by poor presentation by the rider or inexperience of the horse can all be put in the same category of inadequate training, for even the way the rider approaches his fences can indicate a gap in his own education. A mistake of this type can always be blamed directly or indirectly on the rider, whether the run out be due to immediate error or inadequate training at some stage. A difficult fence, such as a combination, needs accurate riding both in line and pace to avoid any problems.

*Treatment*: A solid background of correct training leaves little margin for error and if the horse is schooled over fences jumped on the angle, he will become accustomed to jumping wherever he is asked. At all times the rider must jump a precise point on a fence and not allow the horse to drift either one way or the other. The horse should be channelled to a particular spot and the rider should aim precisely for that point. With a line of fences, it is important that the rider firstly ascertains his correct line through, and it is helpful to line up with some object beyond, such as a tree, to be absolutely certain that the approach is the chosen one (*see* diagram 52). Situations can alter considerably from the leisurely pace of

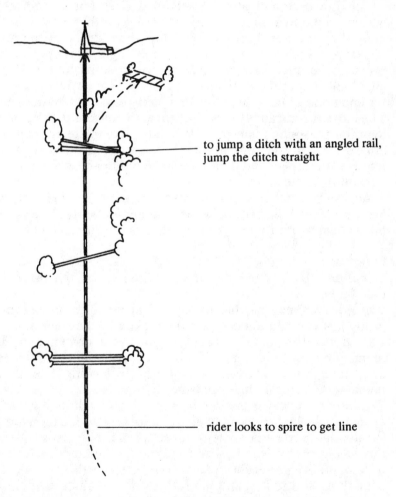

to jump a ditch with an angled rail, jump the ditch straight

rider looks to spire to get line

**52 Aiming for a particular spot beyond a line of fences** — *despite the angles at which the fences are placed, search for a point in the distance*

walking the course to the fast speed of the cross-country and it is of assistance if the rider has various landmarks to confirm his line of approach. The rider must look ahead to avoid any chance of deviation throughout the line of fences, as if he looks down, even briefly, he will lose his direction, which may permit the horse to run out. Riding a horse is the same as riding a bicycle or driving a car, in that the line of travel is dictated by the direction in which the rider's eyes are looking; immediately one looks away, the forward drive is temporarily halted, which invites wandering.

The horse should also be schooled over fences representing corners, not only for his education but also for the rider's practice in presenting the horse on a correct line. Provided that the horse is conversant with jumping fences on the angle, corners should not prove to be any great problem, although siting and wideness of angle will affect their difficulty, and the rider must remember to aim for one point directly over the ideal take-off point (*see* diagram 53). The more technically testing the fence, the more the horse must be between the rider's hand and leg and in complete control. Speed affects this control, and the rider has to approach these demanding fences with respect and therefore in the right pace with the requisite amount of impulsion.

Always remember that any short-cuts taken at early stages in a horse's career will materialise eventually and, when they do, the horse must be returned to the basics until they are correct.

### Slow

*Symptoms*: By not meeting the required speed the horse incurs time faults.

*Causes*: This may be due to a physical inability of the horse to gallop fast enough, unnecessary time taken by the rider in his turns and approaches to the fences, or the horse wasting time in his jumping by either backing off too much, ballooning his fences and so spending time in the air, or otherwise by landing flat-footed and taking time to regain his speed and rhythm.

*Treatment*: However fast the horse is able to gallop, it is far more economical in expenditure of energy and wear and tear on the horse to take the shortest possible distance when riding cross-country. In this way the horse is not asked to gallop flat out and the fences can be jumped from a sensible pace. In order to be able to make short, tight turns into fences and jump them on the angle, a premium is placed on the horse's response and obedience to the aids, and this is a test of the rider's training of his horse. It is with time and patience that the precision of his approach can be perfected and the horse

## 53 The corner fence — riding the correct line over the fence

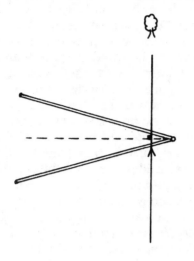

a *the line of take-off stands at 90°
to the line dividing the arms of
the angle; this should be lined up
with a landmark*

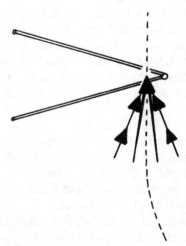

b *channel all the energy into one
pinpoint to avoid running out*

must be given the chance to gain valuable experience and confidence
before he can be asked to perform with the necessary speed of
reaction. The most time- and energy-saving method of riding cross-
country is to maintain the same rhythm throughout; much time is
wasted by a rider over-checking on the approach to a fence to 'look

for a stride'. Provided that the horse is balanced and in a rhythm, the rider should steady the pace and drive the horse's hocks further underneath him, maintaining the forward movement (forwards does not mean fast), and allowing the fence to arrive so that the horse can jump out of his rhythm. Further time can be saved – more than is widely appreciated – on the landing side if the horse can immediately pick up his rhythm and pace. To do this, both horse and rider must be perfectly balanced, as it is the re-adjustment of this balance which takes so long. When the rider is not sitting in the correct place over the fence or·on landing, and the horse pecks, the rider is in no position to assist the horse in regaining his own balance and it will not be until several strides later that the rhythm and pace can be re-established. Picking up this rhythm will help the horse who jumps high over his fences, and giving him a little kick on landing will help to flatten him out, or at least reclaim the time that has been wasted in the air. I do not regard jumping too big as a problem in itself, as it is far preferable to the horse hitting his fences.

Most horses are capable of returning a fast enough time to put them in the money, if not win, at one-day level, but it is important that the horse is fit, and the less 'blood' he has, the fitter he must be, for whereas he will be going almost flat out, a thoroughbred horse will be 'cantering' to move at the same speed. In a three-day event, a less quality horse will be unable to go flat out all the way, which is why a thoroughbred, or near thoroughbred, is sought after for the higher levels of eventing. However, by the rider walking courses with his own horse in mind and working out how to save seconds by economical routes both to and away from fences, he should be able to complete the course with a minimum number of time faults.

### Spooking

*Symptoms*: The wavering lines of approach which the spooking horse will try to take will make angled fences more likely to cause run outs, refusals or falls. Once the horse has become accustomed to the variety of fences he is liable to meet cross-country, he should straighten his approach.

*Causes*: The horse has to become used to a wider variety of fences and terrain on the cross-country than the show-jumping, where the fences are similar apart from the colours. A horse's character has the main bearing on whether he is spooky or not and during his training he must be taught how to overcome his caution by learning to trust himself and his rider. A horse will be naturally suspicious of the new things he meets on the cross-country but must be sufficiently obedient to the rider's aids to jump despite his fears.

A more experienced horse may spook at the first fence on the cross-country, especially on his first outing of the season, but this is him displaying fresh, playful behaviour which the rider must be ready to cope with!

*Treatment*: A young or inexperienced horse must be familiarised with ditches, water, drops, steps and banks so that he becomes confident and happy about tackling them. Some horses remain suspicious all their lives and, if they cannot overcome this caution when going cross-country, are unlikely to make top event horses. The majority of horses soon learn how to cope with the various obstacles as long as they are introduced to them correctly and not presented either too fast or without impulsion. The rider must ride fences likely to cause spooking with a strong and determined attitude and let the horse realise that he has no choice but to jump the fence. It is important that a spooky horse does not adopt the habit of stopping once and then jumping at the second attempt. In the early stages of training the rider must insist that the horse jumps the fence on the first time of asking, albeit from a standstill provided that the fence is very small, to establish in the horse's mind that if he is presented at a fence he must jump it. It is always the rider's job to make that possible by correct training and riding.

## Standing off too far

*Symptoms*: By taking off too far away, the parabola of the jump will be long and flat, which may cause balance problems on landing and will make the distances in combination fences too short, often resulting in a fall (*see* Flat, page 252).

*Causes*: A horse with a naturally long stride will be tempted to stand off his fences simply because there will be no room for another stride unless the rider intervenes. It is the rider's task to prepare the horse for a fence, and unless he sets the horse up by driving him together and gathering the energy, the horse will arrive at the fence on his forehand and will be unable to shorten his stride if required (*see* diag. 50, p. 253).

*Treatment*: Firstly, the horse must be taught, by working through grids and exercises, that he can jump from a deeper take-off position. Secondly, the rider must present the horse to his fences in the correct way – on a medium-length stride, balanced, going forward in a rhythm and on the right line for each particular fence. In this way, the horse is in a position to be able either to stand off a little if he needs to, without launching himself in an unbalanced way or throwing a flat jump, or to pop in a short stride and still jump the fence with ease. Most horses only stand off too far if the rider commits them to doing so by pushing them out of a rhythm and sending them onto their forehands. The horse must always jump out of his rhythm and in this way will be able to maintain his balance throughout the jump.

### Strong/Pulling

*Symptoms*: The rider is out of control either between or on the approach to fences, resulting in falls, refusals or run outs due to the lack of obedience.

*Causes*: The speed of cross-country will exacerbate any problems of this sort and increased speed puts more demands on control and the training necessary to obtain it. Most horses enjoy galloping and jumping at speed, and this enthusiasm, coupled with inadequate training, will make control difficult for the rider. It is of paramount importance that the horse is not taken too fast too soon. He must first learn discipline at the slower paces. All too often, one sees young horses being ridden cross-country at speeds beyond their present mental and physical capabilities, and this can easily affect their future performance.

*Treatment*: Discipline, and training to achieve it, is the only solution. The horse has to be established in his ground work and his jumping from a slower pace before he can be asked to go faster. This will mean that he will collect some time faults initially but, as the speed can be gradually built up when the rider feels the horse is able to cope, there should be no problems encountered and no set-backs in the training programme. All set-backs are to be avoided, and thought from the rider should prevent them.

If, despite re-schooling and patience, the horse remains strong when ridden cross-country, a change of bit is advised. It may then be a matter of trial and error to find a bit suitable for that particular horse, but it is vital that the horse is comfortable and does not finish the course with a sore mouth. If the bit causes him discomfort, the horse is all the more likely to pull, and steering will also be more difficult.

I am perfectly willing to accept that some horses do require strength to control them and may therefore not be suitable rides for women. Struggling to hold a horse is exhausting and potentially hazardous if the horse cannot be controlled in the approach to his fences. My firm belief is that a horse should never be allowed to pull in the first place, and that with patient training he should learn obedience not only in walk, trot and canter, but in gallop as well. But I regret to say that theory does not always work out in practice!

# SIX

# Steeplechase

Although the steeplechase occupies only a fraction of the time spent on the speed and endurance day of a two- or three-day event (occupying from two to four and a half minutes), it is nevertheless most important that both horse and rider feel confident and proficient about performing Phase B. So that they can make the necessary time with minimum effort, it is vital that both horse and rider are trained to gallop and to jump steeplechase fences at speed. Lack of practice is all too evident when one watches Phase B at an average three-day event.

Anyone proposing to compete in three-day events should study the top steeplechase jockeys in action and the way in which they present their horses at the fences. John Francome was the master of this, and he rarely met a fence wrong, even when racing in earnest over the last few fences. The difference between racing and the steeplechase phase of an event is that there are no other horses: it is much easier for a horse to remain 'on the bridle' (strongly up to the rider's hand) when he is galloping *with* other horses because he naturally begins to race them and this helps to draw him into the fences. He is likely to lose enthusiasm on his own, particularly as he becomes slightly tired towards the end. Despite this, the principles are exactly the same for steeplechasing whether one is racing or on one's own: these are, of course, rhythm and balance . . . the same as for jumping any fence. The speed at which the horse travels will accentuate any problems he may have, although the partnership will generally stay intact because the very nature of the fences allows for a certain margin of error: the construction of a steeplechase fence makes it possible for the horse either almost to tread on the fence before taking off or to stand back and brush through the fence, without causing him to fall. The horse will expend more effort (and therefore energy) if he meets a fence wrong, even if he does avoid the penalty of falling, and this may take its toll later (on the cross-country) when the horse's last reserves are required. The rider has to learn how to minimise the harm caused by meeting a fence on a bad stride, and this is where schooling and practice are required. It is not a phase which can be practised *ad infinitum*, because the galloping carries with it an increased risk of injury; it has to be fitted into the horse's general training programme.

It depends on the experience of both horse and rider as to how often schooling sessions will be needed. When the horse is ready for a two- or three-day event, he will know how to jump the fences, but the partnership still have to be taught how to negotiate them at the necessarily increased speed. Some horses benefit by jumping 'upsides' another if they are lacking in enthusiasm (a racing term meaning working two or more horses side by side), whereas the easily excitable horse is best schooled on his own. It is sufficient to jump only two or three fences if the distance is long enough to allow speed and rhythm to be established; indeed it is more beneficial to school three times up a line of three fences than to complete a circuit when the horse may become weary and therefore susceptible to strain.

The rider must be aiming for the horse to be in a balanced rhythm throughout the steeplechase phase. To achieve this, the rider must drive the horse up to a firm contact and at no time should that contact be lost, otherwise there is a danger that the horse will drop onto his forehand and the balance will be lost. A horse will lower his outline when he is galloping and should be encouraged to stretch into this natural shape. The rider must help him not only to establish his balance but also to readjust it as he approaches the fences. The position of the rider has an even greater influence on the horse's balance at steeplechase speed than it does at the slower pace of the cross-country. He should tuck himself behind the horse's head and neck in a forward position between the fences in order to obtain the best possible streamlining – sitting (or standing) bolt upright with arms and legs flapping is hardly conducive to good aerodynamics. In order to allow the horse to jump the fence most efficiently, the balance should be adjusted: raising the shoulders slightly on the approach ought to be enough, combined with a slightly forward lower leg. This is the ideal position to maintain over the fence. From here it is very simple to adopt the 'safety seat' – feet forward and head up with slipping reins – in emergencies, when the horse hits the fence or pecks on landing, for instance.

The rider should practise slipping the reins and gathering them up again as quickly as possible; if the rider holds a bridge, this task is made much easier. It is advisable to hold a bridge throughout the steeplechase phase (*see* diag. 36, p. 181), because the rider can use it as a support both for himself and for the horse. By resting the bridge across the horse's withers or neck the rider can keep a steady contact, which gives the horse the support he needs when travelling at high speeds; it is also a great help on landing if the horse should peck. The sudden reduction in forward motion when a horse hits a fence will cause the unprepared rider to lose his balance or even to be shot out of the saddle: a bridge will prevent the hands from dropping either side of the horse's neck and will therefore stop the rider flopping forward. All jockeys hold bridges. The unpopularity of the bridge amongst event riders seems to stem from a fear of not being able to steer whilst holding one. Steering when holding a bridge does indeed require practice, but once mastered it actually helps enormously. At steeplechase pace, remembering that speed exaggerates problems, it is important that the outside hand is used in the bridge to control the shoulder, preventing the horse from swinging out wide on the turns. One of our top show-jumpers often rides with a bridge, in the first round and against the clock, which disproves the theory that one cannot steer *and* hold the reins this way. It is not always possible, however, to maintain a straight line from the horse's mouth through the rein up to the rider's hand, and the rider must put his hand up the horse's neck to allow him some freedom. The Americans advocate the 'Crest release system' which means that the hands move up the crest (rather than down either side of the neck) to allow the horse to use himself, and this method would not be affected by holding a bridge. Obviously the choice is a personal one. There is no one right or wrong method as both ways are successful – a situation encountered quite often when solving training problems – but what is important is that the method adopted works for the individual horse and rider.

As the rider raises his shoulders on the approach to a fence, he should also be driving the horse strongly up to his hand in order to gather enough energy for the fence ahead. There should be no loss of speed as this is done, but there should be an increase of impulsion; through this the horse is able either to maintain his stride pattern, or to back off (shorten his stride) a little to arrive at a suitable take-off point. Do not confuse backing off to meet a correct take-off point with over-backing off when the horse slows down and loses impulsion (*see* diag. 54, p. 270). If a rider sees that he is meeting a fence on a bad stride he should keep coming, rather than steadying up or allowing the horse to slow down, and he should tighten the contact by driving the horse up to the hand, thus maintaining the important rhythm. The horse in this position is able either to stand off or to back off, whichever he feels he can do better at the time: if the horse makes the decision to stand off a fence, he will probably make more effort to clear it than if it is the rider who asks for a long stride. If the rider had asked for 'a long one' (asking the horse to lengthen

**54 Approaching a steeplechase fence — the importance of driving the horse forward and maintaining his rhythm**

long stride — easily possible    correct stride — ideal

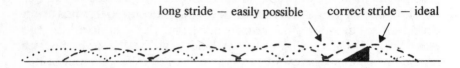

a *the most economical way of steeplechasing is to jump out of a rhythm with no change of stride length but when rhythm is maintained any alteration needed is possible without loss of energy or speed*

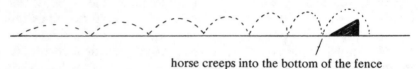

horse creeps into the bottom of the fence

b *if the rider alters the horse's stride length and show-jumps the fence, he is losing valuable time and wasting energy*

his stride to meet a fence at a better take-off point) and the horse had not responded appropriately, the horse might well have fallen. He must go for 'a long one' without losing his rhythm or balance, but, even then, every time this happens, the horse is expending more energy than if he were jumping out of his natural stride, and this is particularly important to consider with the horse who has doubtful stamina – these maximum efforts must be kept to a minimum.

Knowing that balance and rhythm are a vital part of the steeplechase phase – not only improving the chances of jumping all the fences but also economising on the energy expended – it is easy to see why it is so important that there are no changes of pace at all, around the bends, between and over the fences. It is advisable to start at the required speed as it is very difficult to catch up time, especially if the horse should jump slowly or make a mistake, which loses valuable seconds. Many event horses have to travel constantly near or at their top speed to make the time on the steeplechase, and so it may be impossible to increase the pace at all. It is important, therefore, to establish a speed and constant rhythm immediately so that as little time as possible is lost (*see* Slow, page 275).

Although the problems likely to be encountered on the steeple-chase phase are being discussed separately it must not be forgotten that, even though the horse is travelling at a faster speed, all his early training must be kept in mind. All those hours spent schooling on the flat over poles, and riding exercises, are a means to an end; they will produce a horse who is a pleasure to ride over a variety of fences at whatever speed. The relevant sections in the show-jumping, cross-country and dressage chapters should be referred to where applicable.

## Problems encountered

### Creeping into the bottom
*Symptoms*: The horse loses impulsion on the approach, which causes him to back off to such an extent that he ends up almost climbing over the fence. He will waste valuable time not only on the approach, but also in the air and on landing, because he will take time to gather speed again.

*Causes*: A cautious or inexperienced horse may well show these tendencies and, whereas the inexperienced horse will learn to keep going forward to his fences, the cautious horse may be unnerved jumping fences at speed and the problem may get worse.

The rider must ensure that the horse maintains his rhythm and forward movement all the way to the fence; if he does not there will be a loss of impulsion which will cause the horse to prop into his fences. A rider who steadies on the approach to his fences will encourage the horse to back off too much if he is already inclined to do so.

*Treatment*: Both the inexperienced and the cautious horse will obviously gain confidence from practice and schooling. The rider has to exert a strong influence on both these types of horses; he has to insist that the horse keeps coming to his fences and he must not allow his horse to slow down on the approach. Strong driving may be required to maintain the rhythm and create the impulsion which, if lost, is the cause of a horse creeping into the bottom of his fences.

If the horse should jump his fence slowly or stickily, the rider should be ready, on landing, either to give him a kick or a reminder with the whip, which will teach him that he must pick up his rhythm immediately and be quick away from his fences, even if he jumps the occasional one less fluently. Studying the racing on television it is interesting to notice that the horse's speed away from the fences is as important as his speed elsewhere. It is even preferable to be a little slower on the approach and in the air – so avoiding a mistake – than to be fast, hitting the fence and either falling, or, at best, taking time to regain balance and rhythm.

### Falling

*Symptoms*: The horse can hit the top of the fence either having stood off too far, or having taken off at too deep a point, but in both cases the horse is likely to overbalance on landing. The worst type of fall occurs when the horse meets a fence on a bad stride and scarcely rises at the fence, turning a somersault as a result. The horse may, of course, peck and then fall on landing without having hit the fence, and the rider may fall off when the horse does not actually come down at all.

*Causes*: The horse must be presented at a fence by the rider in rhythm and balance at all times: the faster the pace, the more demands there are on this correct approach. If a horse approaches a steeplechase fence unbalanced he will have little chance either of re-arranging his stride to arrive at the fence at a more suitable take-off point (should he be meeting the fence wrong), or of staying on his feet – particularly if he has hit the fence when his speed and impetus are likely to cause him to peck or topple over. Whether or not the horse manages to stay upright having hit a fence is influenced by a variety of factors, from the state of the going, to the experience and condition of the horse . . . whether he is fresh or tired. There are far more falls in novice chases (and even more when the going is heavy or soft) than in any other races: the horses have not yet developed the quick reaction speed which they need to adjust their stride or alter their balance according to their speed and the state of the ground. A seasoned campaigner, on the other hand, will know how to counter-balance himself, as the experienced jockey will know how to ride under different sets of circumstances and, although there is no substitute for experience, knowledge of the theory behind jumping at speed can only be of assistance.

The influence of the rider's weight can make the difference between a horse regaining his balance on landing or falling. If a rider's weight is too far forward, for instance, it can 'tip the scales', particularly if he loses contact at the same time, so that the horse has no support at a critical moment. A horse–rider combination may get away with several mistakes if they are travelling slowly, but this will not be possible when the pace is fast and any flaws will be exposed.

If the horse has no impulsion in his hocks to stand off when he meets a fence wrong, he will 'dive' at the fence and probably fall himself or shoot the rider out of the saddle. He will not have the necessary power in his hocks to back-off either (remember this is the same theory behind lengthening and shortening the stride in flat work when preparation is all important) and he will run deep into the fence on his forehand, which will mean he will hit it hard. If the rider – jumping at speed – asks the horse for a long stride and the horse tries to put in a short stride and hits the fence very hard, he will undoubtedly fall. Jumping an open ditch the horse may put his feet in the ditch itself and this will result in a bad fall; open ditches probably cause more falls than plain fences because of the extra width of the fence and the ditch on the take-off side. It is indecision on the part of either horse or rider which most commonly causes a fall; if the partnership is positive in what they do, they will remain in balance, and the horse will jump the fences in a committed, confident manner. The cautious or inexperienced horse, lacking determination, is more likely to hit a fence steeplechasing – as he is across country – than the bold horse, who will jump from less ideal take-off positions and who will always 'have a go'. Thus the timid jumper, being less committed, and the horse lacking scope, are much more likely to fall.

*Treatment*: A horse is unlikely to fall if he meets a fence right, so it must be decided quickly how best to cope with less than perfect situations. When a horse is meeting a fence on a bad stride, a decision must be made about whether to stand off or put in a short stride before take-off: the rider's task is to present the horse at the fence in such a way that the horse has the choice. He does this by driving the horse strongly together on the approach, increasing the hold-and-drive action if he can see that the horse is meeting the fence wrong. This will increase the horse's impulsion and he can then either pick up and jump without diving over the fence, or, because he has his hocks underneath him, back off and pop over. If the rider throws the horse at the fence with a loose rein, he is asking for a fall, because he is sending the horse onto his forehand and not giving him a proper chance; he must *keep hold* at all times to help the horse, keeping him balanced and between hand and leg. He should offer the horse a long stride if he wants to take it, but should also give him the chance to fiddle at the fence if he prefers. It is really important to understand the horse one is riding when a decision has to be made about whether he prefers to stand off or to pop.

When the rider asks for 'a long one' and does not obtain the necessary response from the horse a fall is probable. It is important to consider at this stage that, if the horse is going at maximum speed, his stride will be at its maximum length. This means that although he will be able to stand off (assuming the rider has created the necessary impulsion), he will *not* be able to lengthen his stride into a fence, which means that the possible limits of the take-off area become further restricted. If the horse is not responding because of greenness, tiredness, caution or lack of scope the rider must drive the horse up very strongly – without dropping the contact – to create potential energy. As the horse grows more tired, he will become more unbalanced (and lacking in scope): not only will the rider find it more difficult to create the necessary energy for a jump, but he will also need to be extra careful on the landing side. Possibly he should shorten up the horse, allowing him to pop the fence, rather than asking him to stand off and fly . . . particularly as the chances of overbalancing on the landing side of a fence increase on a tired horse.

The rider should refrain from asking the horse to stand off at the open ditch, if possible, in order to avoid the danger mentioned above (under Causes). However, even the boldest horse may be surprised by the ditch, so the rider must drive the horse strongly up to his hand on the approach in order to keep him in rhythm and balance at all costs: he is then offered a long stride or given the chance to back off. The rider must stay in behind the horse in perfect balance himself, by being in the correct position throughout not only the approach and the jump but also on landing, so that he can help the horse maintain his balance. On landing he should keep his weight slightly back; from this position he is more able to absorb any impact, if the horse hits a fence, by slipping the rein and bracing the lower leg forward against the stirrup (*see* diag. 49, p. 249). Should the horse peck when the rider is in this position, not only is he less likely to overbalance the horse, he will also tend to stay in the saddle himself.

The rider's fitness is as important as that of the horse, a certain amount of physical strength being required to keep any horse balanced throughout a steeplechase course. The rider of a 'stuffy' horse will have to work harder than someone on a quality scopey horse, and bad going will also put heavier demands on the rider's stamina because the horse will need more help. If the rider becomes weak through tiredness, he will be unable to help his horse and he will also be more easily unseated if the horse makes a mistake . . . and of course the horse is more liable to make mistakes if the rider cannot gather him on the approach to the fences.

## Off the bridle

*Symptoms*: The horse will not take up a contact and is reluctant to go at the requisite speed. The rider will have difficulty in meeting the fences on good strides as a result because the horse will not have impulsion enough to jump his fences from anything but the perfect natural take-off point.

*Causes*: The rider may be asking the horse to gallop faster than he is capable of going, so that all his energy is being used in the gallop itself and no more can be created on the approach to the fences unless the rider is really driving him together, keeping the horse between hand and leg. The horse may be unfit and, of course, heavy or testing going will place demands on the horse's stamina and energy reserves, or he may just not enjoy going at the required speed. A young horse may not understand how to gallop and is unbalanced when going fast; as yet, he does not have a reason (or desire) to go at that speed anyway. A lazy horse will drop the bridle and pretend that he is tired or unable to maintain his speed; but knowing whether the horse is being lazy depends largely on the rider knowing and understanding each individual horse.

*Treatment*: Galloping alongside another horse will help in many ways. It will encourage him to be enthusiastic and to work, which, in turn, will both teach him how to gallop on a contact, and get him fitter at the same time. Most horses enjoy the challenge of another horse beside them and discover their racing instincts. This is where hunting can benefit the phlegmatic horse enormously, giving him a purpose in his mind for galloping and jumping fast. The horse must want to attack his fences with gusto, because otherwise the rider will be sitting on a horse with no power, which will feel similar to driving a car with no acceleration.

Energy must be contained at all times, and the more the horse tries to drop the contact, the more the rider must keep hold of him and drive him together. Watch the racing: when a racehorse comes off the bridle, the jockey will 'change hands' (shorten the reins), and kick the horse up to a renewed contact, never allowing him to be on a loose rein. Remembering that it takes two to pull, the rider merely has to try to take hold and encourage the horse to do the same in order to make him take a contact in this case. It follows that if the rider drops his hands he is indicating to the horse that he can slow down – something to remember when getting carted!

## Slow

*Symptoms*: Obvious perhaps but mentioned as a problem because, remember, faults are incurred for every second exceeding the optimum time.

*Causes*: The horse may not be able to maintain the necessary speed for the length of the course because he is unfit; he may waste time either over his fences, in the approach or on landing; or the rider may have steering problems (*see* page 279), which will mean that time will be wasted on the turns. The rider may be entirely to blame for the time faults, either because he does not realise the speed required, or because he travels an unnecessarily long distance by riding sweeping turns. Of course deep or holding going must also be considered as this will affect a horse's speed and test his stamina.

*Treatment*: Most horses are capable of *reaching* the speed of 690 metres per minute: the difference between a quality horse and a more common animal lies in the possession of stamina, which will allow the horse either to maintain that speed, or to increase it, for several minutes. Slower horses must be given every assistance to make the time on the steeplechase, without (bearing in mind that they still have to perform on the cross-country) completely exhausting them. If every ounce of their energy is used on this phase, they will be sapped before they ever get to the demanding phase D.

The horse must be very fit, carrying no excess weight, and he must be generally confident about how to tackle the steeplechase. It is necessary to teach some horses *how* to gallop and it is good to work them upsides another horse, and preferably one with a longer stride who will act as an incentive, encouraging the greener horse to stretch out and match the bigger strides. The rider must teach him how to extend his form to use himself to the full and to maximise the length of his stride, keeping an even contact to balance him: a short, choppy stride will waste time and energy. Developing a horse's gait with some fast work alongside another horse on straight, level ground will help not only on the steeplechase but also on the cross-country. Mistakes on the approach may often be caused by this speed, which can unnerve either horse or rider; but this, with more practice, need not occur. Any mistake at a fence means that there will be a loss of rhythm and, therefore, a waste of precious seconds. However, if this does happen, the rider must be in a balanced position, ready to recover the speed and rhythm immediately, so losing the minimum amount of time. Invariably most time is lost on the landing: either horse or rider takes too long to recover their balance; the rider fumbles for his reins, or maybe even a stirrup (which should be kept on the ball of the foot, not the toe, remember

. . . and there are occasions when the foot can be even further into the stirrup for safety). All of these take time and, multiplied by the number of fences, can result in several time penalties. The rider must drive the horse up to the hand on the approach, ride strongly into the fences without going for 'long ones', sit in balance, and then drive on the moment the horse has landed.

The optimum time is fast and there is little opportunity to make up time, particularly on a horse which lacks speed, so it is most important that the horse is made to start picking up speed as soon as the starter says 'Go'. Be very careful not to allow the horse to start before the 'Go', as a false start can be very costly. If necessary, face backwards and only turn as the starter reaches 'one' on his count-down, so that you are ready for the off the moment he says 'Go'. Starting your stop-watch as he says 'five' on the countdown saves time: there is time to check that the watch is going, and there is no further need to fiddle with the reins which could lead to problems if left until the last second.

It is amazing how much time can be lost by riding a bad line around the steeplechase course, and although the inside rail defines the shortest distance, it does not necessarily represent the quickest. The course must be walked very thoughtfully at least twice, and the competitor should be careful not to lose concentration, becoming involved in the general chit-chat which seems so often to be part of the official course walk. It is also impossible to see the lines to the fences and around the bends when walking in a crowd of people, so it is better to drop behind, or lead the way, or perhaps to concentrate on the lines later, when alone, walking the course again. The rider should note the state of the going, any undulations which might unbalance the horse, and the bends and their angles. Nothing must endanger the balance or rhythm, as this will mean loss of speed. A sharp bend will probably require a wide approach so that the horse swings out steadily from the inside rail before entering the bend; and in order to approach the next fence straight or reduce any chance of slipping up, it could be necessary to drift out after the bend too (*see* diag. 55, p. 278).

The rider must aim not only to ride the shortest possible distance without any loss of rhythm or balance, but also to present his horse correctly at each fence. In this way, the horse will be given the greatest possible chance of getting within the time, provided that he is fit and the going is not too testing. Always bear in mind that, if the going is soft or heavy, it is worth getting a few time faults on the steeplechase if it means that problems caused by an exhausted horse

**55 Steeplechase turns — how to ride them correctly**

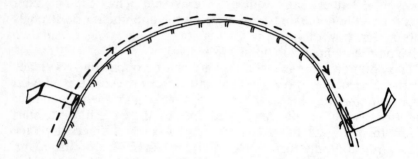

a *if the turn is shallow, the rider should 'hug the rails' and take the shortest route*

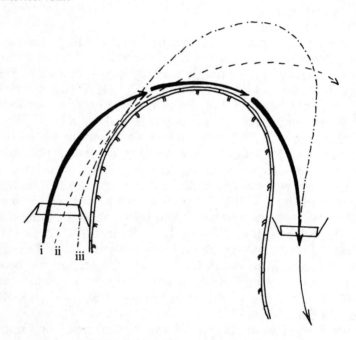

b *if the turn is sharp there is more room for error:*
  i *correct track — approach the corner wide, only touching the rail on the lip of the bend, swinging out again after it*
  ii *incorrect track — bouncing off the corner too early, the horse will miss the next fence*
  iii *incorrect track — hugging the rail around the first corner the horse will lose a lot of time trying to come around the turn — making a long detour*

are to be avoided on the cross-country. The rider's skill is put to the test here, as he must gauge how much energy the horse possesses and how best to utilise it.

## Standing off too far

*Symptoms*: The horse takes off further away from the fence than his scope will allow; he either hits the fence, falling or unseating his rider, or, at best, expends excess energy.

*Causes*: The rider may be asking the horse to stand off too far, combined with the fact that the horse is losing impulsion on the approach. This loss of power is caused either by a lack of preparation by the rider, or by heavy going, or by tiredness, caution or, finally, exuberance or lack of concentration on the part of the horse.

*Treatment*: If the horse stands off through choice, and he is jumping from a balanced form with impulsion, he is unlikely to make a mistake; it is the rider's task to ensure that the horse always meets the fence in this way. By keeping hold, raising the body slightly and keeping the legs on, the rider simultaneously keeps the horse balanced and gives him energy; he gives the horse the scope to jump the fence from any suitable take-off point. In the case of an open ditch, the rider must think – holding and driving as he does so – about running the horse right up to the guard rail. On no account should the rider pull at the horse to try to prevent him from standing off; this will result in a hollow, powerless jump, with no drive from behind, and this may cause a fall.

## Steering, problems with

*Symptoms*: The rider is unable to turn the horse on the corners; he has to cover extra distance and this means not only an expenditure of unnecessary energy but also possible time penalties. The horse may hang towards home but the rider will be unable to correct him.

*Causes*: Lack of control is the root of the problem. The horse may just be too strong for the rider so that he is unable to hold or steer the horse. This lack of control may stem from inaccurate riding, however, the rider being unable to contain the horse's shoulder on the bends and then allowing him to swing wide.

*Treatment*: It is imperative that the rider learns how to turn a horse correctly at the slower gaits before he is expected to turn him at the gallop with any degree of control. The horse must learn too, at these slower paces, to turn in response to the correct aids and to understand the importance of the outside hand in particular. The horse cannot be turned by the inside hand alone at gallop, because the force of the pace encourages the outside shoulder to swing out

on the corner while, in fact, before the horse is able to turn, this
shoulder must be contained. Watching racing on television, one can
see how the horses gallop around their corners bent to the outside,
but inevitably on the correct lead. The show-jumpers work in the
same way when they are turning in the jump-off – where controlling
the outside shoulder is all-important. More outside hand is needed
as the turns become sharper on the steeplechase course, and this is
where holding a bridge is so helpful. Of course it is perfectly
possible to ride with a bridge at home and to practise turning at
canter (or even faster). (If we imagine the cutting ponies herding
cattle and the way in which they are turned – by neck-reining – the
importance of the outside rein becomes apparent; on a turn of 180
degrees, the inside rein is virtually loose.) Any horse who is ignorant
of the outside rein aid is going to resist turning with his shoulder
under control but, if the rider perseveres, he will discover that it is
not only possible to turn the horse with the correct aids – inside
hand guiding, outside hand controlling the shoulder, outside leg
behind the girth to control the quarters, and inside leg on the girth
to maintain forward movement – but also easier than just using the
inside hand. These are, of course, the basic dressage aids for turning
any corner whether it be in walk or gallop: any fault in a slow pace is
merely exaggerated in a faster pace . . . underlining, once again, the
need for correct basic schooling.

## Strong

*Symptoms*: The rider has difficulty holding the horse during the
steeplechase phase which may mean that the horse is using more
energy than necessary (by going faster that the required speed). The
rider lacks control to the extent that he has problems on the
approach to the fences and also on the turns.

*Causes*: There are many possible contributing factors to a horse's
becoming strong: the rider may be weak, unfit, or inexperienced, or
the horse may lack discipline. Some horses only grow very strong
once they start galloping, and the rider may not know how to hold a
horse at speed. He may be difficult to hold because he is over-keen,
but a nervous horse, or one who is running away from discomfort,
may also seem to be strong. When the horse is galloping on his
forehand he will appear strong, because he is relying heavily on the
rider's hand for support.

*Treatment*: A strong horse is actually easier to ride on this phase
than one who will not take hold of the bridle. As long as the rider
keeps a contact, the horse is creating his own impulsion by pulling,
so the rider can sit against the horse and allow him to jump out of

his hand. The rider must not panic, standing up in his stirrups and hauling, although it is quite common to see a rider trying to stop a horse by dropping his hands and then heaving and hauling repeatedly, with no response whatever from the horse; instead he should maintain a firm contact. The best way to learn how to hold a horse is to ride out for a racehorse trainer, and I strongly recommend that everyone should do this at some stage in their riding career. It is possible to learn so much from 'riding work': it teaches one how to balance oneself and the horse at the gallop, to ride straight, and how to control a fit thoroughbred!

However strong a hold the horse may be taking, the rider must remember the golden rule of rhythm and balance and he must try to impose this upon the horse, even if it requires a supreme effort. If the rider is completely unable to hold the horse and he is actually dangerous, it may be advisable to experiment with stronger varieties of bit, and of course it will be a matter of trial and error to find the best one for each particular horse.

A horse who is unbalanced in his gallop needs assistance from the rider. This is particularly on the approach to his fences when the rider must alter his weight ratio, driving the hocks under the horse to lighten his forehand. The rider should allow the horse to find his own balance to a certain degree between the fences, but, by holding a bridge and allowing the horse to rely on that if necessary, he should give him the support of his hand. In this way the rider will not be exhausted by trying to hold the horse together, because the horse is in fact resting on himself and not the rider.

There is no denying that galloping can 'blow some horses' minds'. On the whole, however, provided that the faster paces are introduced in the same way as the slower ones – as part of the horse's training programme – there is no need for him to become overexcited but merely enthusiastic because he is enjoying himself.

# Summary — Final Thoughts

Before I embarked on this tome, I had doubts in my mind as to whether I would have enough to write about to warrant a book. Once I began writing in earnest, I realised just how much there was to discuss, and I also found it amazing and comforting to think that I could churn out this number of words entirely from my own head without the need to resort to any reference book. In trying to explain everything clearly and succinctly, John and I were forced to scratch our heads many times as it made us re-examine at length exactly what we were doing and why. I am hoping that the reader too will find the book proves to be thought-provoking, if nothing else!

There are two major recurring constants in my thoughts: understanding a problem is halfway to solving it, and that individual horses require different training approaches. It has been fascinating to see how many of the problems in the book have cropped up in the various horses we have trained while I was writing it: this has not only assisted me in my explanations, but it has also underlined one point which emerges on re-reading the manuscript – that the solution to almost every problem is the same. One tends to imagine that one's horse has a special problem that is due to a specific fault, but really it just comes down to a matter of good basic schooling, and while some horses require taxing in their work to make them try their utmost, others almost need treating with kid gloves to bring the best out in them.

The emphasis of this whole book lies on the importance of establishing balance and rhythm in whatever the horse is being asked to do because unless they characterise the horse's movement, he is unable to proceed correctly in his training. There are no hard-and-fast rules about when the horse should be asked a particular question: sometimes the horse needs to be asked to perform a movement beyond his present capabilities even though he is unable to do so correctly, because – providing that he tries without losing confidence – it will help to consolidate his immediate work and will build up, in the meantime, a basis for his future work. Each time he is asked the same question, the horse's answer should be a little nearer to perfection; one cannot expect a horse to perform a new movement correctly straight away as he will not understand exactly what is required. Many people are diffident about asking a question of a horse and, consequently, end up by asking nothing at all, worried lest they lose what they have achieved already. Perhaps 'try' is the key word in progression, for a rider must always be mindful of the need of his horse to try for him. In general terms, if the horse's previous work has been correct he will try something new because he will find it easy, but if the horse does not try of his own accord, then the rider will have to tell him that he *will* try.

Horses do possess a very good memory and once they have been taught something, they rarely forget it: their physical fitness may restrict their ability to perform something, however. Do not forget that a horse will be as quick to pick up bad habits as good ones: without exception the easier option leads to a bad habit, and once again the emphasis must be prevention rather than cure.

My final comment is that there is no substitute for hard work, dedication and patience, however galling that may seem on numerous occasions. For me, though, the pleasure and satisfaction in producing a well-trained horse more than compensates for the time and effort involved in achieving that end.

# *Index*

M